SYLLOGE OF COINS
OF THE BRITISH ISLES

44

SYLLOGE OF COINS OF THE BRITISH ISLES

A British Academy Research Project

THE British Sylloge project was first promoted in the early 1950s by Christopher Blunt and other members of the British and Royal Numismatic Societies. An informal committee was formed under the chairmanship of Sir Frank Stenton, who in 1956 secured its admission as a Committee of the British Academy. The first volume, on Anglo-Saxon coins in the Fitzwilliam Museum, Cambridge, was published by the British Academy in 1958, since when more than forty volumes have appeared.

The aim of the series is to publish detailed and fully illustrated catalogues of coins of the British Isles in British and foreign collections. The volumes range in scope from Ancient British coins to seventeenth-century tokens, with most detailed coverage of the Anglo-Saxon coinage. The collections recorded include those of national, university and provincial museums in Britain and Ireland and of museums in Scandinavia, Germany, Poland and the United States of America.

Chairmen of the Sylloge Committee
- Sir Frank Stenton, F.B.A. (1956-66)
- Professor Dorothy Whitelock, C.B.E., F.B.A. (1966-79)
- Professor H. R. Loyn, F.B.A. (1979-93)
- Lord Stewartby, P.C., F.B.A. (1993-)

General Editors
- C. E. Blunt, O.B.E., F.B.A. (1956-87)
- Professor M. Dolley, M.R.I.A. (1956-83)
- M. A. S. Blackburn (1980-)

The present members of the Sylloge Committee are:
- Miss M. M. Archibald
- M. A. S. Blackburn (*General Editor and Secretary*)
- Professor C. N. L. Brooke, F.B.A.
- Professor N. P. Brooks, F.B.A.
- Professor P. Grierson, F.B.A.
- Professor H. R. Loyn, F.B.A.
- C. S. S. Lyon
- Dr D. M. Metcalf
- H. E. Pagan
- Dr Veronica Smart
- Lord Stewartby, P.C., F.B.A. (*Chairman*)

A full listing of the series is printed at the end of this volume.

SYLLOGE OF COINS OF THE BRITISH ISLES

44

THE NORWEB COLLECTION
CLEVELAND, OHIO, U.S.A.

TOKENS OF THE BRITISH ISLES
1575–1750

PART IV

NORFOLK TO SOMERSET

BY

R. H. THOMPSON and M. J. DICKINSON

LONDON
PUBLISHED BY SPINK & SON LIMITED
1993

PUBLISHED BY SPINK & SON LIMITED

LONDON

1993

ISBN 0 907605 46X

Production of this volume has been financed
through foundation grants made available
to the American Numismatic Society
in memory of Mrs R. Henry Norweb

Typeset from the authors' disks by Quorum Technical Services, Sandford Park Trading Estate,
Corpus Street, Cheltenham, Gloucestershire GL52 6XH
Printed in Great Britain on acid-free paper at the University Press, Cambridge

CONTENTS

Frontispiece: Henry Gutch, mercer in Glastonbury, 1653 (as 4048), Somerset County
   Museum specimen, obverse x 2½. See Introduction

PLATES

viii

PREFACE

PART IV has maintained the practices and procedures set up for Part III. Mr R. Henry Norweb Jr continues to support the project in memory of his mother. Mr Mark Blackburn has edited the volume for the Sylloge Committee. Mr Douglas Liddell in his retirement has overseen matters at Spink's, and Mr Douglas Saville has attended to the practical details of publication. Mr Matthew Weait carried out the weighing of the tokens long ago. Mr John Spink or his Brighton firm took the initial photographs, additional prints were made by Mr Steve Wakeham, and photographs of Somerset County Museum specimens were supplied by Mr Stephen Minnitt. The photographs were cut out and mounted by Mrs D. C. Thompson. We are grateful to all.

As previously announced, London and Middlesex have been postponed, and the old ambiguity over the English or Welsh allegiance of Monmouthshire having been resolved in favour of Wales this volume covers eight counties from Norfolk to Somerset. From the small series of Northumberland and Rutland there is almost a complete representation. The 'difficult' counties of Nottinghamshire and Shropshire have good runs, the rarity of the former emphasized by the presence of only 68 entries despite Mr Ambassador Norweb's particular interest in the county in which (in 1894) he had been born. Northamptonshire is quite good, containing the only silver striking in the parts of the collection arranged by counties (3408d). Somerset is extensive, adding to Williamson the localities of Godney and Stogumber, although the condition of this series is disappointing. Oxfordshire has been well published, yet apart from thirteen entries not in Williamson there are additions and corrections to be made both to Leeds and to Milne, including the restoration of Thomas Barret's Duns Tew halfpenny over which Milne was misled by Blundell.

Norfolk is a revelation, with 358 entries as against 353 Williamson numbers. The Yarmouth Borough farthings of 1667-9 exhibit no less than 20 obverses and 21 reverses, but obscure tradesmen also rise into prominence for their numbers of dies, especially Clare Shewell of Harleston with a chain of four obverses plus five reverses dated from 1656 to 1666. His obverses bear the Grocers' Arms, as does the extraordinary total of 81 Norfolk entries. There is a remarkable number of merchants' marks (as also in Somerset). The device of Thomas Hering in Yarmouth, here classified as a merchant's mark, might relate to his trade of pulley maker; and many other trades are newly documented. There are die-links between Norwich and Swanton Abbott, and between Norwich and Pulham Market, the latter referring in an earlier state to Pulham St Mary; this requires explanation, since Pulham Market was alternatively Pulham St Mary

Magdalene, while Pulham St Mary the Virgin was only a mile away. It has proved possible to suggest an identity for A. L. at the Post Office in Norwich (3221-2).

Augustine Briggs of Norwich, grocer, is one issuer in this volume who was sufficiently grand to appear in the *History of Parliament*, and for his portrait to survive; he died in 1684 leaving £9,000 and extensive holdings of land (Le Strange 1913, facing p. 49; Henning 1983, i. 719-20; Priestley 1985, pp. 5-6). Amongst the Oxford token-issuers is the famous clockmaker Joseph Knibb (1640-1711), although IX in the dial on his token must serve both VIII, IX and X if the hours are to be complete. William Walker d. 1695, mercer at the Bird and Hand in Oxford, was knighted through the happy accident of being mayor when James II was crowned.

THE LEGEND OF THE
GLASTONBURY THORN

by R. H. Thompson

Fig. 1

HENRY Gutch, mercer in Glastonbury, is the only recorded token-issuer of that surname. Snelling included Gutch in his list of surnames that had come to his notice (1766, p. 20), but he neither illustrated nor described the device on Henry Gutch's tokens. The first to do so, it appears, was Boyne (1858, p. 395), with pl. 27 fig. 8 reproduced above as Fig. 1, and the description 'The Glastonbury thorn' for the obverse field of his catalogue number Somersetshire 113.

This entry is followed by a long note on Joseph of Arimathea who, after he had laid the body of Christ in the tomb, departed with some companions to teach the Gospel to the heathen, and founded a religious establishment at Glastonbury, not far from Wearyall Hill where, arriving with his companions 'weary, all', he had thrust in the earth his walking-staff of hawthorn; there it immediately germinated, and bloomed constantly on Christmas Day. The legend of the Thorn evolved at some point after the Dissolution of the monasteries; the last trunk of the bush identified as the Glastonbury Thorn was cut down during the Civil War (Collinson 1791, ii. 265; Carley 1988, pp. 181-4).

Gill added for Henry Gutch the variety dated 1653 (1879, no. 22), but made no comment on Boyne's entry. The same description of the 1666 token was given by Bidgood, curator of the Taunton museum (1886, pp. 131-2). Accepting that the device was intended for the Thorn, he suggested in a note even longer than Boyne's that Gutch would have witnessed the destruction of the Sacred Thorn, and very naturally adopted it as his sign. The same text was contributed by Bidgood to Williamson (pp. 980-1), and the identification of the Glastonbury Thorn has been unquestioned ever since. Whiting, for example (1971, p. 40), devoted eight lines to it.

Through the propagation of cuttings there are now several Glastonbury Thorns. That on Wearyall Hill stands within a protective fence, which is of course modern, and the lattice-work trunk of Gutch's device resembles no type of tree on other Norweb tokens (classification numbers 4.1, 4.2), nor the presumed thorn-bush on Norweb 325. A normal bush illustrates *[Crataegus] oxyacantha* in the herbal by William Turner (d. 1568), dean of Wells, who actually refers to the Glastonbury Thorn. Another problem with the description, pointed out by Gray (1915, p. 123), is that the thorn is inverted: inverted, that is, when the tokens are placed with the start of the legend at 12 o'clock, so that the legend must start at 6 o'clock for the thorn to be observed upright. While tokens do occur with legends starting thus, they are most unusual.

A legend starting at 12 o'clock is very much the norm, and tokens should be so positioned if at all possible. Let the grammar of the tokens be followed, and instead let the identification of the thorn be questioned (Figs. 2-3). They who are not dazzled with visions of the Holy Grail will see, not the Glastonbury Thorn, but Glastonbury Tor, that extraordinary oval hill a mile from the abbey, topped by the fourteenth-century tower of St Michael's church; this tower, though disproportionately large on the tokens, is at least represented as a structure.

Fig. 2. *Obv.* ·HENRY·GVTCH·MERCER around Glastonbury Tor
Rev. ·IN·GLASTONBVRY·1653 around ·G·|H·A
BW Somerset 148; Somerset County Museum specimen

Fig. 3. *Obv.* ·HENRY·GVTCH·MERCER ❖ around Glastonbury Tor
Rev. ·IN·GLASTONBVRY·1666 around ·G·|H·A| ⋯
BW Somerset 147; Somerset County Museum specimen

So Glastonbury's Thorn should be turned upside down, like the Irish Royal Crown (that was a bowl from the Late Bronze Age: Piggott 1951, p. 216). The legend of the Glastonbury Thorn on Henry Gutch's tokens can be replaced with the reality of the issuer's own locality. As it happens, this reality could hold its own resonance, for the Tor may have been the pre-Saxon Christian nucleus of Glastonbury, and the earliest Christian monastic site in the west of Britain (Rahtz 1991, pp. 33-4).

Two views of Glastonbury by Wenceslaus Hollar date from no later than 1655 (not *c.*1670 as given by Carley 1988, p. xviii), the year in which they were published in Volume I of the *Monasticon Anglicanum* of Roger Dodsworth and Sir William Dugdale. The view facing page 2, taken from Compton Hills about three miles to the south, is mentioned by Bidgood for the tree (with normal trunk) growing on Wearyall Hill and captioned 'Sacra Spina'. The Tor is shown, but is more prominent on the second engraving (see Fig. 4). On this the caption to letter L, confusing Tor and Tower, notes that Richard Whiting, the last abbot, was hanged there. While such a note was appropriate to the *Monasticon*, it perhaps should not be assumed to have been every contemporary's first association when considering the Tor.

Omitted from Fig. 4, but present in the original state of the engraving above Hollar's name, was *Ric:Newcourt delin:*, i.e. drawn by Richard Newcourt the elder (d. 1679). Newcourt lived at Somerton about eight miles away, and it is possible that his drawing had existed for some time before publication of a work which had been in preparation since 1638 (Douglas 1951, pp. 32-5). Indeed, it has been proposed that the drawing probably pre-dates 1652, if the engraving were done after Hollar's return to England (Batten 1880, p. 119). Thus the view in Fig. 4 might even be the model for the central punch on Gutch's 1653 obverse.

This punch was curved in base to fit into an inner circle. The 1666 obverse, which is likely to have been copied from a specimen of the 1653 token, makes the Tor quite spherical and less realistic. These devices are unique to Glastonbury, and are rather remarkable. Castles in different towns could be represented by the same punch (Thompson 1986, pp. 575-6), yet here is an individual and distinctive landscape, represented as early as 1653 by a purpose-made punch. Only London's Royal Exchange (see Norweb 3325 in this volume) appears otherwise to have provided in the sixteen-fifties a topographical illustration on tokens.

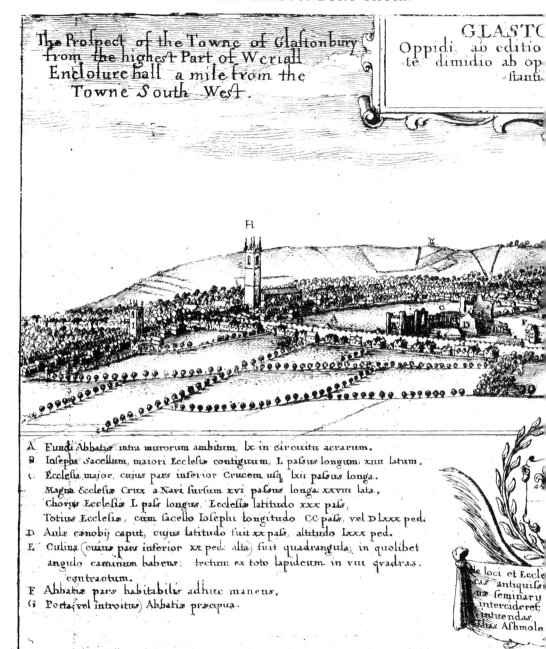

The Prospect of the Towne of Glastonbury from the highest Part of Weriall Enclosure hall a mile from the Towne South West.

GLASTO
Oppidi ab editio
te dimidio ab op
stanti

A   Fundi Abbatiæ intra murorum ambitum, lx in circuitu acrarum.
B   Iosephi Sacellum, maiori Ecclesiæ contiguum, L passus longum xiiii latum.
C   Ecclesia major, cujus pars inferior Crucem usq lxii passus longa.
    Magna Ecclesiæ Crux a Navi sursum xvi passus longa xxviii lata,
    Chorus Ecclesiæ L pass longus, Ecclesiæ latitudo xxx pass,
    Totius Ecclesiæ, cum sacello Iosephi longitudo CC pass, vel Dlxxx ped.
D   Aulæ cænobij caput, cujus latitudo fuit xx pass, altitudo lxxx ped.
E   Culina (cujus pars inferior xx ped alta) fuit quadrangula, in quolibet
    angulo caminum habens, tectum ex toto lapideum in viii qvadras
    contractum.
F   Abbatiæ pars habitabilis adhuc manens.
G   Porta (vel introitus) Abbatiæ præcipua.

e loci et Eccle
as antiquiss
ue seminary
intercideret
intuendas
llius Ashmole

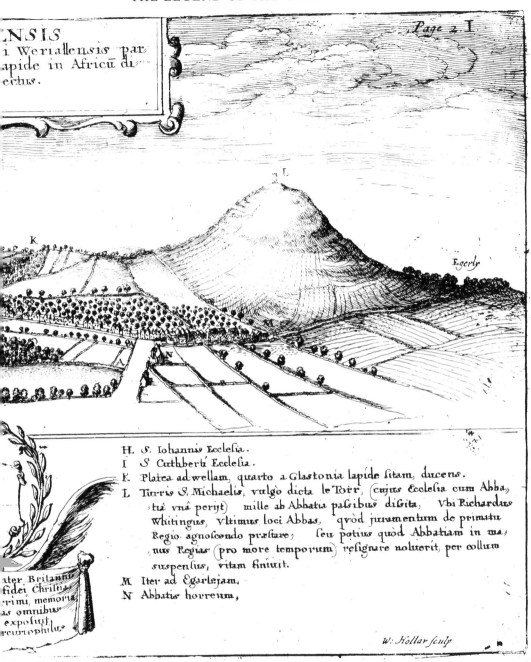

Fig. 4. *Glastoniensis Oppidi ab editiori... prospectus*; central cartouche 'Ne loci... Elias Ashmole ... Anglicus'; signed *Ric:Newcourt delin:|W:Hollar sculp.*; undated. Reproduction courtesy of the Somerset Archaeological and Natural History Society.

ARRANGEMENT

THE attributions of the tokens have been assessed in the light of published information known to the authors, and those which seem Uncertain have been relegated to the end of the topographical arrangement, as have Forgeries. The purpose of the publication, in accordance with Sylloge practice, is to put the tokens in the Norweb Collection at the service of those who would base studies on them, and not itself to publish documentary research, something which, on a national basis, would hardly have been possible.

The tokens are arranged within an alphabetical sequence of the historic English counties, to be followed by Ireland, the Isle of Man, Scotland, and Wales. A reference has been made where a locality was shared by more than one county, and where county boundaries were altered after the seventeenth century; but no attempt has been made to indicate the local government reorganizations of 1965 and 1974. The indispensable authority for the English parishes of the seventeenth century is Youngs 1979 and 1991 (for bibliographical references see Abbreviations, C). Bartholomew 1972 has normally been followed for the form of a place-name, although hyphens have been on principle omitted from compound names.

Within each county the arrangement is alphabetical by the specific locality in which tokens were issued, with the addition in brackets of the civil parish or chapelry where the locality did not give its name to a parish. The intention is to represent every indication of place appearing on the tokens, and separate headings are provided for subordinate localities, e.g. 'KING'S LYNN. Lathe Street', 'BRIDGWATER. High Cross neighbourhood'. By logical extension, tokens which name a sign are placed in an alphabetical sequence of 'Named signs'; if an adjective alone is in the legends, a noun is supplied from the device in square brackets and with a query, e.g. *Red* [*?Lion*]. Readers accustomed to a single sequence under simple place-names will need to remember to look under any subsequent sub-headings; a concordance to Williamson is envisaged for the final volume.

Below each heading the various readings for the place-name are given, normally in order of their frequency on the tokens, but for brevity the occurrences of the commonest form may not be enumerated. Incomplete and uncertain readings are spelled out, a point below a character being used to mean that that reading is possible but no more than that. A dash indicates a single illegible character, three stops an indeterminate number of missing characters. The same treatment applies to any readings given in the entries.

The tokens are numbered in a single sequence, continued from Part III. Die-duplicates are not separately numbered but distinguished by the addition of a lower-case letter, which coincides with Mrs Norweb's intention to dispose of duplicates, and will minimise the number of five-figure entries. The number alone is used for references to the dies, and for indexing; and it is recommended that Norweb references for other specimens should omit the lower-case letters.

Weights were obtained in grams and corrected to the nearest centigram, 0.005 being rounded up in accordance with the 1989 *SCBI Guidance for Authors*. These metric figures have been multiplied by 15.432358 to convert them to grains, and the result corrected to one place of decimals. Metals are described from their appearance on a scraped edge as brass (Br) or copper (Cu); silver is 'Ar', lead or pewter 'Pb', and tin 'Sn'. Between the yellow of high-zinc brass and the brown of what must be called not copper but low-zinc brass there is a whole range of tones about which it is difficult to be precise, and the abbreviation 'M' (mixed metal) has been applied to any intermediate tone. Die-axes are expressed in degrees, as recommended by the 1989 *Guidance*.

Under each heading any corporate issues are placed first, and personal issues follow alphabetically, except that two issuers distinguished only as senior and junior are placed in that order. Several entries for one issuer are arranged chronologically, with undated tokens normally at the beginning. In the same chronological position tokens which do not name a denomination precede those which do.

The catalogue entries consist of the following elements.

(a) *Issuer statement* For corporate issuers this takes the form of the place-name and 'City', 'Borough' etc., whether or not this appears on the tokens. Personal issuers, following any sign named on the token, have the surname spelled as on the token, except where related dies represented in the collection prescribe another spelling. Forenames are normalized, although either of the following is accepted as they remain alternatives: Ann or Anne, Edmond or Edmund, Gervase or Jarvis, Laurence or Lawrence, Nathanael or Nathaniel. As regards abbreviated forms, suspensions such as THO: are not extended, except where the full name is documented; contractions such as SAM^{LL}, however, are silently extended where this can be done with confidence. Readings which differ from the chosen form are added in brackets. To surname and forename is added any trade or other description of the issuer mentioned on the token.

(b) *Issue statement* The date, or 'nd' if the token is not dated; the denomination if named; and any legend such as 'hearty double token'.

(c) *Types* The obverse and reverse fields, separated by a semicolon, are identified by means of a class number (see below), by the transcription of individual letters, or by the word 'date'. A triangular arrangement of letters is transcribed in two lines separated by '|', the letter at the apex being taken to be one line. Readings not in Williamson are added in brackets, the presence of ornamental stops being indicated but not their form.

(d) *References* This is normally a number in Williamson (BW), with the county understood when it is the same as in the present arrangement. The reference applies only, of course, to the wording as printed in Williamson, and moreover pays no attention to the indicator of denomination at the end of his entries. Norweb variations from a published reading are introduced by 'but . . .', which is not intended to assert necessarily that the published reading does not exist. However, in this volume 'but . . .' following Leeds or Milne, which are fully illustrated, means that their text does require correction. Tokens not in Williamson are given as 'BW —', followed where possible by the number in Dickinson (see Abbreviations, C). References to other works may be added if they have distinguished varieties, or have simply added information. An asterisked reference means that the published reading is not wholly confirmed by the Norweb specimen(s).

(e) *Provenance* This copies the source recorded on the envelope in which each specimen is stored, and/or on Mrs Norweb's record cards. A provenance inferred from the accession number, or from an accompanying ticket, is placed in square brackets. From the tickets or other information it has been possible in many cases to take the provenance beyond the immediate source.

(f) *Notes* These cover notes of die-links within the collection (die-links outside the Norweb Collection have not been sought); evidence for attribution; documentation of an issuer which has a direct bearing on the token, such as his trade (where none is mentioned on the token), and the name of the sign used on the token, and if the token is undated the date of the issuer's death if within the token-issuing period; and any contemporary record of a private token. Also noted are legends starting at irregular positions, by numbers o'clock; 12 o'clock is the norm, but 11 o'clock is not considered irregular.

As regards the plates it was intended originally that, for ease of handling, the photographs should be taken x $1\frac{1}{2}$, to be reduced in printing to 1:1. Subsequently, by measuring tokens and converting the result, it was discovered that different batches of tokens were photographed at varying magnifications, most at slightly less than $1\frac{1}{2}$:1. Checks throughout have eliminated extreme examples, but it remains possible that illustrations in this volume are 2% too small, or 2% too large. A letter added to the catalogue number identifies which of any die-duplicates has been illustrated.

CLASSIFIED INDEX OF TYPES

OBVERSE and reverse types are described by means of a class number, except in the case of letters (which are transcribed) and dates (for which see 5.77). The class numbers identify the types according to their appearance, and so avoid the imprecision and the often unwarranted certainty involved in putting a name to them. Their explanations can encompass both description and a possible name or names, both the modern wording and a contemporary name such as 'Flower-de-Luce'. The classified arrangement can relate types of uncertain identity to others which may have a contemporary name, and relax the grip of earlier identifications which are not certainly right but which cannot be disproved. Above all, the class number in the catalogue briefly identifies a type which can be elaborated below. These advantages outweigh the slight complication of having to refer from the catalogue to the classification for more information about a token illustrated on a facing plate.

The classification employed is that of Neubecker 1974, in which Rentzmann's numismatic material (alphabetical by the German) has been re-arranged into an ordinary of arms with a systematic notation. For a few types there is no provision, but generally the tokens fit in well; and the differences hold out the opportunity for comparing the devices chosen for tokens with more formally heraldic representations.

There are five main categories, here numbered 1 to 5:

> GEOMETRICAL
>
> UNIVERSE
>
> LIVING BEINGS
>
> PLANTS
>
> INANIMATE OBJECTS

Neubecker's numbered classes within these five categories have been adopted in their entirety, with occasional modifications of his English wording. The following classes have been added to Neubecker's: 4.15, and 5.82 to 5.88. This notation has been extended to specify subdivisions of the classes which, though sometimes present in Neubecker, are not there numbered. For example, 1.33.10 is a subdivision of 1.33, Checky, which falls within category 1, Geometrical. Related devices are brought together as far as possible within each class.

Except for charges on shields (5.14, 5.15), numismatic left and right are used and not heraldic dexter and sinister. Heraldic conventions are, however, often assumed, for example that a Lion rampant faces to left.

3.95	Two-headed eagle
3.95.1	A two-headed eagle displayed — 3569, 3941-2
3.99	Stilt-bird
3.99.1	A stilt-bird close. Crane — 3326
3.101	Cock, hen
3.101.1	A cock close. Gamecock. Heathcock. Moorcock — 3135, 3681
3.101.4	A cock close and in base a dexter hand appaumé fesswise — 4079
3.101.21	A hen couchant accompanied by smaller birds. Hen & Chickens — 3723
3.102	Swan, goose
3.102.1	A swan close perhaps water in base — 3372, 3463, 3542, 3855-6
3.102.11	A swan rising wings elevated and addorsed unchained or apparently so perhaps rushes in base — 3502-3
3.103	Duck, martlet
3.103.1	A duck close — 3138
3.107	Plume of feathers
3.107.2	Out of a crest-coronet a plume of three feathers. The Feathers. Prince of Wales' Feathers — 3089
3.108	Bird unspecified
3.108.2	A bird close accompanied by letters ( ). Pigeon — 3412
3.108.10	A bird close in the beak a branch of olive. Dove — 3360, 3426-7
3.108.16	Three birds close two and one. Three Blackbirds — 3763
3.108.20	Three birds close two and one in the beak a branch of olive. Three Doves. Cf. 5.14 Tallow Chandlers — 3060, 3532, 3724
3.108.21	Three birds close two and one in the beak a branch of olive and in chief a ragged staff. [Otherwise a staff *raguly* (Fox-Davies 1907, p. 91); Preston-Morley (p. 35, no. 115) corrects the description 'ragged staff' to 'a tree-trunk with four branches lopped off', but *raguly* means jagged or notched like the trunk or limbs of a tree lopped of its branches (see Fox-Davies 1985, pp. 74-5)] — 3548
3.108.27	A bird rising wings elevated and displayed in the beak a branch of olive. Dove — 3155, 4185
3.108.30	A pelican standing above its nest and vulning its breast with its beak to nourish its young with its blood. Pelican in her Piety — 3439
3.109	Fish, cetacean
3.109.1	A dolphin embowed — 3346, 3652
3.109.10	A fish naiant. Salmon — 3756
3.109.16	Three fishes fretted in a triangle. Three Salmons — 3765
3.109.17	A whale naiant and blowing in chief water in base — 3341
3.111	Crayfish
3.111.1	A lobster palewise — 3708-11

5 INANIMATE OBJECTS

arms of the Worshipful Company of Barbers and Surgeons of London (Bromley 1960, p. 14) — 3654-5

5.14 Bath   A shield party per fess embattled the base masonry in chief two bars wavy over all a sword erect the point upwards; the arms of the City of Bath, *Party per fesse embattled azure and argent the base masoned in chief two bars wavy of the second over all a sword in pale gules hilt and pommel or* (Fox-Davies 1915, p. 66) — 3948-54

5.14 Blacksmiths   On a shield a chevron between three crowned hammers; the arms of the Worshipful Company of Blacksmiths of London (Bromley 1960, p. 22) — 3012, 3498

5.14 Brewers   A shield: on a chevron perhaps engrailed between six barley-sheaves in saltire three kilderkins; the arms of the Worshipful Company of Brewers of London (Bromley 1960, p. 28) — 3738-9

5.14 Clothworkers   On a shield a chevron ermine between in chief two havettes and in base a teasel cob; the arms of the Worshipful Company of Clothworkers of London (Bromley 1960, p. 46) — 3835, 4137, 4152

5.14 Coopers   A shield gyronny of eight on a chevron between three annulets a royne between two broad axes on a chief three lilies; the arms of the Worshipful Company of Coopers of London (Bromley 1960, p. 55) — 3071

5.14 Cordwainers   On a shield a chevron between three goats' heads erased; the arms of the Worshipful Company of Cordwainers of London (Bromley 1960, p. 60) — 3378, 3450, 3924

5.14 Cordwainers 2   On a shield three goats' heads erased; for the arms of the Worshipful Company of Cordwainers of London; the chevron is omitted — 3730

5.14 Drapers   On a shield [three clouds] perhaps with sunbeams issuing crowned with imperial crowns; the arms of the Worshipful Company of Drapers of London (Bromley 1960, p. 72) — 3028, 3049-51, 3257, 3270-1, 3443, 3469, 3526, 3547, 3592, 3646, 3793, 3988

5.14 Dyers   On a shield a chevron between three bags perhaps corded; for the arms of the Worshipful Company of Dyers of London, *Sable a chevron engrailed argent between three bags of madder argent corded or* (Bromley 1960, p. 79) — 3157, 3464-6

5.14 Goldsmiths   A shield quarterly in the first and fourth a leopard's head in the second and third a covered cup between two buckles; the arms of the Worshipful Company of Goldsmiths of London (Bromley 1960, p. 126) — 3718, 3968

5.14 Grocers   On a shield a chevron between nine cloves; the arms of the Worshipful Company of Grocers of London (Bromley 1960, p. 130) — 3006, 3008, 3013-14, 3025-7, 3029, 3031-2, 3034-5, 3042, 3052-9, 3061-2, 3080-1, 3084, 3097, 3099-3100, 3104-5, 3132, 3134, 3139-40, 3156, 3158, 3160, 3165, 3167, 3170-1, 3175-9, 3181, 3183, 3186, 3188-90, 3192-4, 3201, 3203,

3206-7, 3209, 3212-13, 3215, 3234-5, 3244, 3249, 3252, 3255, 3272, 3322-4, 3337-8, 3342-3, 3348, 3358-9, 3371, 3373-4, 3379, 3386, 3421, 3428, 3438, 3447-8, 3452, 3454, 3473, 3477-9, 3496, 3505, 3509, 3512, 3559, 3593, 3602, 3625, 3632, 3648, 3693, 3767-72, 3780, 3785, 3794-5, 3813-14, 3821, 3857, 3859, 3872-3, 3997, 4041, 4058, 4155-6

5.14 Haberdashers — A shield barry wavy of six on a bend a lion passant guardant; the arms of the Worshipful Company of Haberdashers of London (Bromley 1960, p. 137) — 3260-2, 3901, 3972, 4019

5.14 Innholders 2 — On a shield a chevron party per pale and per chevron argent and — between three garbs; for the arms of the Worshipful Company of Innholders of London c.1588-1634 *Azure a chevron per pale and per chevron argent and gules between three oatsheaves or* (Bromley 1960, pp. 144-6) — 4000

5.14 Ironmongers — A shield: on a chevron between three gads of steel three swivels; the arms of the Worshipful Company of Ironmongers of London (Bromley 1960, p. 148) — 3037-9, 3143, 3405-6, 3504, 3518, 3541, 3578, 3591, 3732-3, 3865, 3900, 3936

5.14 King's Lynn — On a shield three dragons' heads erased and erect in the mouth of each a cross crosslet fitchy also erect; the arms of King's Lynn (Fox-Davies 1915, p. 414) — 3064-70

5.14 Mercers — A shield: perhaps issuant from a bank of clouds a figure of the Virgin couped at the shoulders the neck perhaps encircled by a jewelled necklace and perhaps wreathed about the temples with a chaplet of roses and crowned with a celestial crown the whole perhaps within a bordure of clouds; the arms of the Worshipful Company of Mercers of London (Bromley 1960, pp. 168-9) — 3040, 3048, 3085, 3251, 3254, 3258, 3264-8, 3388, 3457, 3475, 3486, 3516, 3519-20, 3561, 3566, 3580, 3584, 3586, 3686, 3694-5, 3799-3802, 3806, 3823, 3826, 3849-50, 3890, 3893, 3917, 3928-30, 3940, 3955-7, 3960-1, 3964-6, 4040, 4051-2, 4091

5.14 Merchant Taylors — On a shield a pavilion between two mantles on a chief a lion passant guardant; the arms of the Worshipful Company of Merchant Taylors of London (Bromley 1960, p. 174) — 3043, 3091, 3137, 3429, 3797-8

5.14 Norwich — On a shield a castle in base a lion passant guardant; the arms of the City of Norwich (Fox-Davies 1915, p. 564) — 3108-26, 3162

5.14 Oxford — On a shield an ox passing a ford of water; the arms of the City of Oxford (Chesshyre 1992, p. 212) — 3665-75

5.14 Oxford 2 — On a shield an ox; for the arms of the City of Oxford; the ford of water is omitted — 3610, 3653

5.14 Pewterers — A shield: on a chevron between three strikes as many roses; the arms of the Worshipful Company of Pewterers of London (Bromley 1960, p. 197) — 3590

5.14 Saddlers — On a shield a chevron between three saddles; the arms of the Worshipful Company of Saddlers of London (Bromley 1960, p. 211) — 3510

5.14 Salters — On a shield party per chevron three covered salts the salt shedding on both sides of the salts; the arms of the Worshipful Company of Salters of London (Bromley 1960, p. 215) — 3546, 3986

5.14 Stationers 2 — On a shield a chevron between three books perhaps with clasps; for the arms of the Worshipful Company of Stationers of London *Azure on a chevron between three books with clasps all or an eagle volant gules with a nimbus or between two roses gules leaved vert in chief issuing out of a cloud proper radiated or a holy spirit wings displayed argent with a nimbus or* (Bromley 1960, p. 233); the eagle, roses, and holy spirit are omitted — 3915

5.14 Tallow Chandlers — A shield: on a field of six pieces three doves each holding in its beak an olive branch; the arms of the Worshipful Company of Tallow Chandlers of London (Bromley 1960, p. 237) — 3082, 3086, 3200, 3506-7, 3514, 3841, 3848, 3861, 3912, 3939, 3963, 4092

5.14 Tallow Chandlers 2 — The arms of the Worshipful Company of Tallow Chandlers of London, as above, but the divisions of the field omitted — 3878

5.14 'Upholsterers' — A shield: on a chevron between three tents three roses; cf. the arms of the Company of Upholders or Upholsters *Sable on a cheveron or 3 roses gules between 3 such [pavilions or tents royall] argent fringed or* (Holme 1688, 3.12.40), the arms of the Company of Upholsterers of London (Boyne 1858, pl. 2), and the arms of the Company of Upholders or Upholsterers *Sable on a chevron or between three tents (without poles) ermine lined azure* (another, 1730, *gules) as many roses gules* (Papworth 1874, p. 534); but the arms of the Worshipful Company of Upholders of London are *Sable three spervers ermine garnished azure and gules beneath the sperver in base a lamb couchant argent on a cushion or above the lamb a cross formy fitchy gules*, without a chevron (Bromley 1960, p. 249) — 3092, 3725-6

5.14 Vintners — On a shield a chevron between three tuns; the arms of the Worshipful Company of Vintners of London (Bromley 1960, p. 253) — 3713-14, 3919-20

5.14 Weavers — A shield: on a chevron between three leopards' heads each holding in the mouth a shuttle three roses; the arms of the Worshipful Company of Weavers of London (Bromley 1960, p. 263) — 4129

5.14 Wells — On a shield perhaps on a mount in base a tree between three wells; the arms of the City of Wells *Silver on a mount vert in base an ash-tree proper between three wells gules* (Scott-Giles 1953, p. 325) — 4157-61

5.14 Yarmouth

On a shield party per pale three demi-lions passant guardant conjoined to the bodies of as many herrings; the arms of Great Yarmouth (Fox-Davies 1915, p. 872) — 3273-98

5.14.1 Apothecaries

A shield as at 5.14 Apothecaries, accompanied by letters ( ) — 3567

5.14.1 Grocers

A shield as at 5.14 Grocers, accompanied by letters ( ) — 3047, 3441, 3444

5.14.2 Mercers

A shield as at 5.14 Mercers, accompanied by an inscription — 3559

5.14.5

A shield quarterly the 1st and 4th grand quarters France Modern and England quarterly the 2nd Scotland the 3rd Ireland; the Royal Arms of 1603-88. King's Arms — 4045-6

5.14.52

Rising from the base of a shield a ragged cross of wood between three crowns the lowest encircling the bottom limb of the cross; for the arms of Colchester *Gules two silver ragged staves in the form of a cross its arms and foot pierced by Passion Nails and three golden crowns the bottom one encircling the foot of the cross* (Scott-Giles 1953, pp. 128-9: nails sometimes omitted); and for the arms of Nottingham *Gules rising from the base of the shield a ragged cross of wood proper between three open crowns of gold the lowest encircling the bottom limb of the cross* (Scott-Giles 1953, p. 304) — 3523-4

5.14.86

On a shield a beast or monster rampant — 3023

5.14.87

On a shield nine mullets three three two and one — 3078-9

5.14.88

A shield per pale a saltire wavy; cf. the arms of Water or Waters *Paly of six argent and azure a saltire wavy counterchanged*, and the arms of Waters *Quarterly argent and sable a saltire wavy counterchanged* (Papworth 1874, p. 1062) — 3356

5.14.89

On a shield six cloves three two and one, accompanied in chief by letters ( ) — 3426

5.14.90

On a shield two lions combatant and in chief a ?rose; cf. the arms of Heron of that ilk, co. Kirkcudbright, *Argent two lions rampant affronté supporting between their forepaws a rose gules stalked and leaved vert* (Burke 1884, p. 482); accompanied in chief by an inscription perhaps incorporating letters ( ) — 3472

5.14.91

On a shield three castles of four turrets two and one each charged with the letter L; cf. the arms of Newcastle upon Tyne *Gules three towers triple-towered argent* (Fox-Davies 1915, p. 548) — 3491

5.14.92

On a shield one bend; for the arms of Scrope etc. *Azure a bend or* (Chesshyre 1992, pp. 323-4) — 3557

5.14.93

On a shield a bend ?or — 3609

5.14.94

On a shield six martlets three two and one; for the arms of Appleby etc., co. Leicester, *Azure six martlets three two and one or*, or of Apelby or Apleby, co. Salop and co. Stafford, *Azure six martlets three two and one argent* (Papworth 1874, p. 335) — 3677-8

5.14.95 On a shield a unicorn rampant — 3727-8

5.14.96 A shield: on a bend three fleurs de lis; cf. the arms of Powtrell etc. *Argent on a bend azure three fleurs de lis of the first, Or on a bend azure three fleurs de lis argent,* and *Or on a bend azure three fleurs de lis of the first* (Papworth 1874, p. 239) — 3867-8

5.14.97 A shield: three demi-lions rampant and on a chief three covered cups — 3871

5.14.98 On a shield three mullets pierced impaling ermine on a canton a fleur de lis; for the arms of Wollaston of Shenton, co. Leicester, *Argent three mullets sable pierced of the field,* impaling Anselme, Middlesex, or Aunsam, *Ermine on a canton sable a fleur de lis or* (Papworth 1874, pp. 993, 359) — 3879

5.14.99 On a shield three leopards' faces; for the arms of Shrewsbury *Azure three leopards' faces or* (Fox-Davies 1915, p. 724) — 3913, 3916, 3931

5.14.100 On a shield a fess between three boars' heads couped; cf. the arms of Allaunson of co. York, co. Essex and London *Argent a fess azure between three boars' heads couped sable a martlet for difference* (Burke 1884, p. 11) — 3934

5.14.101 On a shield three crowns; perhaps intended for the Drapers' Arms (see above, 5.14 Drapers) — 3935

5.14.102 A shield: on two bars seven escallops four and three — 3937-8

5.14.103 On a shield a sword erect between two wings conjoined tips upwards — 3994

5.14.104 A shield ermine on a canton a crescent — 4020-3

5.14.105 On a shield a chevron ?or between three fleurs de lis; cf. the arms of Crul or Kyrle, co. Hereford, and Kirle, co. Salop, *Vert a chevron between three fleurs de lis or* (Papworth 1874, p. 422) — 4032-3

5.14.106 On a shield a chevron between three bugle-horns; cf. the arms of Foster, co. Somerset etc., *Argent a chevron vert between three bugle-horns sable* (Papworth 1874, pp. 451-2) — 4071

5.14.107 A shield quarterly first a sinister hand appaumé and erect, second two [?sides of bacon] in pale, third [?a circular tool], fourth three pellets one and two — 4097

5.15 Complete achievement of arms

5.15 Leathersellers 2 On a shield three bucks trippant; the arms of the Worshipful Company of Leathersellers of London incorporating the mistery of Glovers-Pursers (1502-1639) *3 bucks passant,* but omitting the impalement; crest of the Worshipful Company of Glovers *On a wreath argent and sable a ram's head argent armed and issuing from a basket or filled with wool argent between two wings erect gules;* and mantling (Bromley 1960, pp. 119, 157; Chesshyre 1992, p. 291) — 3690

INDEX TO CLASSIFICATION

ABBREVIATIONS

A. GENERAL

IN addition to the usual abbreviations for counties etc., the following are used:

*	(before a reference) Published reading not wholly confirmed by specimen
Ar	Silver
Br	Brass, or any yellowish alloy of copper
Cu	Copper, or an alloy of similar colour
g	Grams
gr	Grains
i.m.	Initial mark
M	A metal intermediate in colour between copper and brass; mixed metal
nd	Not dated
obv.	Obverse
Pb	Lead or pewter
rev.	Reverse
Sn	Tin
var.	Variety

B. COLLECTORS, DEALERS, AND COLLECTIONS
CITED IN THE TEXT

Baldwin	Albert Henry Frederick Baldwin (1889-1970), of Messrs A. H. Baldwin & Sons Ltd, London coin dealers since *c*.1880 [3006b. . . 4187b, at least 529 specimens]
Brand	Virgil Michael Brand (1862-1926), of Chicago, brewer, who built up a collection of more than 350,000 coins. In London he was buying from Spink at least as early as 1895. At his death the collection was divided between his two brothers, and portions have since been dispersed through dealers, auction rooms, and privately. See Bowers 1983, who includes comments by Mrs Norweb [3036c, ?3067e, ?3070f, ?3103a, ?3113a, 3164b, ?3205b, ?3408a, 3522, 3538, 3561, ?3566b, ?3576b, ?3579b, ?3587d, 3634a, ?3660c, ?3750a, ?3768a, ?3785a, ?3846a, ?3976c, ?3977d, ?3978a, ?4044b, ?4111b, ?4185c]
Carthew	Col. Ranulphus John Carthew, JP, Royal Field Artillery (1863-1943), of Woodbridge Abbey, who became a Fellow of the Royal Numismatic Society in 1905 (Pagan 1986, p. 89), and a member of the British Numismatic Society in 1906. His 'magnificent' collection of seventeenth-century tokens was offered in *SCMB*, March 1946 and May 1953. Inexplicably he is named as Col. Thomas Carthew in Preston-Morley, p. 3, in Spink Sale 28, and thence in Manville 1986,

	p. 376 [3361, 3378, 3382, ?3386, 3392, 3403-4, 3407, 3412, 3428, 3435, 3438, ?3447, 3448, 3462, 3473, 3477, 3557, 3862, 3864, 3959a]
Clark	Nigel A. Clark, a coin dealer since 1976, in Brentwood (Essex) then East Grinstead (West Sussex) [3299a, 3373, 3415, 3449, 3453, 3456, 3507, 3545, 3549, 3702, 3903, 3916b, 3934, 3936, 4091, 4107, 4123]
Coins & Antiquities	Coins & Antiquities Ltd, successors to D. J. Crowther Ltd (established 1966), were London dealers in coins, medals and classical antiquities from c.1968 to 1979 [3054, 3400d, 3434a]
Cornell 1986	David L. Cornell sold his collection of Norfolk tokens at Christie's, 18 Feb. 1986, lots 394-462 [cf. 3229]
Daniels	James Herbert Daniels, of Brighton, a coin dealer whose stock was auctioned after his death by Glendining, 25-26 March and 17-18 June 1936 [3417b, 3482a, 3774b, 3832b, 3840c, 3890a, 3934, 4035f]
Deane	Patrick Deane (Coins) Ltd, a London coin dealer since 1973 [3361, 3376, 3378, 3382, ?3386, 3391-2, 3403-4, 3407, 3412, 3428, 3435, 3438, 3447-8, 3461-2, 3473, 3477, 3958b]
Gilbert	William Gilbert, LRIBA (c.1878-1944), a Fellow of the Royal Numismatic Society from 1913 (Pagan 1986, p. 93). See also Abbreviations, C [3006b... 3359b (Norfolk, at least 149 specimens); ?3978a]
Hird	Alderman Horace Hird (d. 1973), of Bradford, FSA, who was a Fellow of the Royal Numismatic Society from 1943, and a Vice-President of the British Association of Numismatic Societies. He gave a spectacular collection of Scottish coins to the Ashmolean Museum in 1953 (see SCBI 35); a second collection was auctioned anonymously by Glendining on 6 March 1974. This sale also included in two lots his collection of Yorkshire seventeenth-century tokens, a series about which he was very possessive. See also Abbreviations, C [3467, 3486b, 3487-93, 3638a, 4191]
Longman 1958	William Longman, FSA (1882-1967), a member of the publishing family of that name, was a Fellow of the Royal Numismatic Society 1911-33 (Pagan 1986, p. 99), and a member of the British Numismatic Society 1915-59/60. See also SCBI 43, p. xliii. He published in 1916 *Tokens of the Eighteenth Century connected with Booksellers & Bookmakers*, and sold a related collection through Glendining on 12-13 March 1958 [3436a, 3969, 4008]
Lowe	Leonard Lowe, of Nottingham; his collection was sold anonymously through Glendining's on 22 Sep. 1971 (lot 306) [3494, 3499, 3502, 3511, 3513, 3533, 3534a, 3536a, 3547, 3550a, 3555]
Lowe, H.	H. Lowe, of Altrincham, Cheshire; his coins were auctioned by Glendining, 19 Oct. 1943, and his tokens anonymously by Spink, 5 Dec. 1979 [3936]
Norwich Castle Museum	The Castle Museum, formed by a private society in 1825 and in public ownership since 1894, has a strong collection of Norfolk and Suffolk tokens. See also SCBI 26, pp. 108-12 [cf. 3270]

Nott   Ralph Augustus Nott (1883-1960): see SCBI 31, pp. xii-xv   [3052b
                              . . . 4190, at least 581 specimens]

Sare   A source for H. Lowe, 1933; unidentified   [3936]

Seaby   B. A. Seaby Ltd, London coin dealers from 1926 until 1991   [3108a,
                              ?3205b, 3344a, 3362a, ?3370b, 3390a, 3408d, 3419, 3432b, 3445a,
                              3467, 3494, 3499, 3502, 3511, 3513, 3533, 3534a, 3536a, 3547, 3550a,
                              3555, 3599a, ?3635, 3638a, 3700a, ?3750a, 3751a, 3840d, 3889, 3920,
                              3938, 3958a, 4042, ?4185c, 4191; cf. 3046]

Selwood [i.e. Sellwood]   'Selwood Coll.' as the source for a silver specimen of BW Northants.
                              85, offered in *SCMB* 1968, p. 364, presumably refers to Percy Hickson
                              Sellwood (d. 1961), Secretary of Newbury Numismatic Society, who
                              published coin finds in the *Berkshire Archaeological Journal*
                              (Manville 1993, p. 242), and 'Newbury Town 17th-century tokens' in
                              SCMB 1950, p. 583   [3408d]

Smallfield   J. Stone Smallfield (*c.*1814-1883), a member of the Numismatic
                              Society of London from 1864 (Pagan 1986, p. 71), and of the Kent
                              Archaeological Society, author of papers on Sussex and London
                              tokens   [3993a n.]

Somerset County   The museum, started by the Somerset Archaeological and Natural
Museum   History Society in 1849 and removed to Taunton Castle in 1874,
                              includes a large collection of seventeenth-century tokens. See also
                              SCBI 24, pp. xxiv-xxxi   [cf. Introduction, and 3941, 3967-8, 3971,
                              3986-8, 4011, 4047, 4058, 4065, 4071-2, 4083, 4085, 4094, 4097,
                              4124, 4126, 4132, 4137-8, 4183]

Sotheby 25 July 1918   Sotheby, 25 July 1918: [Lord Mostyn. . . James Hoole. . . Charles
                              Lilburn. . . E. Hargrave Booth. . . William Greenwell. . .]   [3654]

Spink   Spink & Son Ltd, London coin dealers since 1666   [3243, 3358a,
                              3366, 3379b, 3380, 3387, 3399e, 3402, 3418, 3425, 3479, 3486b,
                              3487-93, 3517, 3532, ?3535a, 3535b, 3537, 3539, 3542, 3550b, 3554,
                              3559, 3598b, 3617c, 3632a, 3632c, 3893-4, 3896, 3898-9, 3901, 3911,
                              3913, 3917, 3919, 3927-8, 3930, 3972, 3981, 4003b, ?4006, 4009,
                              4034, ?4037, ?4039, 4064, 4066-7, 4086, ?4141, ?4148, ?4152, ?4159,
                              4160b, 4184]

Spink Sale 7   Spink Coin Auctions, Sale no. 7, 5 December 1979   [3934, 3936; cf.
                              3883, 3885, 3898, 3907, 3914-15, 3926, 3933]

Spink Sale 28   Spink Coin Auctions, Sale no. 28, 28 April 1983

Stevens [i.e. Stephens]   'Homer Stevens' presumably refers to Homer R. Stephens, who
                              published a *Check List of Conder Tokens* in 1937, and various notes
                              in *The Numismatist* and the *Coin Collector's Journal* of 1936-42 such
                              as 'English tokens relating to America' and 'Sightseeing in the British
                              Isles via Condor [!] tokens'   [3120, 3122b]

Tatton   Thomas Egerton Tatton, J.P. (1846-1924), of Wythenshawe Hall,
                              Northenden, Cheshire, a Fellow of the (Royal) Numismatic Society
                              from 1888 to 1916 (Pagan 1986, p. 73), and a member of the British
                              Numismatic Society from the foundation until 1913, sold a collection
                              of tokens at Sotheby's, 6-7 Nov. 1911 (Manville 1986, p. 222)   [3934]

Taunton	See Somerset County Museum
Young	David M. Young, accountant, of Taunton, Somerset [cf. 4000, 4049, 4098]

C. BIBLIOGRAPHICAL

BNJ =	*The British Numismatic Journal*
NC =	*The Numismatic Chronicle*
NCirc =	*The Numismatic Circular*, subsequently *Spink Numismatic Circular*
SCMB =	*Seaby's Coin and Medal Bulletin* subsequently *Seaby Coin & Medal Bulletin*
Adams 1680	[John] Adams, *Index Villaris, or, An alphabetical Table of all the Cities, Market-towns, Parishes, Villages and private Seats in England and Wales* (London, 1680)
Bardsley 1901	Charles Wareing Bardsley, *A Dictionary of English and Welsh Surnames, with special American Instances*; revised for the press by his widow (London, 1901)
Bartholomew 1972	John Bartholomew & Son Ltd, *Gazetteer of the British Isles*, 9th edn., reprinted with. . . Supplement. . . (Edinburgh, 1972)
Batten 1880	E. Chisholm Batten, 'The Holy Thorn of Glastonbury', *Somersetshire Archaeological and Natural History Society's Proceedings* 26 (1880), 117-25
Beeson 1962	C. F. C. Beeson, *Clockmaking in Oxfordshire 1400-1850* (Banbury, 1962)
Belfast 1913	Belfast Public Art Gallery and Museum, *Catalogue of Irish Tokens, 17th, 18th and 19th centuries. . .* (Belfast, 1913)
Bidgood 1886	William Bidgood, 'Somerset trade tokens of the seventeenth century, and of the period from 1787 to 1817', *Somersetshire Archaeological and Natural History Society's Proceedings* 32 (1886), 115-54
Bird 1992	N. du Quesne Bird, 'West Country goldsmiths, tokens and badges, 1571-1664', *NCirc* 100 (1992), 191-2
Blundell 1928	Joseph Hight Blundell, *Bedfordshire Seventeenth-century Tokens*, new edn. (Ventnor, 1928)
Bourne 1991	*Rutland Hearth Tax, 1665*, introduced and edited by Jill Bourne and Amanda Goode ([Oakham], 1991). Rutland Record Society Occasional Publications, 6
Bowers 1983	Q. David Bowers, *Virgil Brand, the Man and his Era: profile of a numismatist* (Wolfeboro, New Hampshire, 1983)
Boyne 1858	William Boyne, *Tokens issued in the Seventeenth Century. . .* (London, 1858)
Bridgwater 1973	*Bridgwater Official Guide* (Bridgwater, 1973)
Bromley 1960	John Bromley, *The Armorial Bearings of the Guilds of London: a record of the heraldry of the surviving companies with historical notes; with. . . [illustrations] by Heather Child. . .* (London, 1960)

Burke 1884	Sir Bernard Burke, *The General Armory of England, Scotland, Ireland and Wales. . .*; with a Supplement (London, 1884)
BW	See Williamson
Camden 1695	*Camden's Britannia*; newly translated into English with large additions and improvements. . ., by Edmund Gibson (London, 1695)
Carley 1988	James P. Carley, *Glastonbury Abbey: the Holy House at the head of the Moors adventurous* (Woodbridge, 1988)
Challis 1989	C. E. Challis, 'Mint officials and moneyers of the Stuart period', *BNJ* 59 (1990), 157-97
Chesshyre 1992	*Dictionary of British Arms: medieval ordinary*, Vol. 1, ed. D. H. B. Chesshyre, T. Woodcock. . . (London, 1992)
Chinnor 1982	Chinnor Historical & Archaeological Society, *Seventeenth-century Tradesmen's Tokens, with particular reference to Chinnor* ([Chinnor, 1982]). Chinnor Historical & Archaeological Society Occasional Paper no. 6
Collinson 1791	John Collinson, *The History and Antiquities of the County of Somerset* . . . (Bath, 1791). 3 vols.
Cornell 1986	see Abbreviations, B
Cottle 1978	Basil Cottle, *The Penguin Dictionary of Surnames*, 2nd edn. (Harmondsworth, 1978)
Cunnington 1972	C. Willett Cunnington and Phillis Cunnington, *Handbook of English Costume in the Seventeenth Century. . .*, 3rd edn. (London, 1972)
Dickinson	Michael Dickinson, *Seventeenth-century Tokens of the British Isles and their Values* (London, 1986)
Dodsworth	Roger Dodsworth and William Dugdale, *Monasticon Anglicanum. . .* (London, 1655-73). 3 vols.
Douglas 1951	David C. Douglas, *English Scholars 1660-1730*, 2nd edn. (London, 1951)
Ekwall 1960	Eilert Ekwall, *The Concise Oxford Dictionary of English Place-Names*, 4th edn. (Oxford, 1960)
Elmhirst 1959	Edward Mars Elmhirst, *Merchants' Marks*; ed. Leslie Dow (London, 1959). The Publications of the Harleian Society, Vol. cviii
EPNS 1933	J. E. B. Gover et al., *The Place-Names of Northamptonshire* (Cambridge, 1933). English Place-Name Society [Publications], Vol. x
EPNS 1940	J. E. B. Gover et al., *The Place-Names of Nottinghamshire* (Cambridge, 1940). English Place-Name Society [Publications], Vol. xvii
EPNS 1954	Margaret Gelling, *The Place-Names of Oxfordshire*, Part II (Cambridge, 1954). English Place-Name Society [Publications], Vol. xxiv
EPNS 1989	Karl Inge Sandred and Bengt Lindström, *The Place-Names of Norfolk*, Part 1: *The Place-Names of the City of Norwich* ([Nottingham], 1989). English Place-Name Society [Publications], Vol. lxi
Fletcher 1901	Lionel L. Fletcher, '"Mallia Cadreene"', *NCirc* 9 (1900-1), col. 4677

Forrest 1924   *Shrewsbury Burgess Roll*, abstracted and edited by H. E. Forrest (Shrewsbury, 1924)

Fox-Davies 1907   Arthur Charles Fox-Davies, *Heraldic Badges* (London, 1907)

Fox-Davies 1915   Arthur Charles Fox-Davies, *The Book of Public Arms. . .*, new edn. (London, 1915)

Fox-Davies 1985   A. C. Fox-Davies, *A Complete Guide to Heraldry*; revised and annotated by J. P. Brooke-Little (London, 1985)

Frankel 1983   *Norfolk Hearth Tax Assessment, Michaelmas 1664*, transcribed by M. S. Frankel & P. J. Seaman. . . ([Norwich, 1983]). Norfolk Genealogy, Vol. xv

Frey 1947   Albert R. Frey, *Dictionary of Numismatic Names. . .* ([New York], 1947)

Gibson 1977   *Banbury Corporation Records: Tudor and Stuart*, calendared, abstracted and edited by J. S. W. Gibson and E. R. C. Brinkworth (Banbury, 1977)

Gilbert 1927   W. Gilbert, 'Unpublished seventeenth-century tokens in the collection of William Gilbert', *NC* 5th series 7 (1927), 121-55, 342-69, pls. vi-vii, xv

Gill 1879   Henry S. Gill, 'Seventeenth-century Somersetshire tokens not described in Boyne's work', *NC* new series 19 (1879), 99-107

Gill 1881   H. S. Gill, 'Addenda to Devonshire seventeenth-century tokens, not described in Boyne's work', *NC* 3rd series 1 (1881), 162-9, pl. vii

Gray 1915   H. St George Gray and Henry Symonds, 'Somerset trade tokens, XVII century: new types and varieties, and corrections of former lists', *Proceedings of the Somersetshire Archaeological & Natural History Society* 61 (1915), 115-27

Gretton 1920   R. H. Gretton, *The Burford Records* (Oxford, 1920)

Hearne 1889   *Remarks and Collections of Thomas Hearne*, Vol. III, ed. C. E. Doble (Oxford, 1889)

Hearne 1898   *Remarks and Collections of Thomas Hearne*, Vol. IV, ed. D. W. Rannie (Oxford, 1898)

Henning 1983   Basil Duke Henning, *The House of Commons 1660-1690*; published for the History of Parliament Trust (London, 1983). 3 vols.

Hird 1951   H. Hird, 'Northumberland seventeenth-century tokens', *Transactions of the Yorkshire Numismatic Society* 2nd series 1.1 (1951), 35-40, pl. iv

Hobson 1933   *Oxford Council Acts 1626-1665*, [transcribed] by M. G. Hobson and H. E. Salter (Oxford, 1933). Oxford Historical Society [Publications], Vol. xcv

Holme 1688   Randle Holme, *The Academy of Armory. . .* (Chester, 1688). Contains Book I, chapter 1 to Book III, chapter 13, only

Holme 1905   Randle Holme, *The Academy of Armory. . .*, Second volume . . ., ed. I. H. Jeayes (London, 1905). Contains Book III, chapter 14 to Book IV, chapter 13

Le Strange 1913   *An Address from the Gentry of Norfolk and Norwich to General Monck in 1660: facsimile of a manuscript in the Norwich Public Library*, with

	an introduction by Hamon Le Strange, and biographical notes by Walter Rye (Norwich, 1913)
Lee 1964	Ronald A. Lee, *The Knibb Family, Clockmakers...* (Byfleet, 1964)
Leeds	E. Thurlow Leeds, 'Oxford tradesmen's tokens', in Salter 1923 (q.v.), pp. 355-453, [10] pls.
Lewis 1845	Samuel Lewis, *A Topographical Dictionary of England...*, 5th edn. (London, 1845). 4 vols.
Lloyd 1979	David Lloyd, *Broad Street: its houses and residents through eight centuries* (Birmingham, 1979). Ludlow research papers, no. 3
Manville 1986	Harrington E. Manville, Terence J. Robertson, *British Numismatic Auction Catalogues, 1710-1984* ([London], 1986). Encyclopædia of British Numismatics, Vol. i
Manville 1993	Harrington E. Manville, *Numismatic Guide to British & Irish Periodicals, 1731—1991* ([London], 1993). Encyclopædia of British Numismatics, Vol. ii Part 1
McKinley 1977	Richard McKinley, *The Surnames of Oxfordshire* (London, 1977). English Surnames series, iii
Mellows 1937	*Peterborough Local Administration...*, ed. W. T. Mellows (Kettering, 1937). Northamptonshire Record Society Publications, Vol. x
Milne	Ashmolean Museum, *Catalogue of Oxfordshire Seventeenth-century Tokens*, ed. J. G. Milne (Oxford, 1935)
Milne 1945	J. G. Milne, 'Oxfordshire traders' tokens', *Oxoniensia* 10 (1945), 104-5
Milne 1946	J. G. Milne, 'Berkshire tradesmen's tokens of the seventeenth century', *Berkshire Archaeological Journal* 49 (1946), 17-22, plate
Monks forthcoming	Simon Monks and Robert Thompson, 'Hawkins of Masham, Marsham, and Aylsham', *S&B's Coin & Medal Bulletin* forthcoming
Morden 1695	Robert Morden, [County Maps]. In Camden 1695 (q.v.)
Neubecker 1974	Ottfried Neubecker, Wilhelm Rentzmann, *Wappen-Bilder-Lexikon = Dictionnaire héraldique = Encyclopaedia of heraldry* (München [=Munich], 1974)
Norfolk 1910	Norfolk and Norwich Archaeological Society, *A Calendar of the Freemen of Great Yarmouth 1429-1800*, compiled from the records of the Corporation... (Norwich, 1910)
Norfolk 1913	Norfolk and Norwich Archaeological Society, *A Calendar of the Freemen of Lynn 1292-1836*, compiled from the records of the Corporation... (Norwich, 1913)
Nottingham 1900	*Records of the Borough of Nottingham*, published under the authority of the Corporation of Nottingham, Vol. v (London etc., 1900)
Ogilby 1675	John Ogilby, *Britannia, volume the first, or, An illustration of the Kingdom of England and Dominion of Wales by a geographical and historical description of the principal roads thereof...* (London, 1675)
Owen 1984	*The Making of King's Lynn: a documentary survey*, ed. Dorothy M. Owen (London, 1984)

Pagan 1986   H. E. Pagan, 'Record of members and Fellows', in *A History of the
                    Royal Numismatic Society, 1836-1986*, by R. A. G. Carson...
                    (London, 1986), pp. 51-143

Papworth 1874   John W. Papworth, *An alphabetical Dictionary of Coats of Arms...
                    forming an extensive Ordinary of British Armorials...*, ed. ... Alfred
                    W. Morant (London, 1874)

Piggott 1951   Stuart Piggott, 'William Camden and the *Britannia*', *Proceedings of
                    the British Academy* 37 (1951), 199-217

Plomer 1907   Henry R. Plomer, *A Dictionary of the Booksellers and Printers who
                    were at work in England, Scotland and Ireland from 1641 to 1667*
                    (London, 1907)

Preston-Morley   Peter Preston-Morley & Harry Pegg, *A Revised Survey of the
                    Seventeenth-century Tokens of Nottinghamshire* ([London], 1983).
                    Reprinted from *BNJ* 51 (1981), 134-96, pls. xvi-xxiii

Priestley 1985   Ursula Priestley and Alayne Fenner, *Shops and Shopkeepers in
                    Norwich 1660-1730* (Norwich, 1985)

Rahtz 1991   Philip Rahtz, 'Pagan and Christian by the Severn Sea', in *The
                    Archaeology and History of Glastonbury Abbey*, ed. Lesley Abrams
                    and James P. Carley (Woodbridge, 1991), pp. 3-37

Reaney 1976   P. H. Reaney, *A Dictionary of British Surnames*, 2nd edn... by R. M.
                    Wilson (London, 1976)

Reaney 1991   P. H. Reaney, *A Dictionary of English Surnames*, 3rd edn... by R. M.
                    Wilson (London, 1991)

Rising 1959   *An Index of Indentures of Norwich Apprentices enrolled with the
                    Norwich Assembly, Henry VII—George II*, compiled by Winifred M.
                    Rising and Percy Millican ([Norwich], 1959). Norfolk Record Society
                    [Publications], Vol. xxix

Room 1983   Adrian Room, *A Concise Dictionary of Modern Place-Names in Great
                    Britain and Ireland* (Oxford, 1983)

Rutledge 1979   *A Calendar of Great Yarmouth enrolled Apprenticeship Indentures,
                    1563-1665*, by Paul Rutledge ([Norwich, 1979]). Norfolk Genealogy,
                    Vol. xi

Salter 1923   *Surveys and Tokens...*, ed. H. E. Salter (Oxford, 1923). Oxford
                    Historical Society [Publications], Vol. lxxv

Saxton 1576   Christophorus Saxton, 'Northamton, Bedfordiae, Cantabrigiae,
                    Huntingdoniae et Rutlandiae Comitatuum... descriptio', 1576. In
                    Christopher Saxton's 16th-century Maps...; with an introduction by
                    William Ravenhill (Shrewsbury, 1992), pp. 64-5

SCBI 24   *SCBI 24: Ancient British, Anglo-Saxon and Norman Coins in West
                    Country Museums*, by A. J. H. Gunstone (London, 1977)

SCBI 26   *SCBI 26: Museums in East Anglia...*, by T. H. McK. Clough (London,
                    1980)

SCBI 31   *SCBI 31: The Norweb Collection, Cleveland, Ohio, U.S.A.: Tokens of
                    the British Isles, 1575-1750. Part I: England: Bedfordshire to Devon*,
                    by R. H. Thompson (London, 1984)

SCBI 35	*SCBI 35: Scottish Coins in the Ashmolean Museum, Oxford, and the Hunterian Museum, Glasgow*, by J. D. Bateson and N. J. Mayhew (London, 1987)
SCBI 43	*SCBI 43: The Norweb Collection, Cleveland, Ohio, U.S.A.: Tokens of the British Isles, 1575-1750. Part III: Hampshire to Lincolnshire*, by R. H. Thompson and M. J. Dickinson (London, 1992)
Scott-Giles 1953	C. Wilfrid Scott-Giles, *Civic Heraldry of England & Wales*, revised and reset [edn.] (London, 1953)
Seaman 1988	*Norfolk and Norwich Hearth Tax Assessment, Lady Day 1666*, transcribed and indexed by P. Seaman ([Norwich, 1988]). Norfolk Genealogy, Vol. xx
Sharman 1984	Robert Sharman, 'More unpublished seventeenth-century tokens recovered from the Thames', *Bulletin—Token Corresponding Society* 4.1 (winter 1984), 22-3
Shaw 1906	Wm. A. Shaw, *The Knights of England. . .* (London, 1906). 2 vols.
Sheppard 1982	Francis Sheppard, *Robert Baker of Piccadilly Hall and his Heirs* (London, 1982). London Topographical Society Publication no. 127
Short 1972	J. L. Short, 'An Oxfordshire token reclaimed', *Bulletin—Token Corresponding Society*, 1.7 (October 1972), 147-8
Smith 1879	W. Smith, *The Particular Description of England, 1588. . .* ed. Henry B. Wheatley and Edmund W. Ashbee (London, 1879)
Snelling 1766	Thomas Snelling, *A View of the Copper Coin and Coinage of England . . .* (London, 1766)
Speed 1610	John Speed, 'Northamton shire', 1610. In *The Counties of Britain. . . by John Speed*; introduction by Nigel Nicolson. . . (London, 1988), pp. 134-5
Spelman 1678	Sir Henry Spelman, *Villare Anglicum, or, A view of all the cities, towns and villages in England, alphabetically composed. . .*, 2nd edn. (London, 1678)
Spink Sales	See Abbreviations, B
Sydenham 1905	S. Sydenham, *Bath Token Issues of the 17th century* (Bath, 1905). Reprinted from *Proceedings of the Bath Natural History and Antiquarian Field Club* 10.4 (1905), 423-525
Symonds 1911	Henry Symonds, 'Taunton tokens of the seventeenth century', *Proceedings of the Somersetshire Archaeological & Natural History Society* 57 (1911), part ii, 54-65
Thompson 1986	R. H. Thompson, 'Making before matching: the multiple use of pictorial punches on London-made tokens of the seventeenth century', in *Proceedings of the 10th International Congress of Numismatics, London, September 1986 . . .*, ed. I. A. Carradice with. . . [others] (London, 1986 [*i.e.* 1990]), pp. 575-81, pl. 57
Thompson 1992a	R. H. Thompson, 'An addition to the Derbyshire series of seventeenth-century tokens', *NCirc* 100 (1992), 228
Thompson 1993	R. H. Thompson, 'The Royal Exchange on seventeenth-century tokens', *NCirc* 101 (1993), 78-80

Tillett 1882   Edward A. Tillett, *The Tokens of Norfolk issued in the Seventeenth, Eighteenth and Nineteenth centuries...* (Norwich, 1882)

Trinder 1980   *Yeomen and Colliers in Telford: probate inventories for Dawley, Lilleshall, Wellington and Wrockwardine, 1660-1750*, ed. Barrie Trinder & Jeff Cox (Chichester, 1980)

VCH Northants. iii   *The Victoria History of the County of Northampton*, Vol. III, ed. William Page (London, 1930)

Vis. Oxon. 1566-1634   *The Visitation of the County of Oxford taken in the years 1566...1574 ...and in 1634...*, edited and annotated by William Henry Turner (London, 1871). The Publications of the Harleian Society, Vol. v

Vis. Rutland 1681-2   *The Visitation of the County of Rutland*, begun by Fran. Burghill and Gregory King in... 1681; carried on and finished by Tho. May and ...[Gregory King] in... 1682...; ed. W. Harry Rylands and W. Bruce Bannerman (London, 1922). The Publications of the Harleian Society, Vol. lxxiii

Vis. Som. 1672   *The Visitation of Somerset and the City of Bristol 1672*, made by Sir Edward Bysshe; transcribed and edited by G. D. Squibb (London, 1992). The Publications of the Harleian Society, new series Vol. 11

Watkins-Pitchford 1949 *The Shropshire Hearth-Tax Roll of 1672*, [transcribed by Miss L. Drucker]; with introduction by W. Watkins-Pitchford ([Shrewsbury], 1949)

Webster 1988   *Nottinghamshire Hearth Tax 1664 [and] 1674*, ed. W. F. Webster... (Nottingham, 1988). Thoroton Society, Record series Vol. xxxvii

Welford 1911   Richard Welford, 'Newcastle householders in 1665: assessment of hearth or chimney tax', *Archaeologia Æliana* 3rd series 7 (1911), 49-76

Wells   William C. Wells, *Seventeenth-century Tokens of Northamptonshire* (London, 1914). Reprinted from *BNJ* 6 (1909), 305-55, pl.; 7 (1910), 269-330, ii-iv pls.; 8 (1911), 303-60

Wells 1915   William C. Wells, *Seventeenth-century Tokens of Northamptonshire: addenda et corrigenda* (London, 1915). Reprinted from *BNJ* 10 (1913), 319-24

Wells 1924   William C. Wells, 'Northamptonshire seventeenth-century tokens', *NCirc* 32 (1924), cols. 411-12

Wells 1931/3   William C. Wells, 'The Hartwell token', *BNJ* 21 (1931-3), 103-10

West 1976   Vincent West, 'Berkshire seventeenth-century tokens', *NCirc* 84 (1976), 270-2

Wetton 1969   J. L. Wetton, *Seventeenth-century Tradesmen's Tokens* (Newcastle upon Tyne, 1969)

Whiting 1971   J. R. S. Whiting, *Trade Tokens: a social and economic history* (Newton Abbot, 1971)

Whittet 1986a   T. D. Whittet, 'A survey of apothecaries' tokens, including some previously unrecognised specimens', *Pharmaceutical Journal*.
                       Part 14: Norfolk to Rutland, 237 (1986), 111-13
                       Part 15: Shropshire to Suffolk, 237 (1986), 198-200

Whittet 1986b	T. D. Whittet, 'Somerset apothecaries' tokens and their issuers', *Somerset Archaeology and Natural History* 130 (1985/6), 127-33
Whittet 1987a	T. Douglas Whittet, 'Norfolk apothecaries' tokens and their issuers', *Norfolk Archaeology* 40 (1987), 100-09
Whittet 1987b	T. D. Whittet, 'A medical trade token of Oakham', *Rutland Record* 7 (1987), 249-51
Whitty 1934	R. G. Hedworth Whitty, *The Court of Taunton in the 16th and 17th Centuries* (Taunton, 1934)
Williamson	George C. Williamson, *Trade Tokens issued in the Seventeenth Century. . .; a new and revised edition of William Boyne's work* (London, 1889-91). 2 vols.
Withycombe 1977	E. G. Withycombe, *The Oxford Dictionary of English Christian Names*, 3rd edn. (Oxford, 1977)
Young 1913/14	Joseph Young, 'The token coinage of Leicestershire and Rutland in the XVII century', *Transactions of the Leicestershire Architectural and Archaeological Society*, 11.1&2 (1913-14), 115-34, pl.
Youngs 1979	Frederic A. Youngs, *Guide to the Local Administrative Units of England*, Vol. I: Southern England (London, 1979)
Youngs 1991	Frederic A. Youngs, *Guide to the Local Administrative Units of England*, Vol. II: Northern England (London, 1991)

CORRECTIONS TO PART III (*SCBI* 43)

Page xliii:	*To* Hird. . . 2622 *add* 2801a
2022:	*For* WHITCHVRC[H] *in text and heading read* WHITTCHVRC[H]
2033:	*To* BW 222 *add* BW 231 but MICHILL
2281:	Readings, including Y^E, all confirmed from a superior specimen now in Dacorum Museum
2309:	On Plate 22 obv. and rev. have been transposed
2415a:	*Add* Obv. legend starts at 6 o'clock
2789/2:	For reattribution to Grindlow, in Hope parish, Derbyshire, see Thompson 1992a

PLATES

MONMOUTHSHIRE *see* WALES including MONMOUTHSHIRE

NORFOLK

The county occurs as NORFOLK on 3023, 3040-1, 3047 (NOR|FOLK), 3061, 3091, 3104-5, 3233, 3260 (NOR:|FOLK), 3261-2 (NOR|FOLK), 3272; NORFOLKE on 3018, 3046, 3099-3100, 3236, 3265-8; NORFELKE on 3037-9; NOFOCKE on 3004-5; NORF on 3234-5; NORFOL^K on 3012, 3244; NORFOLK^E on 3266-7; NORFFOLK on 3075; NORFV on 3249. The hundred of Holt occurs as HOVLT HONDRED on 3017

ALDBOROUGH

	Weight		Die	
	g	gr	axis	

Briggs, John *see* ALDEBURGH (Suffolk)

ALDEBY

The reading is ABY IN NOFOCKE on both

| 3004 | 0.93 | 14.4 | Br | 180° | *Robats,* Philip (PHILLIP). nd. 3.39.3; R|PM. BW 2. Nott [?Baldwin ex Gilbert]. Attributed to Philip Roberts, of Gillingham St Mary near Aldeby, 1664 (Frankel 1983, p. 7) |
| 3005 | 1.46 | 22.5 | Br | 180° | *Robats,* Philip (PHILLIP). nd. 3.39.3; R|PM. BW 2. Nott [?Baldwin ex Gilbert] |

ASHBY ST MARY

Sherwood, Joseph *see* 2806 (Leics.: Ashby de la Zouch)

AYLSHAM

The reading is ALISHAM on 3009-10; AYLSHAM on 3006, 3008; *A-SHAM on 4191; ALYSHAM on 3007

3006a	1.59	24.5	Br	0°	*Empson,* Thomas, grocer. 1665. 5.14 Grocers; E	TA. BW 5 but GROCER. [?Nott]
3006b	1.27	19.6	Br	0°	Same dies. Baldwin [ex Gilbert]
3007	0.85	13.1	M	270°	*Flaxman,* Jeffrey (IAPHERY). 1664. 3.2.9; F	IA. BW 6 but ALYSHAM. Baldwin [ex Gilbert]
					Haukins, Michael *see* 4191 (Addendum)
3008	0.77	11.8	M	270°	*Thexton,* Lancelot (LANSALET), grocer. 1666. 5.77; 5.14 Grocers. BW 8. Baldwin [ex Gilbert]
3009	1.18	18.2	Br	30°	*Watts,* William. nd. 3.52.6; W	WM. BW 9. Baldwin [ex Gilbert]
3010	0.61	9.4	Br	0°	*Watts,* William. nd. 3.52.6; W	WM. BW 9*. Baldwin [ex Gilbert]

BAWDESWELL

The reading is BAVDSWELL

| 3011 | 0.84 | 12.9 | Br | 270° | *Bowrne,* Thomas. 1667. 3.54.10; B|TE. BW 11 but BOWRNE·IN. Baldwin [ex Gilbert] |

'BLAKY'

Wilson, James *see* 'BLAKY' (Uncertain I)

BRANCASTER

The reading is BRAN CASTELL NORFOL^K

| 3012 | 0.78 | 12.0 | Br | 90° | *Rix,* William. 1667. 5.14 Blacksmiths; R|WC. BW 12. Baldwin [ex Gilbert] |

BUCKENHAM, New

The reading is NEWBVCKENHAM on 3013; NEW BVCKENHAM on 3014

| 3013 | 0.82 | 12.7 | M | 180° | *Watts,* Francis. 1657. 5.14 Grocers; F W. BW 109. Baldwin [ex Gilbert] |
| 3014 | 0.87 | 13.5 | Cu | 270° | *Youngman,* Tho—, grocer. 1667. 5.14 Grocers; date|T Y. BW 110 but THO:, BVCKENHAM = I667|T · Y.Baldwin |

BURNHAM WESTGATE [*otherwise* BURNHAM MARKET]

The reading is BVRNHAM MARKET on both

3015a	1.03	15.9	Br	150°	*Tucke,* John. nd. 5.64.1; T	IM. BW 13. Baldwin. Obv. legend starts at 6 o'clock
3015b	0.97	15.0	Br	150°	Same dies. [?Nott]
3016a	1.24	19.2	M	180°	*Tucke,* Martin. nd. M T; 5.37.16. BW 14. Nott [?Baldwin ex Gilbert]
3016b	0.90	13.8	M	180°	Same dies. [?Nott]

[continued overleaf]

PLATE 1

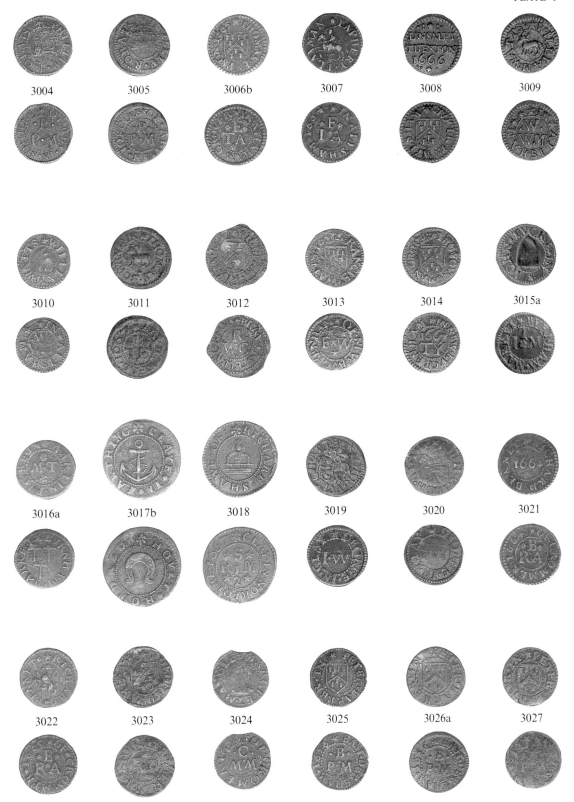

3004 3005 3006b 3007 3008 3009

3010 3011 3012 3013 3014 3015a

3016a 3017b 3018 3019 3020 3021

3022 3023 3024 3025 3026a 3027

Plate 1 (*cont.*)

CAISTER NEXT YARMOUTH / CAISTER ST EDMUND

	Weight		Die
	g	gr	axis

Hanson, William *see* 2924 (Lincs.: Caistor)
Lathorp, John *see* 2925 (Lincs.: Caistor)

CARLETON, East / CARLETON FOREHOE / CARLETON RODE / CARLETON ST PETER

Hancocke, John *see* 'CARLTON' (Uncertain I)

CLEY NEXT THE SEA (Holt hundred)

The reading is CLAY on 3018-20, with IN NORFOLKE on 3018; CLAYE IN HOVLT HONDRED on 3017

3017a	2.34	36.1	Br	270°	*Cley,* [Parish]. nd Cley (CLAYE) in Holt hundred (HOVLT HONDRED) ¼d. 5.38.20; 5.68.10. BW 19. [?Nott]. It might be better to transpose obv. and rev. and understand the legends as 'Holt hundred (Cley in) farthing', Cley being the issuing address for the Holt Hundred token
3017b	1.56	24.1	Br	270°	Same dies. Baldwin
3018	1.48	22.9	Cu	90°	*Shawe,* Richard. 1667 ½d. 3.3.13; S|RM|½. BW 20 but S|R½M. Baldwin [ex Gilbert]

Named signs

3019	1.14	17.5	Br	150°	*George* (AT THE): Wilch, John. nd. 3.2.8; I W. BW 21 but AT[no stop]THE. Nott [?Baldwin ex Gilbert]. Obv. legend starts at 2 o'clock. Same rev. die as 3020
3020	1.15	17.7	M	180°	*George* (AT THE): Wilch, John. nd. 3.2.8; I W. BW 21. Baldwin [ex Gilbert]. Same rev. die as 3019

CROMER

The reading is CROMER on 3023-4, with IN NORFOLK on 3023; CROMMER on 3021-2

					Beaney, Richard *see* Bennet, Richard
3021	1.29	19.8	Cu	0°	*Bennet,* Richard. 1664. Date (I664; ·RICHARD·BENNET around); B|RA (·B·|RA; ·OF·CROMMER·I664 around). BW —; Dickinson 24A. Baldwin
3022	1.03	15.9	M	90°	*Bennet,* Richard. 1665. 3.11; B|RA. BW 24. Baldwin [ex Gilbert]
3023	0.64	9.9	Br	0°	*Drake,* Robert. nd. 5.14.86; R D. BW 25 but AT· = Arms: a beast or monster rampant, rev. CROMER·IN·NORFOLK. Baldwin [ex Gilbert]
	(chipped)				
3024	0.65	10.0	Br	0°	*Mangles* (MANGLES), Margaret (MARGRET). 1666. 4.1.1; C|MM [*sic*]. BW 26 but MANGLES. Baldwin [ex Gilbert]

DEREHAM, East

The reading is EAST DEREHAM on 3025-7, 3033; EAST DEARHAM on 3028, 3031-2; EASTDEARHAM on 3029; EAST DEAREHAM on 3030; DEERHAM on 3034 and ?3035 (DEE. . .)

3025	0.72	11.1	Br	180°	*Barker,* Peter. 1656. 5.14 Grocers; B|PM. BW 31. Nott [?Baldwin ex Gilbert]. Same rev. die as 3026-7
3026a	1.03	15.8	Br	180°	*Barker,* Peter. 1656. 5.14 Grocers; B|PM. BW 31. [Baldwin ex Gilbert]. Same rev. die as 3025, 3027
3026b	0.88	13.5	Br	180°	Same dies. [?Nott]
	(pierced)				
3027	0.54	8.3	Br	90°	*Barker,* Peter. 1656. 5.14 Grocers; B|PM. BW 31. [?Nott]. Same rev. die as 3025-6

NORFOLK (*cont.*)

DEREHAM, East (*cont.*)

	Weight			Die	
	g	gr		axis	
3028	1.09	16.8	Br	0°	*Blyfer,* Tho—, draper. nd. 5.14 Drapers; B|TA. BW 32 but THO:. Baldwin [ex Gilbert]
3029	1.14	17.6	M	0°	*Boddy,* Henry (HENREY), grocer. nd. 5.14 Grocers; B|HS. BW 33 but EASTDEARHAM. Baldwin [ex Gilbert]
3030	1.42	21.9	M	180°	*Halcott,* John. nd. 5.41.1; H|IC. BW 34 but OF · EAST · DEAREHAM. Baldwin [ex Gilbert]. John Halcott, 'gent.', d. March 1678 (BW 34 n.)
3031	0.88	13.5	Br	180°	*Jessup,* Thomas, grocer (G–O). nd. 5.14 Grocers; T –. *BW 36 (GRO, T.I.). Baldwin [ex Gilbert]
3032	0.76	11.7	Br	180°	*Jessup,* Thomas. 1660. 5.14 Grocers; T I. BW 35. Baldwin [ex Gilbert]
	(chipped)				
3033	0.74	11.4	Br	180°	*Moore,* Thomas. nd. 5.84.7(· THOMAS · MOORE · OFaround); TM(T · M; · EAST · DEREHAM around). BW —; Dickinson 37A. Baldwin
3034	0.72	11.1	Br	0°	*Waller,* Frances. nd. 5.14 Grocers; 5.65.1. BW 38. Baldwin [ex Gilbert]. Same obv. die as 3035. The forename FRANCES may mean Francis, though the distinctive spellings for the male and female names came in during the 17th century (Withycombe 1977, p. 120)
3035	0.89	13.7	Br	90°	*Waller,* Frances. nd. 5.14 Grocers; 5.65.1. *BW 38 (DEERHAM). [?Nott]. Same obv. die as 3034 (q.v. for forename). Attribution to this Dereham as the only market town (Adams 1680)

DISS

The reading is DISS throughout, with IN NORFELKE on 3037-9

3036a	2.11	32.5	Cu	0°	*Diss,* [Parish]. 1669 Diss ¼d. 5.15.20; 5.77. BW 27 but obv. and rev. transposed. [Baldwin ex Gilbert]. Diameter 20.5 mm
3036b	2.01	30.9	Cu	0°	Same dies. [?Baldwin]. Diameter 21.5 mm
3036c	1.38	21.3	Cu	0°	Same dies. Brand. Diameter 20.5 mm
3036d	1.08	16.7	Cu	0°	Same dies. [?Nott]. Diameter 20.5 mm
3036e	0.97	15.0	Cu	0°	Same dies. [?Baldwin]. Diameter 20 mm
3037a	1.06	16.3	Br	180°	*Burton,* Thomas. nd. 5.14 Ironmongers; T B. BW 28. Nott [?Baldwin ex Gilbert]. Same rev. die as 3038
3037b	1.00	15.4	Br	180°	Same dies. [?Baldwin]
3038	1.09	16.8	Br	180°	*Burton,* Thomas. nd. 5.14 Ironmongers; T B. BW 28*. Baldwin [ex Gilbert]. Same rev. die as 3037
3039a	1.07	16.6	Br	180°	*Burton,* Thomas. nd. 5.14 Ironmongers; T B. BW 28*. [?Nott]
3039b	0.97	15.0	Br	180°	Same dies. [Baldwin ex Gilbert]

DOWNHAM MARKET

The reading is DOWNHAM MARKET IN NORFOLK on 3041, . . . MARKETT. . . on 3040

3040a	1.62	24.9	Br	270°	*Ray,* Will—. 1666. R|WA|date; 5.14 Mercers. BW 29 but WILL:. Nott [?Baldwin ex Gilbert]
3040b	1.08	16.6	Br	0°	Same dies. [?Nott]
	(chipped)				
3040c	0.78	12.1	Br	0°	Same dies. [?Nott]
	(pierced)				
3041a	1.34	20.7	Br	90°	*Trott,* Jo'n (IOᴺ). nd. 5.68.10; T|IE. BW 30. Baldwin [ex Gilbert]
3041b	1.01	15.5	Br	270°	Same dies. [?Nott]

EAST DEREHAM *see* DEREHAM, East

EAST HARLING *see* HARLING, East

EMNETH (Norfolk *and* Cambridgeshire, Isle of Ely, Elm parish)

The reading is EMNETH

3042a	1.18	18.2	Br	180°	*Whyting,* George (GEORG). 1660. 5.14 Grocers; G W. BW 40 but GEORG. Nott [?Baldwin ex Gilbert]
3042b	0.89	13.6	Br	180°	Same dies. [?Nott]

[*continued overleaf*]

PLATE 2

3028   3029   3030   3031   3032   3033

3034   3035   3036a   3037a   3038   3039a

3040a   3041a   3042a   3043c   3044   3045a

3046   3047   3048a   3049a   3050   3051

Plate 2 (*cont.*)

FAKENHAM

The reading is FAKENHAM on 3043-4; FACKENHAM on 3045

	Weight			Die	
	g	gr		axis	
3043a	1.33	20.5	Br	270°	*Peckoner* [i.e. *Peckover*], Edmond, grocer (GROCR). 1667. 5.14 Merchant Taylors; date. BW 42. [?Nott]. 'Edmund Peckeover gentillmane' 1655 (BW 42 n.)
3043b	1.31	20.2	Br	270°	Same dies. [?Nott]
3043c	1.08	16.6	Br	180°	Same dies. Nott [?Baldwin ex Gilbert]
3044	0.52	8.0	Br	0°	*Sheldrake,* Robert. 1667. 5.14 Apothecaries; R S. BW 43. Baldwin [ex Gilbert]. Robert Sheldrock of Fakenham, 'pharmacopola' *i.e.* apothecary, 1697/8 (Whittet 1987a, p. 104)
3045a	1.11	17.1	Br	0°	*Shildrack,* William. 1657. W S; date. BW 44. Nott [?Baldwin ex Gilbert]. 'William Sheldrake druggist' 1648, 'apothecary' 1662 (Whittet 1987a, p. 104)
3045b	0.84	13.0	Br	180°	Same dies. [?Nott]

FORDHAM

Badcock, John *see* 1783 (Cambs.)

FORNCETT ST PETER

The reading is FON|SET PETER IN NORFOLKE

| 3046 | 1.36 | 21.0 | Br | 270° | *Plowman,* Robert. 1668 ½d. 5.77; P|RM. BW 46 but SET · PETER. Baldwin [ex Gilbert]. Reading confirmed from a photograph of a specimen recorded at Seaby's |

FOULSHAM

The reading is FOVLSHAM on both, with IN NOR|FOLK on 3047

3047	1.24	19.1	Br	0°	*Atthill,* John, grocer. nd. 5.14.1 Grocers (A	IM); 5.77. BW 47 but GROCER = IN. Baldwin [ex Gilbert]
3048a	1.05	16.2	Br	0°	*Benn,* Edward, mercer. 1668. 5.14 Mercers; B	ER. BW 48. Baldwin [ex Gilbert]
3048b	1.04	16.1	Br	0°	Same dies. [?Nott]

GILLINGHAM ALL SAINTS / GILLINGHAM ST MARY

?C—, R— *see* 2571 (Kent: Gillingham)

HARLESTON (Redenhall with Harleston parish)

The reading is HARLSTON on 3049-51, 3059; HARLSTONE on the remainder

3049a	1.22	18.8	Br	0°	*Freeman,* Stephen. 1666. 5.14 Drapers; S F. BW 49. Nott [?Baldwin]. 'Stephen Freeman, gent.' 1684 (BW 49 n.)
3049b	0.80	12.4	M	0°	Same dies. [?Nott]
3050	1.30	20.1	Cu	180°	*Freeman,* Stephen (STEVEN). 1666. 5.14 Drapers; S F. BW 50. Baldwin. Same rev. die as 3051
3051	1.17	18.1	Cu	180°	*Freeman,* Stephen (STEVEN). 1666. 5.14 Drapers; S F. BW 50. [Baldwin ex Gilbert]. Same rev. die as 3050

HARLESTON (*cont.*)

	Weight			Die	
	g	*gr*		*axis*	
3052a	1.27	19.6	Br	180°	*Shewell,* Clare (CLEARE). 1656. 5.14 Grocers; C S. BW 52. [Baldwin ex Gilbert]. Same rev. die as 3053-4
3052b	1.09	16.8	Br	0°	Same dies. [Nott]
3053	1.41	21.7	Br	180°	*Shewell,* Clare (CLEARE). 1656. 5.14 Grocers; C S. BW 52. Nott [?Baldwin ex Gilbert]. Same rev. die as 3052, 3054
3054	1.19	18.3	Br	0°	*Shewell,* Clare (CLEARE). 1656. 5.14 Grocers; C S. BW 52. Coins & Antiquities 1977. Same obv. die as 3055; same rev. die as 3052-3
3055	1.12	17.3	Br	180°	*Shewell,* Clare (CLEARE). 1656. 5.14 Grocers; C S. BW 52. Baldwin [ex Gilbert]. Same obv. die as 3054; same rev. die as 3056
3056	1.40	21.5	Br	180°	*Shewell* (SHEWEL), Clare (CLEARE). 1656. 5.14 Grocers; C S. BW 51. Baldwin [ex Gilbert]. Same obv. die as 3057-9; same rev. die as 3055. Form of surname from 3052-5
3057a	1.44	22.2	Br	180°	*Shewell* (SHEWEL), Clare (CLEARE). 1656. 5.14 Grocers; C S. BW 51. [Baldwin ex Gilbert]. Same obv. die as 3056, 3058-9. Form of surname from 3052-5
3057b	1.04	16.1	Br	180°	Same dies. [Nott]
3057c	0.99	15.2	Br	180°	Same dies. [Nott]
3058	0.97	15.0	Br	180°	*Shewell* (SHEWEL), Clare (CLEARE). 1656. 5.14 Grocers; C S. BW 51. [Baldwin ex Gilbert]. Same obv. die as 3056-7, 3059. Form of surname from 3052-5
3059	1.18	18.2	Cu	270°	*Shewell* (SHEWEL), Clare (CLEARE). 1666. 5.14 Grocers; C S. BW 53. Baldwin [ex Gilbert]. Same obv. die as 3056-8. Form of surname from 3052-5

HARLING, East

The reading is EAST HARLING

| 3060 | 0.93 | 14.4 | M | 30° | *Hilton,* John. 1660. Date; 3.108.20. BW 39 but HILTON · AT. Baldwin [ex Gilbert] |

HILGAY

The reading is HELLGAY IN NORFOLK

| 3061 | 1.48 | 22.9 | Cu | 0° | *Dey,* John. 1664. 5.14 Grocers; I D. BW 54. Nott |

HINGHAM

The reading is HINGHAM

| 3062a | 1.08 | 16.7 | Br | 180° | *Rix,* William, grocer (GROSER). 1659. 5.14 Grocers; R|WA. BW 56. [?Nott] |
| 3062b | 0.99 | 15.3 | Br | 180° | Same dies. Nott [?Baldwin] |

HOLT

The reading is HOLT

| 3063 | 0.78 | 12.0 | Br | 90° | *Roll,* Daniel. 1666. 5.64.110; D R. BW 57. Baldwin [ex Gilbert] |

KING'S LYNN

The reading is LYN on 3064-70 (KINGS LYN), 3078-9 (LYN REGIS), 3081, 3088, 3091 (LYN REGIS NORFOLK); LINN on 3071, 3072-3 (LINN REGIS), 3080, 3084, 3087, 3089 (KINGS LINN), 3090, 3095, 3097; LYNN on 3074 (KINGS LYNN), 3076 (LYNN REGIS), 3082, 3083 and 3086 (LYNN REGES), 3093, 3094 and 3096 (LYNN REGIS), 3101; LIN on 3085 (LIN REGIS), 3092, 3099-3100 (LIN REGES IN NORFFOLKE); LYNNE REGIS on 3102-3; LINNE REGIS on 3077; KINGS LYNE on 3098. On 3075 the place is unnamed, reading only IN NORFFOLK. Note on 3064-70: The arms of King's Lynn are *Azure three dragons' heads erased and erect or in the mouth of each a cross crosslet fitchée also erect of the last (Fox-Davies 1915, p. 414)*

3064a	2.86	44.1	Cu	180°	*King's Lynn,* [Borough]. 1668 King's Lynn (LYN) ¼d. 5.14 King's Lynn; 5.77. BW 64 but i.m. a pierced cinquefoil, obv. and rev. transposed. Nott [?Baldwin ex Gilbert]. Same rev. die as 3065-6
3064b	1.90	29.3	Cu	180°	Same dies. [?Nott]
3065	1.56	24.0	Cu	180°	*King's Lynn,* [Borough]. 1668 King's Lynn (LYN) ¼d. 5.14 King's Lynn; 5.77. BW 64 but i.m. a pierced cinquefoil, obv. and rev. transposed. Baldwin [ex Gilbert]. Same rev. die as 3064, 3066
3066	1.69	26.1	Cu	180°	*King's Lynn,* [Borough]. 1668 King's Lynn (LYN) ¼d. 5.14 King's Lynn; 5.77. BW 64 but i.m. a pierced cinquefoil, obv. and rev. transposed. [?Nott]. Same rev. die as 3064-5

[*continued overleaf*]

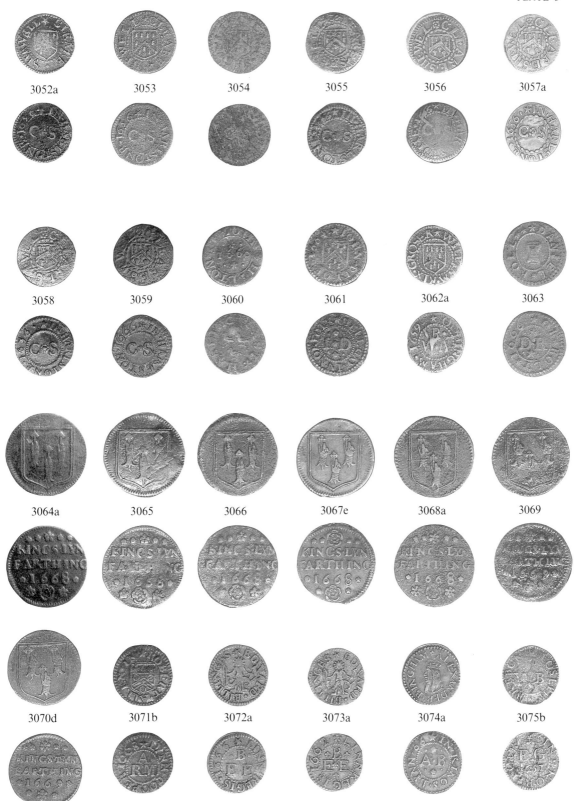

PLATE 3

3052a 3053 3054 3055 3056 3057a

3058 3059 3060 3061 3062a 3063

3064a 3065 3066 3067e 3068a 3069

3070d 3071b 3072a 3073a 3074a 3075b

Plate 3 (*cont.*)

	Weight			Die	
	g	gr		axis	
3067a	3.30	51.0	Cu	0°	*King's Lynn,* [Borough]. 1668 King's Lynn (LYN) ¼d. 5.14 King's Lynn; 5.77. BW 63 but obv. and rev. transposed. [?Baldwin]
3067b	3.11	48.0	Cu	0°	Same dies. [?Baldwin]
3067c	3.06	47.2	Cu	0°	Same dies. [?Baldwin]
3067d	2.21	34.1	Cu	0°	Same dies. [?Baldwin]
3067e	2.16	33.4	Cu	0°	Same dies. Brand [or Baldwin ex Gilbert]
3067f	2.15	33.2	Cu	0°	Same dies. [?Nott]
3067g	1.40	21.6	Cu	0°	Same dies. [?Baldwin]
3068a	2.89	44.6	Cu	180°	*King's Lynn,* [Borough]. 1668 King's Lynn (LYN) ¼d. 5.14 King's Lynn; 5.77. BW 63-4 but i.m. a pierced sexfoil, obv. and rev. transposed. Nott [?Baldwin ex Gilbert]
3068b	1.58	24.4	Cu	180°	Same dies. Baldwin
3069	2.01	31.0	Cu	0°	*King's Lynn,* [Borough]. 1669 King's Lynn (LYN) ¼d. 5.14 King's Lynn; 5.77. BW 65 but obv. and rev. transposed. [?Baldwin]. Same rev. die as 3070
3070a	2.82	43.5	Cu	0°	*King's Lynn,* [Borough]. 1669 King's Lynn (LYN) ¼d. 5.14 King's Lynn; 5.77. BW 65 but obv. and rev. transposed. [?Baldwin]. Same rev. die as 3069
3070b	2.62	40.4	Cu	180°	Same dies. [?Nott]
3070c	2.45	37.8	Cu	0°	Same dies. [?Baldwin]
3070d	2.30	35.5	Cu	0°	Same dies. [?Baldwin]
3070e	1.92	29.7	Cu	0°	Same dies. [Baldwin ex Gilbert]
3070f	1.82	28.1	Cu	0°	Same dies. [?Brand]
3071a	0.92	14.2	Br	0°	*Allen,* Robert, cooper. 1668. 5.14 Coopers; A|RM. BW 66 but LYNN. [?Nott]
3071b	0.64	9.8	Br	90°	Same dies. Nott [?Baldwin ex Gilbert]
3072a	1.08	16.7	Br	180°	*Billinges,* Edward. 1656. 3.10.12; B|EE. BW 67. [?Nott]. Same obv. die as 3073. Edward 'Biddings', apot., 1654/5; Edward Billings, gent., 1678/9 (Whittet 1987a, p. 103)
3072b	0.71	11.0	Br	0°	Same dies. Nott [?Baldwin ex Gilbert]
3073a	0.85	13.1	Br	180°	*Billinges,* Edward. 1662. 3.10.12; B|EE. BW 68. Nott [?Baldwin ex Gilbert]. Same obv. die as 3072
3073b	0.75	11.6	Br	0°	Same dies. [?Nott]
3074a	1.22	18.8	Br	180°	*Bingham,* Alexander. [16]66. 3.5.105; A B. BW 69. Nott [?Baldwin ex Gilbert]. Alexander Bingham, vintner, 1667-8 (Norfolk 1913, p. 175)
3074b	1.10	17.0	Br	180°	Same dies. [?Nott]
3074c	0.97	15.0	M	180°	Same dies. [Baldwin]
3075a	1.04	16.1	Br	180°	*Braban* (BREBON), Joseph. 1657. W B [*sic*]; E G|date. BW 71. [?Nott]. Attribution and form of surname from 3076
3075b	0.81	12.5	Br	180°	Same dies. Nott [?Baldwin]

	Weight		Die	
	g	*gr*		*axis*
3076a	0.85	13.1	M	0°	*Braban,* Joseph, hosier (HOSYER). 1666. 3.7.2; B|IM. BW 70 but obv. device a leg. [?Nott]. Diameter 14.5-15.5 mm
3076b	0.80	12.3	M	180°	Same dies. Baldwin [ex Gilbert]. Diameter 16.5 mm
3076c	0.61	9.5	Br	0°	Same dies. [?Baldwin]. Diameter 16.5 mm
3077a	1.05	16.2	Br	180°	*Bridgman,* Giles. 1650. B|GS; B|GS. BW 73. [?Nott]. Giles Bridgman, merchant, 1646-7 (Norfolk 1913, p. 160)
3077b	1.00	15.5	Br	180°	Same dies. Baldwin [ex Gilbert]
3078a	1.24	19.1	Cu	270°	*Bridgman,* Giles (GYLES). nd. 5.14.87; B|GS. BW 72. Baldwin [ex Gilbert]. Placed after 3077 for stylistic reasons. Same rev. die as 3079
3078b	0.81	12.5	M	270°	Same dies. [?Nott]
3079a	0.84	13.0	M	180°	*Bridgman,* Giles (GYLES). nd. 5.14.87; B|GS. BW 72. Baldwin [ex Gilbert]. Same rev. die as 3078
3079b	0.79	12.2	M	180°	Same dies. [?Nott]
3080	1.17	18.0	Br	180°	*Brown,* Hilary (HILEARD). 1654. 5.14 Grocers; B|HK. BW 74 but BROWN. Baldwin [ex Gilbert]. Hillery Browne, grocer, 1659-60 (Norfolk 1913, p. 169)
3081	1.06	16.4	M	180°	*Browne,* John, grocer. nd. 5.14 Grocers; I B. BW 75 but BROWNE. Baldwin [ex Gilbert]
3082	0.77	11.8	M	0°	*Denman,* Thomas. 1665. 5.14 Tallow Chandlers; D|TI. BW 80. Baldwin [ex Gilbert]
3083a	1.07	16.5	Cu	0°	*Fraunces,* Robert. nd. 5.14 Apothecaries; R F. BW 81 but REGES. [?Nott]. Issuer either Robert Frauncis, free as an apothecary, 1633/4, or Robert Frauncis, apoth., free 1657/8 (Whittet 1987a, pp. 103-4). Rev. legend starts at 6 o'clock
3083b	1.02	15.8	Cu	0°	Same dies. Baldwin [ex Gilbert]. Overstruck on another token
3084a	1.28	19.8	Br	0°	*Garrard,* Seth, grocer. 1652. 5.14 Grocers; G|SM. BW 82. Nott [?Baldwin ex Gilbert]
3084b	0.87	13.4	Br	180°	Same dies. [?Nott]
3084c	0.69	10.6	Br	–	Same dies. Baldwin [ex Gilbert]. Rev. brockage
3085a	0.96	14.9	Cu	180°	*Harwick,* Thomas, mercer. nd. 5.14 Mercers; 5.76.67 (T H ?E). BW 84. [?Nott]
3085b	0.60	9.3	Cu	30°	Same dies. Baldwin [ex Gilbert]
3086a	1.01	15.6	M	90°	*Hatfeild,* Will. 1666. 5.14 Tallow Chandlers; H|WA. BW 85 but HATFEILD. Nott [?Baldwin]. William Hatfield, grocer, 1667-8, 1677-8; tallow-chandler, 1682-3 (Norfolk 1913, pp. 176, 188, 193)
3086b	0.62	9.6	M	90°	Same dies. [?Nott]
3087a	2.97	45.8	Cu	270°	*Houell* or *Hovell,* Jeremiah. 1666 ½d. 3.1.46; 5.77. BW 86. [?Baldwin]. Jeremiah 'Hovell' (BW 86 n.); Jeremiah (-my) 'Howell', brasier 1655-6, brassier 1674-5 (Norfolk 1913, pp. 166, 185)
3087b	2.01	31.0	Cu	180°	Same dies. Baldwin [ex Gilbert]
3088	1.10	17.0	Br	180°	*Howard,* John. 1660. 3.6.37; H|ID. BW 87 but LYN. Baldwin [ex Gilbert]
3089a	0.99	15.3	Cu	180°	*Howlett,* Rebekah (REBECKAH). nd. 3.107.2; R H. BW 88. Baldwin [ex Gilbert]
3089b	0.58	0.9	Cu	180°	Same dies. [?Nott]
3090	0.98	15.2	Br	180°	*Leak,* Robert, wool-comber (WOLLCOMER). nd. 4.12.1; L|RM. BW 89 but IN = Rose, rev. LINN · WOLLCOMER. Baldwin [ex Gilbert]
	(chipped)				
3091	0.86	13.3	M	270°	*Midletun,* Brian (BRYAN). nd. 5.14 Merchant Taylors; M|BM. BW 90. Baldwin [ex Gilbert]. Brian Middleton, taylor, 1666-7 (Norfolk 1913, p. 174)
3092a	1.57	24.3	Cu	90°	*Preston,* William, upholsterer (VPHOLSTER). nd. 5.14 'Upholsterers'; P|WB. BW 91. Nott [?Baldwin ex Gilbert]. Struck from clashed dies
3092b	1.44	22.2	Cu	90°	Same (clashed) dies. [?Nott]
3093	0.62	9.5	Cu	270°	*Quash,* Edmond. 1667. 5.38.1; 5.76.68. BW 92 but Q enclosing a letter I. Baldwin [ex Gilbert]. Edmund Quash, mariner, 1667-8 (Norfolk 1913, p. 176)
3094a	1.09	16.8	Br	90°	*Ringstead,* John, chandler. 1658. 3.3.13; R|IF. BW 95. [?Nott]
3094b	0.99	15.2	Br	90°	Same dies. Baldwin [ex Gilbert]
3095	1.12	17.3	Br	180° ·	*Roberts* (ROBERTS), Richard. 1660. Date; R|RG. BW 96 but R.G.R. Baldwin [ex Gilbert]
3096a	2.15	33.1	Cu	270°	*Sharpe,* William. 1668 ½d. 5.14 Bakers; 5.77. BW 99. [?Nott]. William Sharpe, apprentice baker, 1660-1 (Norfolk 1913, p. 170)
3096b	1.81	27.9	Cu	270°	Same dies. Nott [?Baldwin ex Gilbert]
3097	0.57	8.8	Br	0°	*Thetford,* Robert, grocer. [16]67. 5.14 Grocers; T|RM. BW 100. Nott [?Baldwin ex Gilbert]
3098	0.92	14.2	Br	0°	*Tilson,* Edward. 1668. 5.14 Bakers; date. BW 101. Baldwin [ex Gilbert]. Edward Tilson, baker, 1664-5 (Norfolk 1913, p. 173)
3099a	1.16	17.9	Br	180°	*?W—,* N—. nd. 5.14 Grocers; W|NR. BW 102-102*. Baldwin [ex Gilbert]. Same rev. die as 3100
3099b	1.16	17.8	Br	180°	Same dies. [?Nott]

PLATE 4

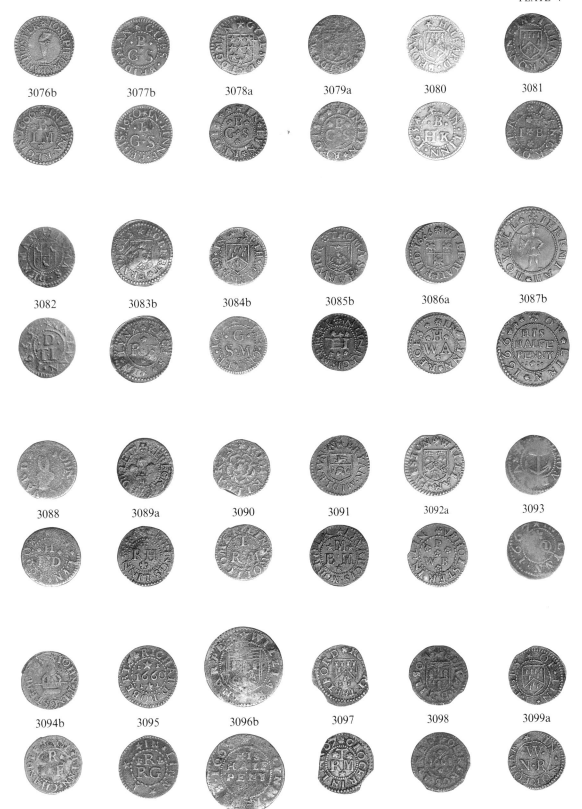

3076b   3077b   3078a   3079a   3080   3081

3082   3083b   3084b   3085b   3086a   3087b

3088   3089a   3090   3091   3092a   3093

3094b   3095   3096b   3097   3098   3099a

NORFOLK (*cont.*)

KING'S LYNN (*cont.*)

	Weight		Die	
	g	*gr*	*axis*	
3100	1.17	18.1	Br 180°	*?W—, N—*. nd. 5.14 Grocers; W|NR. BW 102-102*. Baldwin [ex Gilbert]. Same rev. die as 3099
3101a	1.17	18.1	Br 180°	*Wolterton,* Richard. 1656. 5.83.43; R W. BW 103. [?Nott]
3101b	1.03	15.9	Br 180°	Same dies. Nott [?Baldwin]
3101c	0.90	14.0	Br 180°	Same dies. [?Nott]

KING'S LYNN. Lathe Street

The reading is LATH STREETE IN LYNNE REGIS on both, cf. *Lathstrete* 1506 (Owen 1984, p. 201)

3102	0.87	13.4	Br 180°	*?D—, E—*. 1660. Date; E D. BW 79. [Baldwin ex Gilbert]. Same obv. die as 3103
3103a	0.80	12.3	Br 90°	*?D—, E—*. 1660. Date; E D. BW 79. Brand [or Baldwin ex Gilbert]. Same obv. die as 3102
3103b	0.73	11.2	Br 90°	Same dies. [?Baldwin]
	(pierced)			

LODDON

The reading is LODDON IN NORFOLK on both

3104	0.84	12.9	M 180°	*Burrough,* Henry. 1667. 5.14 Grocers; H B. BW 61. Baldwin [ex Gilbert]. Same rev. die as 3105
3105	1.14	17.7	M 270°	*Burrough,* Henry. 1667. 5.14 Grocers; H B. BW 61. [Baldwin ex Gilbert]. Same rev. die as 3104

LYNN REGIS *see* KING'S LYNN

MARSHAM

Hawk, Michael *see* 4191 (Addendum)

MASSINGHAM, Great

The reading is MASSINGGAM

3106	1.10	16.9	Br 270°	*Childerhouse,* Tho—. 1657. Date; T C. BW 105 but THO:. Baldwin [ex Gilbert]. Attribution to
	(pierced)			this Massingham from the presence of 'Tho Childershowse' 1664 (Frankel 1983, p. 29)

MENDHAM (Norfolk *and* Suffolk) *see* Suffolk

MILEHAM

The reading is MILEHAM

3107a	1.15	17.7	Br 0°	*Ladly,* Francis. 1666. 5.76.69 (F L); L|FC. BW 107. [?Nott]
	(pierced)			
3107b	0.85	13.1	Br 0°	Same dies, after clashing. Nott [?Baldwin ex Gilbert]. Later tinned or silvered

NEW BUCKENHAM *see* BUCKENHAM, New

NORWICH

The reading is NOR|WICH on 3191, 3202; NORWITCH on 3132, 3195, cf. *Norwitch* 1599 (EPNS 1989, p. 1); NORWICH on the remainder. Note on 3108-26: The arms of the City of Norwich are *Gules a silver castle and below it a gold lion passant guardant* (Scott-Giles 1953, p. 290)

3108a	3.55	54.8	M 180°	*Norwich,* [City]. 1667 Norwich ¼d. 5.14 Norwich; 5.77. BW 225 but obv. and rev. transposed.
				Seaby 1961. Same obv. die as 3109-10
3108b	2.67	41.2	M 180°	Same dies. [?Baldwin]
3109a	3.67	56.7	M 180°	*Norwich,* [City]. 1667 Norwich ¼d. 5.14 Norwich; 5.77. BW 225 but obv. and rev. transposed.
				[?Baldwin]. Same obv. die as 3108, 3110
3109b	3.61	55.7	M 180°	Same dies. [?Baldwin]
3109c	3.14	48.5	M 180°	Same dies. [?Baldwin]
3109d	2.78	42.9	M 180°	Same dies. [?Baldwin]
3110a	3.55	54.8	M 180°	*Norwich,* [City]. 1667 Norwich ¼d. 5.14 Norwich; 5.77. BW 225 but obv. and rev. transposed.
				[?Baldwin]. Same obv. die as 3108-9; same rev. die as 3111-12
3110b	3.53	54.5	M 180°	Same dies. [?Baldwin]
3110c	2.95	45.5	M 180°	Same dies. [Baldwin ex Gilbert]

[*continued overleaf*]

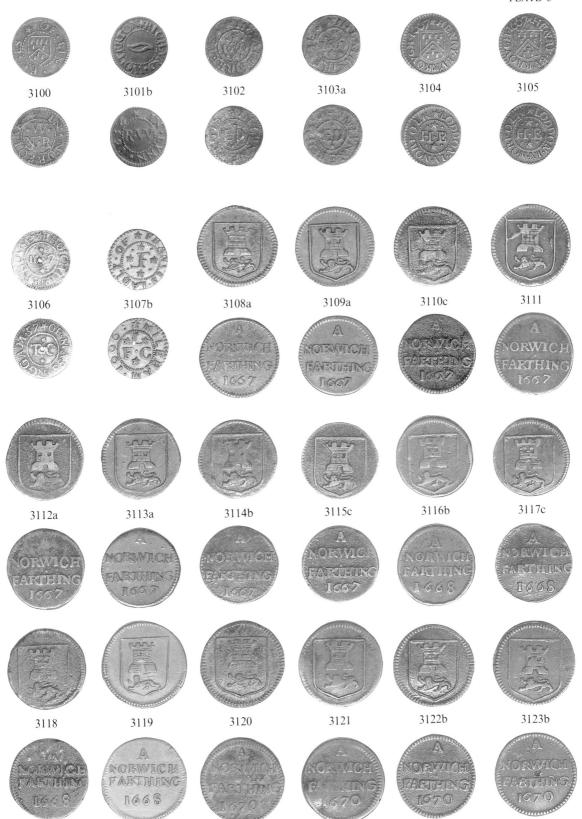

PLATE 5

3100 3101b 3102 3103a 3104 3105

3106 3107b 3108a 3109a 3110c 3111

3112a 3113a 3114b 3115c 3116b 3117c

3118 3119 3120 3121 3122b 3123b

Plate 5 (*cont.*)

	Weight			Die	
	g	gr		axis	
3111	3.92	60.6	M	180°	*Norwich*, [City]. 1667 Norwich ¼d. 5.14 Norwich; 5.77. BW 225 but obv. and rev. transposed. [Baldwin ex Gilbert]. Same rev. die as 3110, 3112
3112a	3.78	58.4	M	180°	*Norwich*, [City]. 1667 Norwich ¼d. 5.14 Norwich; 5.77. BW 225 but obv. and rev. transposed. [?Nott]. Same obv. die as 3113-14; same rev. die as 3110-11
3112b	3.68	56.8	M	180°	Same dies. [?Baldwin]
3113a	4.26	65.8	M	180°	*Norwich*, [City]. 1667 Norwich ¼d. 5.14 Norwich; 5.77. BW 225 but obv. and rev. transposed. Brand [or Baldwin ex Gilbert]. Same obv. die as 3112, 3114
3113b	4.07	62.8	M	180°	Same dies. [?Nott]
3113c	3.73	57.5	M	180°	Same dies. [?Baldwin]
3113d	3.52	54.3	M	180°	Same dies. Nott
3114a	4.09	63.1	M	180°	*Norwich*, [City]. 1667 Norwich ¼d. 5.14 Norwich; 5.77. BW 225 but obv. and rev. transposed. [?Baldwin]. Same obv. die as 3112-13
3114b	3.74	57.7	M	180°	Same dies. [?Baldwin]
3114c	3.48	53.6	M	180°	Same dies. [?Baldwin]
3114d	3.28	50.6	M	180°	Same dies. [?Baldwin]
3115a	4.10	63.3	M	180°	*Norwich*, [City]. 1667 Norwich ¼d. 5.14 Norwich; 5.77. BW 225 but obv. and rev. transposed. [?Baldwin]
3115b	3.42	52.8	M	180°	Same dies. [Baldwin ex Gilbert]
3115c	3.19	49.3	M	180°	Same dies. [?Baldwin]
3116a	6.46	99.7	Cu	0°	*Norwich*, [City]. 1668 Norwich ¼d. 5.14 Norwich; 5.77. BW 226 but obv. and rev. transposed. [?Baldwin]. Same obv. die as 3117-18
3116b	5.42	83.6	Cu	0°	Same dies. [Baldwin ex Gilbert]
3116c	3.61	55.7	Cu	0°	Same dies. [?Baldwin]
3116d	3.31	51.0	Cu	0°	Same dies. [?Baldwin]
3116e	3.17	49.0	Cu	0°	Same dies. Nott
3116f	2.74	42.3	Cu	0°	Same dies. [Baldwin]
3117a	4.07	62.8	Cu	0°	*Norwich*, [City]. 1668 Norwich ¼d. 5.14 Norwich; 5.77. BW 226-7 but obv. and rev. transposed. [?Baldwin]. Same obv. die as 3116, 3118
3117b	3.59	55.3	Cu	0°	Same dies. [?Baldwin]
3117c	3.27	50.5	Cu	0°	Same dies. [Baldwin ex Gilbert]
3118	4.44	68.5	Cu	0°	*Norwich*, [City]. 1668 Norwich ¼d. 5.14 Norwich; 5.77. BW 227 but obv. and rev. transposed. [?Baldwin]. Same obv. die as 3116-17; same rev. die as 3119
3119	4.38	67.6	Cu	0°	*Norwich*, [City]. 1668 Norwich ¼d. 5.14 Norwich; 5.77. BW 227 but obv. and rev. transposed. Nott [?Baldwin ex Gilbert]. Same rev. die as 3118
3120	3.77	58.1	Cu	180°	*Norwich*, [City]. 1670 Norwich ¼d. 5.14 Norwich; 5.77. BW 228 but obv. and rev. transposed. Stevens -1965. Same obv. die as 3121
3121	4.79	73.9	Cu	180°	*Norwich*, [City]. 1670 Norwich ¼d. 5.14 Norwich; 5.77. BW 228 but obv. and rev. transposed. [Baldwin ex Gilbert]. Same obv. die as 3120
3122a	3.80	58.6	Cu	90°	*Norwich*, [City]. 1670 Norwich ¼d. 5.14 Norwich; 5.77. BW 228 but obv. and rev. transposed. [Baldwin ex Gilbert]. Same rev. die as 3123
3122b	2.95	45.6	Cu	90°	Same dies. Stevens -1965
3123a	5.66	87.4	Cu	0°	*Norwich*, [City]. 1670 Norwich ¼d. 5.14 Norwich; 5.77. BW 228 but obv. and rev. transposed. [?Baldwin]. Same obv. die as 3124-5; same rev. die as 3122
3123b	4.00	61.8	Cu	0°	Same dies. [Baldwin]

	Weight			Die	
	g	gr		axis	
3124a	4.44	68.5	Cu	0°	*Norwich,* [City]. 1670 Norwich ¼d. 5.14 Norwich; 5.77. BW 228 but obv. and rev. transposed. [?Baldwin]. Same obv. die as 3123, 3125
3124b	3.93	60.6	Cu	0°	Same dies. [Baldwin ex Gilbert]
3125	2.36	36.5	Cu	0°	*Norwich,* [City]. 1670 Norwich ¼d. 5.14 Norwich; 5.77. BW 228 but obv. and rev. transposed. [?Baldwin]. Same obv. die as 3123-4; same rev. die as 3126
3126a	4.08	63.0	Cu	0°	*Norwich,* [City]. 1670 Norwich ¼d. 5.14 Norwich; 5.77. BW 228 but obv. and rev. transposed. [Baldwin ex Gilbert]. Same rev. die as 3125
3126b	3.26	50.2	Cu	0°	Same dies. [?Baldwin]
3126c	2.68	41.4	Cu	0°	Same dies. [?Baldwin]
3126d	2.30	35.5	Cu	0°	Same dies. [?Baldwin]
3127a	1.26	19.5	Br	0°	*Arbree* (AVBREE), James. 1667. Date; A|IM. BW 115. [?Nott]. Same rev. die as 3128, whence form of surname; 'Jacobus Arborey dyer' 1647, 'James Arbree' 1662 (Tillett 1882, p. 15)
3127b	1.07	16.6	Br	0°	Same dies. [Baldwin ex Gilbert]
3128	1.08	16.7	Cu	270°	*Arbree,* James. 1667. Date (I·6|6·7; ·IAMES·ARBREE· around); A|IM (·A·I M·; ·IN·NORWICH ❖ around). BW —, cf. 115. Baldwin [ex Gilbert]. Same rev. die as 3127
3129a	1.35	20.8	Br	0°	*Atwood,* John. nd. A|IK; A|IK. BW 112-14. [Baldwin]. Issuer a haberdasher (Tillett 1882, p. 15)
3129b	1.07	16.5	Br	270°	Same dies. Nott
3129c	1.01	15.5	Br	180°	Same dies. [Nott]
3129d	0.83	12.7	Br	0°	Same dies. Baldwin [ex Gilbert]. Restruck after turning over
3130a	0.67	10.3	Br	0°	*Baker,* Michael (MICHAELL). 1667. Date; B|MA. BW 116. [?Nott]. 'Michaell Baker taylor' 1645 (Tillett 1882, p. 16)
3130b	0.40 (chipped)	6.1	Br	0°	Same dies. Baldwin [ex Gilbert]
3131a	1.29	20.0	Cu	0°	*Benton,* Violet (m.). 1664. 5.66.10; B|VR. BW 118 but V.R.B. [?Nott]. 'Violett Benton cordyn'' i.e. cordwainer, 1633 (Tillett 1882, p. 16)
3131b	1.11	17.1	Cu	0°	Same dies. Nott [?Baldwin ex Gilbert]
3132a	1.35	20.8	Br	0°	*Bilham,* Nicholas. nd. 5.14 Grocers; N B. BW 119 but NORWITCH. Baldwin [ex Gilbert]. Nicholas Bilham, grocer, free 1660, buried 1662 (Tillett 1882, p. 16)
3132b	0.84	13.0	Br	0°	Same dies. [?Baldwin]
3133	0.88	13.6	Br	180°	*Bland,* John. nd. 3.7.6 (R); B|IM. BW 120-1. Baldwin [ex Gilbert]. Cf. 'Joh'es Blankes' woollen draper, 1648 (Tillett 1882, p. 16)
3134a	0.80	12.4	Cu	180°	*Blofeld,* Peter (PEETER). nd. 5.14 Grocers; P B. BW 122. [?Nott]
3134b	0.80	12.3	Cu	180°	Same dies. Baldwin [ex Gilbert]
3135a	1.12	17.3	M	180°	*Bridgs* [i.e. *Briggs*], Augustine, grocer. nd. 3.101.1; A B. BW 123-4. Baldwin [ex Gilbert]
3135b	0.90	13.9	M	180°	Same dies. Nott
3136a	1.09	16.8	Cu	270°	*Brockden,* James. 1664. 5.7.20; B|IR. BW 125. [?Nott]. James Brockden, spurryer, free 1636 (Tillett 1882, p. 17)
3136b	1.09	16.8	Cu	180°	Same dies. Baldwin [ex Gilbert]
3137a	1.42	22.0	Cu	0°	*Brown,* Robert. nd. 5.14 Merchant Taylors; B|RA. BW 126. [?Nott]
3137b	1.08	16.7	Br	270°	Same dies. Baldwin
3138	0.84	13.0	Cu	180°	*Browne,* John. 1657. 3.103.1; B|IS. BW 127 but obv. device corrected. Baldwin [ex Gilbert]
3139a	1.33	20.6	M	180°	*Buxton,* Edward. 1653. 5.14 Grocers; B|EA. BW 128. Baldwin [ex Gilbert]. 'Edwardus Buxton grocer' 1648 (Tillett 1882, p. 17)
3139b	1.18	18.1	M	180°	Same dies. [?Baldwin]
3139c	0.89	13.7	M	180°	Same dies. [?Baldwin]
3140	1.22	18.8	Br	180°	*Camond* (C-MOND), Edmund, grocer (GROC–R). nd. 5.14 Grocers; E C. BW 129. Baldwin [ex Gilbert]
3141	0.76	11.7	Br	180°	*Castle,* James. 1662. Date; C|II. BW 131. Baldwin [ex Gilbert]
3142a	0.96	14.8	Cu	90°	*Castle* (CASTILL), James. 1664. 5.57.33; C|II. BW 130. Baldwin [ex Gilbert]. Form of surname from 3141
3142b	0.77 (chipped)	11.9	Cu	180°	Same dies. [?Baldwin]
3143a	1.08	16.7	Cu	0°	*Clayton,* Robert, ironmonger. 1663. 5.14 Ironmongers; date. BW 132. Baldwin [ex Gilbert]
3143b	1.02	15.8	Cu	180°	Same dies. [?Nott]
3144	0.96	14.7	Br	180°	*Cooper,* William. 1662. 3.5.105; 4.12.1. BW 133. Baldwin [ex Gilbert]. Same obv. die as 3245 (Swanton Abbott)
3145	0.61	9.5	Cu	90°	*Cowper,* Isaac, bricklayer (BRICK|LAYER). nd. 5.34.20; C|IE. BW 134. Baldwin [ex Gilbert]

[*continued overleaf*]

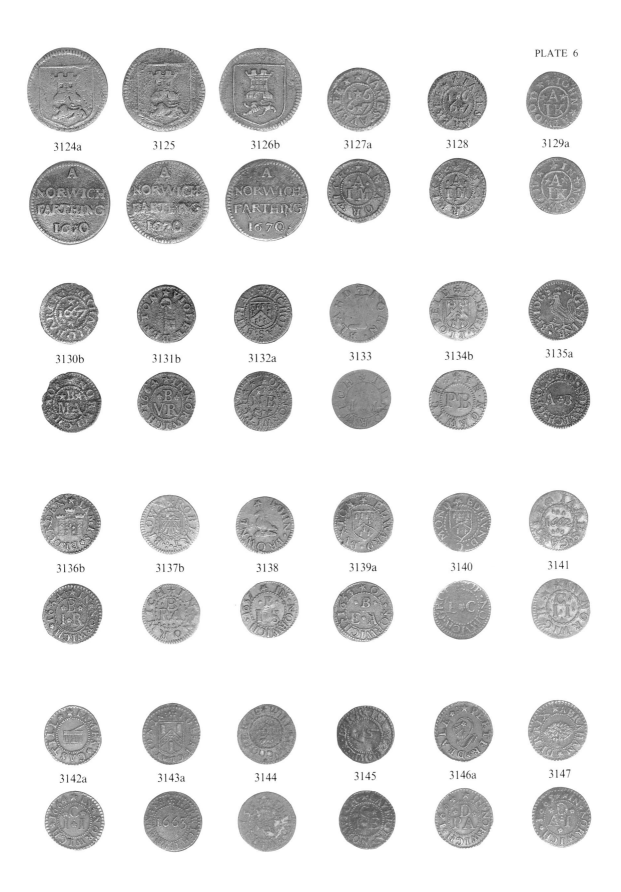

PLATE 6

3124a   3125   3126b   3127a   3128   3129a

3130b   3131b   3132a   3133   3134b   3135a

3136b   3137b   3138   3139a   3140   3141

3142a   3143a   3144   3145   3146a   3147

Plate 6 (*cont.*)

	Weight			Die	
	g	*gr*		*axis*	
3146a	0.96	14.9	Cu	270°	*Deale,* Peter (PEETER). 1664. 5.16.1; D|PA. BW 135. Baldwin. Peter Deale, armourer (Tillett 1882, p. 18)
3146b	0.91	14.0	Cu	270°	Same dies. [?Nott]
3147	0.84	12.9	Cu	0°	*Derrix,* Abraham. 1665. 3.58.9; D|AI. BW 136-7. Baldwin [ex Gilbert]. Same obv. die as 3148; overstruck. Abraham Derricke, worstead weaver, 1651 (Tillett 1882, p. 18)

	Weight			Die	
	g	gr		axis	
3148a	1.11	17.1	M	180°	*Derrix,* Abraham. 1665. 3.58.9; D|AI. BW 136-7. Baldwin [ex Gilbert]. Same obv. die as 3147
3148b	0.59	9.1	M	180°	Same dies. [?Nott]
3149	0.85	13.1	Br	0°	*Dover,* James. 1667. Date; I D. BW 138. Baldwin [ex Gilbert]
3150a	1.33	20.5	Br	150°	*Duglas,* Robert, cutler (CVTTLER). nd. 5.42.30; D|RD. BW 139. [?Nott]. Issuer died 1664 (Tillett 1882, p. 19)
3150b	1.15	17.8	Br	180°	Same dies. Baldwin [ex Gilbert]
3150c	1.10	16.9	Br	0°	Same dies. [?Nott]
3151	0.69	10.7	Cu	0°	*Elmer,* Francis. 1667. 3.66.9; E|FG. BW 140. [Baldwin ex Gilbert]
3152a	0.92	14.2	Br	270°	*Emperor,* Robert. nd. 5.42.1; E|RE. BW 141. [?Nott]
3152b	1.47	22.6	Br	–	Same dies. Baldwin [ex Gilbert]. Rev. brockage
3152c	0.66	10.1	Br	90°	Same dies. Baldwin [ex Gilbert]
3153	1.23	18.9	Cu	180°	*Ferrier,* Thomas. 1664. 5.38.2; T F. BW 142. Baldwin. Thomas Ferrior, grocer, 1665 (Tillett 1882, p. 19)
3154	1.40	21.6	Br	0°	*Flatman,* Thomas. 1664. Date; T F. BW 143. Baldwin [ex Gilbert]. Same obv. die as 3229-30 (Pulham Market), which are from a true pair of dies, and are consequently earlier than this Norwich pairing. Thomas Flatman, tallow-chandler, 1666 [*i.e.* 1667?] (Tillett 1882, p. 19)
3155a	1.14	17.6	M	180°	*Freeman,* Richard. 1657. 3.108.27; R F. BW 144. Baldwin [ex Gilbert]. Richard Freeman, vintner, free 1660; at the sign of the Dove (Tillett 1882, p. 19)
3155b	0.94	14.4	M	180°	Same dies. [?Nott]
	(chipped)				
3156	1.21	18.7	Br	180°	*Greene,* Thomas. 1658. 5.14 Grocers; G|TS. BW 146. Nott [?Baldwin ex Gilbert]. Thomas Greene, grocer, free 1652 (Tillett 1882, p. 20)
	(pierced)				
3157a	0.66	10.1	Br	0°	*Halfknight,* Eliz—. 1667. 5.14 Dyers; 5.76.70 (E H). BW 148 but ELIZ:. Nott [?Baldwin ex Gilbert]. 'Wid. Halfeknights' (Tillett 1882, p. 20)
3157b	0.62	9.6	Br	0°	Same dies. [?Nott]
3157c	0.59	9.1	Br	0°	Same dies. [?Nott]
	(chipped)				
3158a	1.12	17.2	Cu	90°	*Hall,* George. 1664. 5.77; 5.14 Grocers. BW 149. Nott [?Baldwin]. George Hall, grocer, 1668 (Tillett 1882, p. 20)
3158b	0.77	11.9	Cu	90°	Same dies. [?Nott]
3159	0.76	11.7	Cu	180°	*Hanse,* Thomas. 1664. 5.38.1; H|TE. BW 150. Nott [?Baldwin ex Gilbert]
3160	1.18	18.3	M	180°	*Harding,* Edward, grocer. nd. 5.14 Grocers; H|EA. BW 151. Baldwin [ex Gilbert]
3161a	0.91	14.0	Br	0°	*Hatton,* Blythe (BLYTH). nd. 4.12.1; B H. BW 152. [?Baldwin]. Blyth Hatton, widow, buried 1670 (Tillett 1882, p. 20)
3161b	0.89	13.8	Br	0°	Same dies. Baldwin [ex Gilbert]
	(chipped)				
3162	0.64	9.8	Br	180°	*Howlet,* Nathanael (NATHANAELL), worsted-weaver (WOS^{D}WEAVER). nd. 5.14 Norwich; 5.76.71 (N H). BW 154. Baldwin
	(chipped)				
3163	0.84	13.0	M	180°	*Hutton,* John. 1657. 3.7.16; H|IE. BW 156. Baldwin [ex Gilbert]. Same obv. die as 3164. Apprentices of John Hutton, 1638 and 1662, were both haberdashers (Tillett 1882, p. 21)
3164a	1.60	24.7	M	0°	*Hutton,* John. 1657. 3.7.16; H|IE. BW 155. [Baldwin ex Gilbert]. Same obv. die as 3163
3164b	1.33	20.6	M	180°	Same dies. Brand
3164c	1.23	18.9	M	0°	Same dies. [?Nott]
	(chipped)				
3165a	1.31	20.2	Br	0°	*Hyrne,* Edward, grocer. nd. 5.14 Grocers; H|EM. BW 157. Nott [?Baldwin]. Edward Hyrne, free 1655, buried 1658 (Tillett 1882, p. 21)
3165b	1.25	19.3	Br	0°	Same dies. [?Nott]
3165c	1.10	16.9	Br	0°	Same dies. [?Nott]
3166	0.60	9.2	Cu	90°	*Lacey,* Thomas. 1667. 5.66.20; L|TS. BW 162. Baldwin [ex Gilbert]
3167a	1.53	23.6	Br	0°	*Lambert,* William, grocer. nd. 5.14 Grocers; 4.15.9 (L|WA). BW 163. Baldwin [ex Gilbert]
3167b	1.04	16.1	Br	180°	Same dies. [?Nott]
3168a	1.34	20.6	Cu	0°	*Lawrence,* John and *Goodwyn* (GOODWIN), L[aurence]. 1658. 2.4.7; I L|L G. BW 164. [?Nott]. John Lawrence, grocer, 1632; 'salt provisions provided by him and Mr Laurence Goodwyn' 1672 (Tillett 1882, p. 22); see also 3220, whence form 'Goodwyn'
	(chipped)				
3168b	0.85	13.1	M	180°	Same dies. Nott [?Baldwin]

[*continued overleaf*]

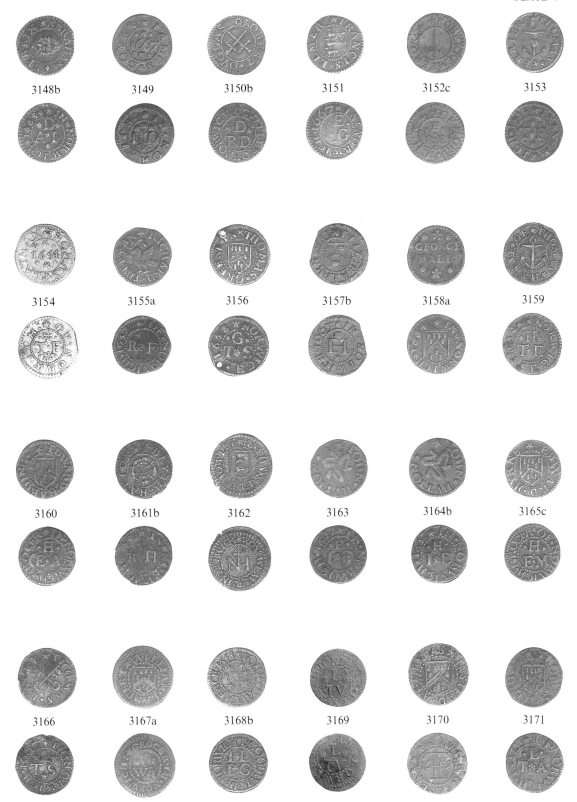

PLATE 7

3148b	3149	3150b	3151	3152c	3153

3154	3155a	3156	3157b	3158a	3159

3160	3161b	3162	3163	3164b	3165c

3166	3167a	3168b	3169	3170	3171

Plate 7 (*cont.*)

	Weight			Die	
	g	*gr*		*axis*	
3169	0.61	9.5	Br	180°	*Leverington,* John. nd. L|IV; L|IV. BW 165. Baldwin [ex Gilbert]
3170	0.72	11.1	Br	0°	*Linstead,* Thomas, grocer (GROSER). 1659. 5.14 Grocers; 5.76.72 (T L). BW 166 but I6[TL monogram]59. Nott [?Baldwin ex Gilbert]. See also 3223-4. Obv. legend starts at 8 o'clock
3171	0.86	13.2	M	180°	*Long,* Thomas. 1657. 5.14 Grocers; L|TA. BW 167. Baldwin. 'Thomas Longe grocer' 1651 (Tillett 1882, p. 22)

	Weight			Die	
	g	*gr*		*axis*	
3172	1.17	18.1	Cu	90°	*Mayes,* John. 1667. 3.3.13; M|IE. BW 168. Baldwin [ex Gilbert]
3173	0.87	13.4	Br	180°	*Mingay,* Anthony (ANTHO:). nd. 5.77; 3.59.2. BW 169. Baldwin [ex Gilbert]. Anthony Mingay, grocer, 1661 (Tillett 1882, p. 22)
3174a	0.87	13.3	Cu	0°	*Morant,* Richard. nd. 5.88.7; R M. BW 172. Nott. Richard Morant, worsted weaver, d. 1666 (Tillett 1882, p. 23)
3174b	0.73	11.3	Cu	180°	Same dies. Baldwin
3175a	1.26	19.4	M	180°	*Morly,* Fra[n]cis. nd. 5.14 Grocers; F M. BW 173. Nott [?Baldwin ex Gilbert]. Diameter 16-16.5 mm. Francis Morl(e)y, grocer, 1633 (Rising 1959, p. 39); buried 1658 (Tillett 1882, p. 23)
3175b	0.75	11.5	M	180°	Same dies. [?Nott]. Diameter 15 mm
	(chipped, corroded)				
3176	0.57	8.8	Br	0°	*Munford,* Ann. nd. 5.14 Grocers; A M. BW 174-174[var.]. Nott [?Baldwin ex Gilbert]. Same rev. die as 3177. The widow Munford, 1659-81 (Tillett 1882, p. 23); see also 3178
3177	0.85	13.1	Br	0°	*Munford,* Ann. nd. 5.14 Grocers; A M. BW 174-174[var.]. Nott [?Baldwin ex Gilbert]. Same rev. die as 3176
3178a	1.24	19.2	Br	0°	*Munford,* George. 1657. 5.76.73 (G M); 5.14 Grocers. BW 175. Baldwin. George Munford fl. 1653-9 (Tillett 1882, p. 23); see also 3176-7
3178b	1.17	18.1	Br	0°	Same dies. [?Nott]
3179a	1.31	20.3	Br	0°	*Newman,* Thomas. nd. 5.14 Grocers; 5.76.74 (T N). BW 176. [?Nott]
3179b	1.05	16.2	Br	180°	Same dies. Baldwin [ex Gilbert]
3180	0.88	13.6	Br	270°	*Norgats,* Elias. 1660. 3.1.56; N|EE. BW 177. Baldwin [ex Gilbert]. Elias Norgate, pinmaker, 1656 (Tillett 1882, p. 23)
3181a	1.09	16.9	M	180°	*Osborn,* John, grocer. nd. 5.14 Grocers; 5.76.75 (I O). BW 178. [?Nott]. John Osborne d. c.1665 (Tillett 1882, p. 23)
3181b	0.95	14.6	M	180°	Same dies. Baldwin [ex Gilbert]
3182	0.97	15.0	Br	180°	*Parker,* John. 1665. 3.55.1; P|IE. BW 179. Baldwin [ex Gilbert]. 'Mr Parker by the Lambe' 1665 (Tillett 1882, p. 23)
3183	1.10	17.0	Cu	180°	*Parmenter,* William. 1654. 5.14 Grocers; P|WS. BW 180. Baldwin [ex Gilbert]
3184	0.69	10.7	Br	0°	*Pearcivale,* Isaac. 1667. 4.1.3; P|II. BW 181. Baldwin. Isaac Persivall, worsted weaver (Tillett 1882, p. 24)
3185a	0.81	12.5	Br	60°	*Price,* William. 1662. P|WS; P|WS. BW 183. [?Baldwin]. William Price or Prike, potter (Tillett 1882, p. 24); Wm Pricke, William Prike, 1666 (Seaman 1988, pp. 75, 85)
	(chipped)				
3185b	0.65	10.0	Br	60°	Same dies. Baldwin [ex Gilbert]
3186	1.16	17.9	Cu	330°	*Pycroft,* Daniel (DANIELL). nd. 5.14 Grocers; D P. BW 184 but NORWECH. Baldwin. 'Daniel Pycroft grocer' 1667 (Tillett 1882, p. 24)
3187a	0.88	13.5	Cu	0°	*Randoll,* Thomas. nd. 5.14 Bakers; R|TE. BW 185. Baldwin
3187b	0.68	10.4	Br	0°	Same dies. [?Nott]
3188	0.64	9.9	Cu	225°	*Rayley,* Augustine (AGVSTINE). 1662. 5.14 Grocers; date. BW 186. Baldwin [ex Gilbert]. Augustin Rayley, grocer, 1669 (Rising 1959, p. 187)
3189a	1.26	19.5	M	180°	*Rayner,* Thomas (THOMOS). 1653. 5.14 Grocers; T R. BW 187. Baldwin
3189b	0.83	12.8	M	180°	Same dies. [?Nott]
3190a	1.27	19.7	M	180°	*Rayner,* Thomas (THOMOS). 1655. 5.14 Grocers; T R. BW 188. Baldwin [ex Gilbert]. Diameter 16 mm
3190b	0.60	9.2	Br	180°	Same dies. [?Baldwin]. Diameter 14.5 mm
3191a	1.13	17.4	Cu	90°	*Reeve,* Charles. 1664. 5.77; 5.77. BW 189. Baldwin [ex Gilbert]. Charles Reeve, cordwainer, 1662 (Tillett 1882, p. 25)
3191b	0.84	13.0	Cu	270°	Same dies. [?Nott]
3192	0.92	14.2	Cu	270°	*Reeve,* George. nd. 5.14 Grocers; R|GR. BW 190, 192-3. Nott [?Baldwin ex Gilbert]. Same rev. die as 3193
3193a	1.22	18.9	Cu	180°	*Reeve,* George. nd. 5.14 Grocers; R|GR. BW 190, 192-3. [?Nott]. Same rev. die as 3192
3193b	1.02	15.7	Cu	180°	Same dies. Nott [?Baldwin ex Gilbert]
3194	1.92	29.6	Cu	0°	*Reeve,* George. nd. 5.14 Grocers; R|GR. BW 191-3. Nott [?Baldwin ex Gilbert]
3195	1.18	18.3	Br	0°	*Robinson,* Will—. 1662. 3.1.75; R|WE. BW 194 but WILL:, pl. xiii.10. Nott [?Baldwin ex Gilbert]. William Robinson, linen draper, 1667 (Tillett 1882, p. 25)

PLATE 8

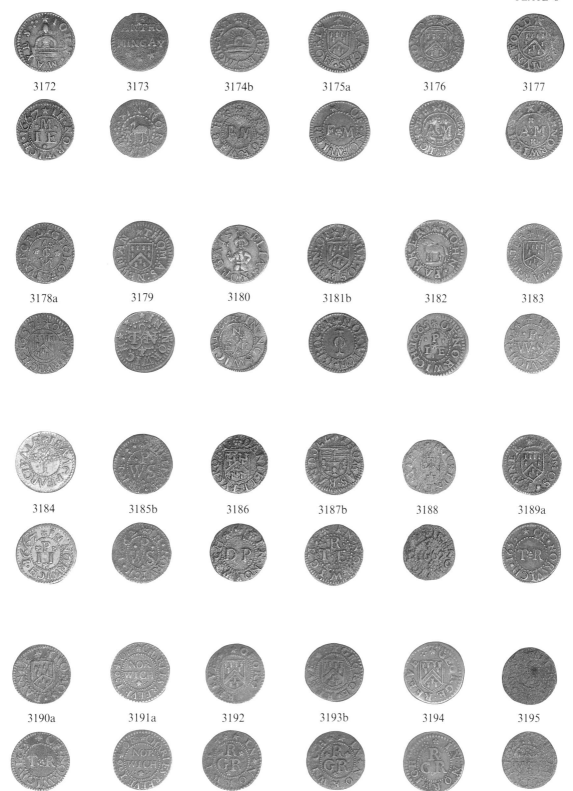

3172	3173	3174b	3175a	3176	3177

3178a	3179	3180	3181b	3182	3183

3184	3185b	3186	3187b	3188	3189a

3190a	3191a	3192	3193b	3194	3195

	Weight			Die	
	g	*gr*		*axis*	
3196	0.95	14.7	Cu	180°	*Sheppard,* John. 1659. 5.76.10 (I S); 5.76.10 (I S). BW 195. Nott [?Baldwin ex Gilbert]. Same obv. die as 3197
3197	0.86	13.2	Br	180°	*Sheppard,* John. 1659. 5.76.10 (I S); 5.76.10 (I S). BW 196. Nott [?Baldwin ex Gilbert]. Same obv. die as 3196
3198	0.85	13.1	Br	0°	*Sidnor,* Henry. 1659. 3.67.20; S|HI. BW 197. Nott [?Baldwin ex Gilbert]. Same obv. die as 3199. 'Henricus Sydnor grocer' 1624; 'Hen Sydnor gent.' 1668 (Tillett 1882, pp. 25-6)
3199a	1.00	15.4	M	180°	*Sidnor,* Henry. 1659. 3.67.20; S|HI. BW 198. Nott [?Baldwin ex Gilbert]. Same obv. die as 3198
3199b	0.90 (chipped)	13.8	Br	180°	Same dies. [?Nott]
3200	0.65	10.0	M	90°	*Sidnor,* Henry. 1667. 5.14 Tallow Chandlers; S|HI. BW 199. Nott [?Baldwin ex Gilbert]
3201	1.47	22.7	Br	270°	*Snowden,* Jonathan. 1660. 5.14 Grocers; S|IE. BW 200-1. Nott [?Baldwin ex Gilbert]
3202	1.21	18.7	M	0°	*Soulter,* Matthew (MATHEW), oatmeal-maker (OATMEALE MAKER). nd. 5.77; S|MB. BW 202. Nott [?Baldwin ex Gilbert]. 'the Oatemeale house of Math: Salter' 1666 (Tillett 1882, p. 26)
3203a	1.01	15.6	M	90°	*Spendlove,* [John], grocer. 1667. 5.76.76 (S); 5.14 Grocers. BW 203 but ★, merchant's mark incorporating first letter of SPENDLOVE|I667. Nott [?Baldwin ex Gilbert]. John Spendlove, grocer, 1654 (Tillett 1882, p. 26)
3203b	0.96	14.8	M	180°	Same dies. [?Nott]
3204a	1.47	22.7	Cu	0°	*Starlin,* Samuel (SAMVELL). 1664. 3.68.4; S S. BW 204. Nott [?Baldwin ex Gilbert]. Samuel Starling, skinner, 1649 (Tillett 1882, p. 26)
3204b	1.08	16.6	Cu	0°	Same dies. [?Nott]
3205a	1.09	16.8	M	180°	*Tabor,* John. 1663. 5.34.1; T|IM. BW 205. [Baldwin ex Gilbert]. John Tabor, gardener, free 1659 [*i.e.* 1660?] (Tillett 1882, p. 26)
3205b	0.79	12.2	M	180°	Same dies. Brand [or Seaby]
3206	1.14	17.6	M	180°	*Tharrold,* Robert, grocer. nd. 5.14 Grocers; R T. BW 206. Nott [?Baldwin ex Gilbert]. Same obv. die as 3207
3207a	1.53	23.7	M	180°	*Tharrold,* Robert, grocer. nd. 5.14 Grocers; R T. BW 206. Nott [?Baldwin ex Gilbert]. Same obv. die as 3206
3207b	1.17 (chipped)	18.0	M	180°	Same dies. [?Nott]
3208	0.65	10.0	Cu	180°	*Thurton,* William. 1665. Date; T|WM. BW 208. Nott [?Baldwin ex Gilbert]. William Thurton, dornick weaver, 1652 (Tillett 1882, p. 27)
3209	0.92	14.2	Cu	180°	*Toft,* Benjamin. 1664. 5.14 Grocers; T|BE. BW 209. Nott [?Baldwin ex Gilbert]
3210	1.16	17.9	M	180°	*Toft,* Daniel (DANEL), grocer. 1653. T|DE; T|DE. BW 210. Nott [?Baldwin ex Gilbert]
3211	1.40	21.5	M	180°	*Tompson,* Robert. 1652. 5.17.13; R T. BW 211. Nott [?Baldwin ex Gilbert]. 'Robtus Tompson grocer' 1638 (Tillett 1882, p. 27)
3212	0.94 (chipped)	14.5	M	180°	*Vyn,* Jeremy (IERIMY). 1657 (ANNO I657). 5.14 Grocers; 5.77. BW 212 but I:VYN. Nott [?Baldwin ex Gilbert]. Same obv. die as 3213
3213a	1.18	18.2	M	180°	*Vyn,* Jeremy (IERIMY). 1657 (ANNO I657). 5.14 Grocers; 5.77. BW 212 but I:VYN. Nott [?Baldwin ex Gilbert]. Same obv. die as 3212
3213b	1.07	16.6	M	180°	Same dies. [?Nott]
3214	0.67	10.4	Br	0°	*Ward,* John. 1667. 5.64.50; W|IE. BW 215. Nott [?Baldwin ex Gilbert]. John Ward, father and son, both wool-combers (Tillett 1882, p. 28)
3215a	1.05	16.2	M	180°	*Warren,* Thomas. nd. 5.14 Grocers; 5.76.77 (T W). BW 217. [?Nott]
3215b	1.01	15.6	M	180°	Same dies. Nott [?Baldwin ex Gilbert]
3216a	0.97	15.0	Br	0°	*Weld,* Tho[mas], hatter. 1657. W|TC; date. BW 218 but THO:WELD:HATTER. Nott [?Baldwin ex Gilbert]
3216b	0.82	12.6	Br	0°	Same dies. [?Nott]
3217	1.08	16.7	Br	0°	*Withers,* Nicholas. 1658. W|NF; W|NF. BW 220 but I658. Nott [?Baldwin ex Gilbert]. Same rev. die as 3218. Nicholas Withers, wool-comber, 1667 (Tillett 1882, p. 28)
3218	0.66	10.2	Br	0°	*Withers,* Nicholas. 1658. W|NF; W|NF. BW 221 but I658. Nott [?Baldwin ex Gilbert]. Same rev. die as 3217
3219a	1.04	16.0	Br	90°	*Youngest,* Will—. nd. 5.57.30; W Y. BW 224 but WILL:. Nott [?Baldwin ex Gilbert]. William Younges, apprentice tailor, 1657 (Rising 1959, p. 187)
3219b	0.99	15.3	Br	90°	Same dies. [?Nott]

Norwich, [City] *see* 3108-26

PLATE 9

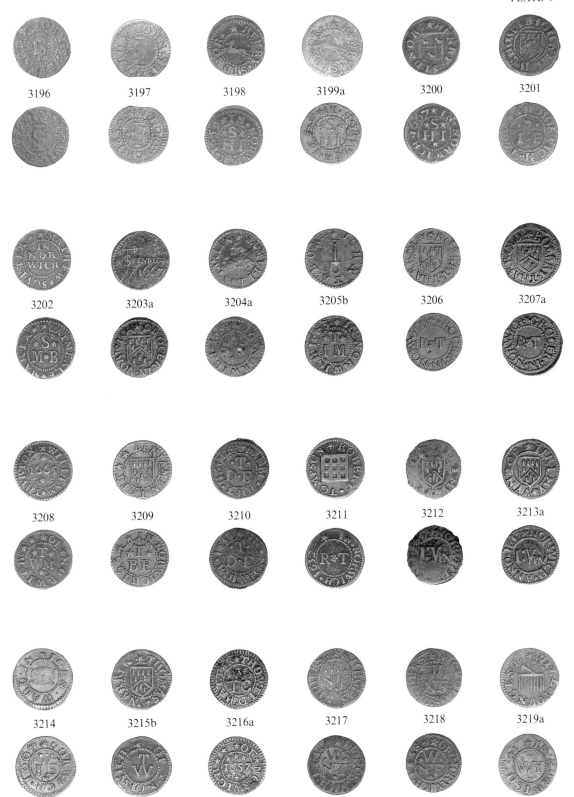

3196 3197 3198 3199a 3200 3201

3202 3203a 3204a 3205b 3206 3207a

3208 3209 3210 3211 3212 3213a

3214 3215b 3216a 3217 3218 3219a

NORWICH (*cont.*)

Named signs

	Weight			Die	
	g	gr		axis	
3220a	1.12	17.3	Cu	180°	*Golden Camel* (AT THE GOLDEN CAMELL): Goodwyn (GOODWY'), L[aurence], confectioner. 1660. 5.76.78 (L G); 3.59.1. BW 145 but [LG monogram]OODWY with tittle above (lacking in 1967 reprint). Nott [?Baldwin ex Gilbert]. For extension of forename see 3168 n.
3220b	0.99	15.3	Cu	180°	Same dies. [?Nott]
3221a	0.93	14.3	Br	90°	*Post Office* (AT Y^E): ?L—, A—. 1661. Date; 3.7.6 (A L). BW 158. Nott. Same obv. die as 3222. Overstruck on Beech Lane (City of London): *Baker*, Peter, q.v. (same dies, axis 90°)
3221b	0.79	12.1	Br	180°	Same dies. [?Nott]. The keeper of a post office in 1661 would have been acceptable to the Restored government; and in a 1660 address to General Monck from the gentry of Norfolk and Norwich, one name (Le Strange 1913, sheet D, col. 2) fits both the initials and the device: Andrew Lightfoote
3222	0.79	12.2	Br	90°	*Post Office* (AT Y^E): ?L—, A—. 1661. Date; 3.7.6 (A L). BW 158 but IN[no stop]NORWICH. Nott [?Baldwin ex Gilbert]. Same obv. die as 3221

NORWICH. Norwich St Andrew parish

The reading is S ANDREWES PARRICH IN NORWICH on both

3223a	1.37	21.1	M	180°	?L—, T—. 1653. L|TD; L|TD. BW 160. Baldwin [ex Gilbert]. Same rev. die as 3224. Possible names in the parish of St Andrew 1666 (Seaman 1988, pp. 78-79) are Thomas Lesingham, and Thomas Linsteed (cf. 3170, which has no elements in common with this token)
3223b	1.02	15.8	Br	0°	Same dies. Baldwin
3224	0.88	13.6	Br	0°	?L—, T—. 1653. L|TD; L|TD. BW 161. Baldwin [ex Gilbert]. Same rev. die as 3223

NORWICH. Red Well neighbourhood [*subsequently* Bank Plain]

The reading is NEAR REDWELL IN NORWICH. The 'red well' had perhaps a red frame or kerb around its top; a pump was placed over it in 1629 (EPNS 1989, p. 131)

3225a	1.00	15.4	Br	0°	*Holbey*, Henry. 1659. 3.6.35; H|HG. BW 153. [?Nott]. Holbey a 'habbidasher of smales wares' (Tillett 1882, p. 20)
3225b	0.76	11.7	Br	0°	Same dies. Baldwin [ex Gilbert]

NORWICH. White Lion Street

The reading is LION LANE^E IN NORWICH on both, cf. *the Lyon Lane* 1626, *White Lyon Lane* 1696..., *White Lion Street* 1819...; the White Lion inn stood about the midst of the north side (EPNS 1989, p. 153)

3226	1.09	16.9	Br	0°	*Mony*, Will—. nd. 3.11; M|WE. BW 170-1 but WILL:. Baldwin [ex Gilbert]. Same obv. die as 3227. William Mon(e)y, apprentice worstead weaver, 1634 (Rising 1959, p. 116); buried 1665 [i.e. 1666?] (Tillett 1882, p. 22)
3227	0.59	9.1	Br	180°	*Mony*, Will—. nd. 3.11; M|WE. BW 170-1 but WILL:. Baldwin [ex Gilbert]. Same obv. die as 3226

OUTWELL (Norfolk *and* Cambridgeshire, Isle of Ely)

The reading is OVTWELL

3228a	1.31	20.3	Cu	180°	*Boyce*, Francis (FRANCES). 1664. 5.65.1; B|FM. BW 232. Nott [?Baldwin ex Gilbert]
3228b	0.84	12.9	Cu	180°	Same dies. [?Nott]

PULHAM ST MARY MAGDALENE [*subsequently* PULHAM MARKET]

The reading is PVLHAM MARKET on 3230; PVLHAM MARKETT on 3231. On 3229 the reading is PVLHAM S^T MARY, but as this was subsequently altered to PVLHAM MARKET it cannot be considered an acceptable form of name; it might have misdirected to the neighbouring village of Pulham St Mary the Virgin, *Pulham Mary* in Spelman 1678, Adams 1680

3229	0.89	13.8	Br	45°	*Flatman*, Thomas. 1664. Date (···|I664|···; ·THOMAS ·FLATMAN around); T F (···|T ·F| ···; ·OF ·PVLHAM ·S^T ·MARY around). BW —; Dickinson 234A. Nott [?Baldwin ex Gilbert]. Same dies as 3230, with rev. in earlier state; extremely rare (Cornell 1986, lot 422), so that 3230 is likely to represent a correction of this rev. legend, and not a change of address from Pulham St Mary the Virgin. Same obv. die as 3154 (see 3230 n.)

[*continued overleaf*]

PLATE 10

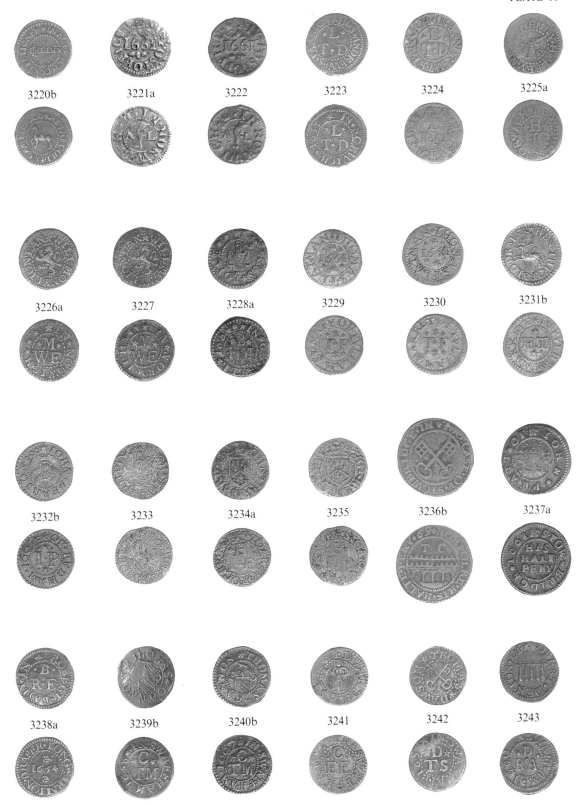

3220b 3221a 3222 3223 3224 3225a

3226a 3227 3228a 3229 3230 3231b

3232b 3233 3234a 3235 3236b 3237a

3238a 3239b 3240b 3241 3242 3243

Plate 10 (*cont.*)

	Weight		*Die*			
	g	*gr*	*axis*			
3230	1.55	23.9	Br	330°	*Flatman,* Thomas. 1664. Date; T F. BW 234. Nott [?Baldwin ex Gilbert]. Same dies as 3229, with PVLHAM · MARKET cancelling PVLHAM S^T MARY; same obv. die as 3154 (Norwich), which is later than this true pair of dies
3231a	1.06	16.4	M	0°	*Theobald,* Hen—, draper. nd. 3.53.7; H T. BW 235 but HEN:. [?Nott]
3231b	0.82	12.7	Br	0°	Same dies. Nott [?Baldwin ex Gilbert]

PULHAM ST MARY THE VIRGIN [*subsequently* PULHAM ST MARY]

Flatman, Thomas *see* 3229 (Pulham St Mary Magdalene)

RUDHAM, East

The reading is RVDHAM

3232a	0.88	13.5	Br	0°	*Pearson,* John. 1667. 3.5.96; I P. BW 236. [?Nott]. Attributed to East Rudham from the presence of John Person 1666 (Seaman 1988, p. 37)
3232b	0.58	8.9	Br	0°	Same dies. Nott [?Baldwin ex Gilbert]

SHIPDHAM

The reading is SHIPDHAM NORFOLK

3233	0.90	13.8	Br	180°	*Golding,* Nicholas. nd. 5.13.15; G|NS. BW 237 but IN · SHIPDHAM. Nott [?Baldwin ex Gilbert]

SOUTHTOWN (Gorleston parish) *see* Suffolk

STOKE FERRY / STOKE HOLY CROSS

The reading is STOAKE NORF on both

3234a	1.02	15.7	Br	180°	*Hubbard,* John, grocer. nd. 5.14 Grocers; H|IE. BW 239. [?Baldwin]. Same rev. die as 3235
3234b	1.02	15.7	Br	0°	Same dies. Nott [?Baldwin ex Gilbert]
3234c	0.81	12.5	Br	180°	Same dies. [?Nott]. The development of the obv. die flaw on these three specimens indicates that they are listed in order of striking
3235	0.90	13.9	Br	180°	*Hubbard,* John, grocer. nd. 5.14 Grocers; H|IE. BW 239. [?Baldwin]. Same rev. die as 3234

STOWBRIDGE (Stow Bardolph parish)

The reading is STOW BRIDGE on 3237; STOWBRIDGE IN NORFOLKE on 3236

3236a	2.23	34.4	Br	180°	*Case,* Tho—. [16]69 ½d. 5.66.20; 5.3.3 (T C). BW 240 but THO:, NORFOLKE. Nott [?Baldwin ex Gilbert]
3236b	1.38	21.3	Br	180°	Same dies. [?Nott]
3237a	2.40	37.1	Br	0°	*Pratt,* John. 1668 ½d. 5.3.2; 5.77. BW 241. Nott
3237b	1.87	28.9	Br	270°	Same dies. [?Baldwin]
3237c	1.64	25.3	Br	0°	Same dies. [?Baldwin]

STRATTON ST MARY [*otherwise* LONG STRATTON]

The reading is LONG STRATTON

3238a	1.11	17.2	Br	180°	*Bayly,* Robert, draper. 1654. B|RE; date. BW 242. Nott [?Baldwin ex Gilbert]
3238b	0.88	13.5	Br	180°	Same dies. [?Nott]

STRATTON ST MARY / STRATTON ST MICHAEL / STRATTON STRAWLESS

Cann, John *see* 572 (Cornwall: Stratton)
Gayer, Samuel *see* 833 (Cornwall: Stratton)

SWAFFHAM

The reading is SWAFHAM on 3242-3; SWAFFHAM on the remainder, with IN NORFOL^K on 3244

3239a	1.25 (chipped)	19.3	M	180°	*Cannon,* Thomas. 1658. 5.15.21; C|TM. BW 244. [?Nott]. Attributed to 'Tho Cannon' 1664 (Frankel 1983, p. 84)
3239b	1.07	16.5	M	180°	Same dies. Nott [?Baldwin ex Gilbert]
3240a	1.00	15.4	M	270°	*Cannon,* Thomas. 1667. 5.15.21; C|TM. BW 245. [?Nott]
3240b	0.84	12.9	M	270°	Same dies. Nott [?Baldwin]

	Weight			Die	
	g	*gr*		*axis*	
3241	1.30	20.0	Br	180°	*Case,* Edward. nd. 3.1.57; C|EE. BW 246. Nott [?Baldwin ex Gilbert]. For attribution cf. 'Eliz Case' 1664 (Frankel 1983, p. 83)
3242	1.26	19.5	Br	180°	*Dawson,* Thomas. 1659. 5.66.20; D|TS. BW 247; BW Cambs. 180 but SWAFHAM. Nott [?Baldwin ex Gilbert]. Attributed to 'Tho Dawson' 1664 (Frankel 1983, p. 84)
3243	0.93	14.4	M	0°	*Denton,* Robert. 1660. 5.32.9; D|RA. BW 248; BW Cambs. 179. Spink 1972. The F of SWAFHAM cancels S. Attributed to 'Robt Denton' 1664 (Frankel 1983, p. 84)

SWAFFHAM (*cont.*)

	Weight			Die	
	g	*gr*		*axis*	
3244	0.57	8.7	Br	90°	*Hooker,* John. 1667. 5.14 Grocers; I H. BW 250. Baldwin

SWANTON ABBOTT

The reading is SWANTON ABBOTT

3245	0.63	9.8	Br	0°	*Cooper,* William. nd. 3.5.105; 4.12.1. BW 251. Nott [?Baldwin ex Gilbert]. Same obv. die as
	(chipped)				3144 (Norwich, 1662)

SWANTON NOVERS

The reading is SWANTON on 3246; SWANTON NOVERS on 3247

3246a	2.08	32.1	Br	180°	*Naylor* (NAILOR), James. 1667 ½d. 5.77; N|IA. BW 252 but NAILOR. [?Nott]. Attribution and
					form of surname from 3247
3246b	1.75	26.9	Br	0°	Same dies. Baldwin
3247	1.61	24.8	Br	180°	*Naylor,* James. 1671 ½d. 5.77; N|IA. BW 253. Nott [?Baldwin ex Gilbert]

THETFORD (Norfolk *and* Suffolk)

The reading is THETTFORD on 3250; THETFORD on the remainder, with NORFV on 3249

3248a	0.91	14.1	M	180°	*Flanner,* William. 1669. Date; F|WM. BW 254. [?Baldwin]
3248b	0.79	12.1	M	180°	Same dies. [?Nott]
3248c	0.72	11.0	M	270°	Same dies. Baldwin
3249	1.07	16.5	Br	180°	*Hetherset,* Wormley (WORMLY). nd. 5.14 Grocers; W H. BW 255. Nott [?Baldwin ex Gilbert]. Final V cancels Ķ; followed by an irregular mark which might be the upper part of a colon, if a mark below is not the leg of the K
3250a	1.05	16.2	Br	180°	*Howlett,* Francis. 1668. 5.64.50; date. BW 256. Baldwin [ex Gilbert]. Francis Howlett the elder, wool-comber (Tillett 1882, p. 36)
3250b	0.71	11.0	Br	180°	Same dies. [?Nott]
3251	0.96	14.8	Br	270°	*Moore,* Edward. 1668. 5.14 Mercers; M|EF. BW 257. Baldwin [ex Gilbert]
3252	1.36	21.0	Cu	180°	*Waymond,* John. 1659. 5.14 Grocers; I W. BW 258. Baldwin

THORNHAM

The reading is THORNVM

3253	1.08	16.6	Br	0°	*Tucke,* Stephen. 1667 ½d. 1.44; T|SM. BW 259 but THORNVM, HALF. Baldwin. Attribution from the presence of Stephen Tucke 1664, 1666 (Frankel 1983, p. 82; Seaman 1988, p. 31)

UPWELL (Norfolk *and* Cambs., Isle of Ely) *see* Cambridgeshire

WALSHAM, North

The reading is NORTH WALSHAM on 3257; NORTH WALSHA^M on 3255; NORTHWALSHAM on 3254; NORWALSHAM on 3256, 3258

3254a	1.09	16.8	Br	270°	*Cooke,* John. nd. 5.14 Mercers; C|IM. BW 266 but NORTHWALSHAM. [?Nott]
3254b	1.05	16.3	M	180°	Same dies. [?Baldwin]
3254c	0.70	10.8	Br	0°	Same dies. Baldwin [ex Gilbert]
3255	0.97	15.0	Br	180°	*Moore,* Thomas. nd. 5.14 Grocers; T M. BW 267 but WALSHA^M. Nott [?Baldwin ex Gilbert]
3256a	1.93	29.8	Br	180°	*Richardson,* Peter. [16]57. 5.15.22; R|PM. BW 268 but NORWALSHAM. Nott [?Baldwin ex Gilbert]
3256b	0.81	12.5	Br	180°	Same dies. [?Nott]
3257	0.56	8.6	Br	270°	*Ruddocke,* Thomas. nd. 5.14 Drapers; T R. BW 269. Nott [?Baldwin ex Gilbert]
3258	1.12	17.3	Br	0°	*Wasey,* Joseph. nd. 5.14 Mercers; I W. BW 270 but NORWALSHAM. Nott [?Baldwin ex Gilbert]

WALSINGHAM, Little

The reading is WALLSINGHAM on 3263, cf. *Walsingham* Adams 1680, a market town, unlike *Walsingham old* otherwise Great Walsingham; LITTLE WALSINGHAM on the remainder, with NOR:|FOLK on 3260, NOR|FOLK on 3261-2

3259a	0.90	13.9	Br	270°	*Framingham,* Will—. nd. 4.12.1; W F. BW 272 but WILL'. Nott [?Baldwin ex Gilbert]
3259b	0.83	12.8	Br	270°	Same dies. [?Nott]

[*continued overleaf*]

PLATE 11

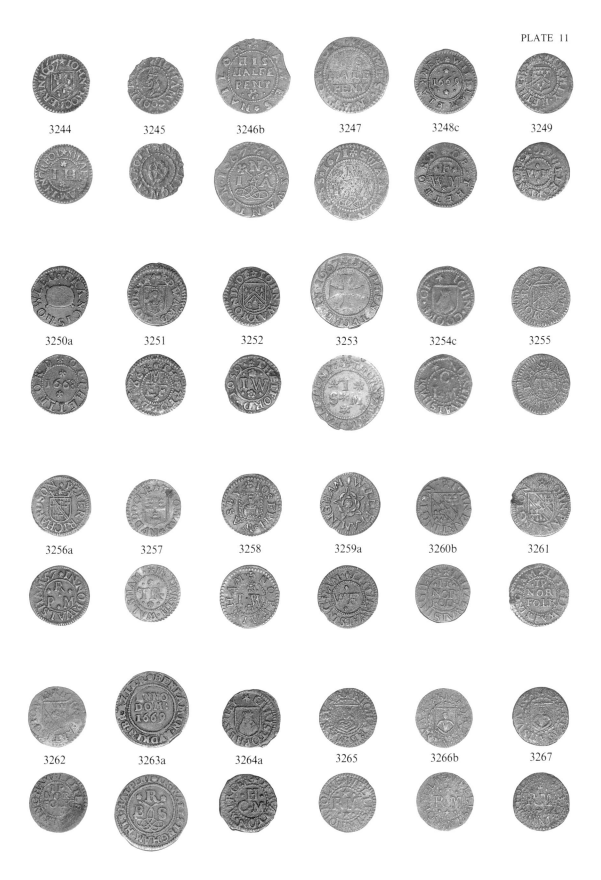

3244 3245 3246b 3247 3248c 3249

3250a 3251 3252 3253 3254c 3255

3256a 3257 3258 3259a 3260b 3261

3262 3263a 3264a 3265 3266b 3267

Plate 11 (*cont.*)

	Weight			*Die*	
	g	gr	Br	axis	
3260a	0.99	15.3	Br	270°	*Partington,* John. nd. 5.14 Haberdashers; 5.77. BW 274 but · IP · |NOR:|FOLK. Nott [?Baldwin ex Gilbert]. Same obv. die as 3261
3260b	0.81	12.5	Br	180°	Same dies. [?Nott]
3261	0.64	9.9	Br	180°	*Partington,* John. nd. 5.14 Haberdashers; 5.77. BW 274 but · IP · |NOR|FOLK. Baldwin. Same
	(chipped)				obv. die as 3260
3262	0.60	9.2	Br	90°	*Partington,* John. nd. 5.14 Haberdashers (· IOHN · PARTINGTON · IN around); 5.77 (· IP · |NOR|FOLK; · LITTLE · WALSINGHAM around). BW —, cf. 274; Gilbert 1927, 316. [?Baldwin]
3263a	2.66	41.0	Br	0°	*Rudkin,* Benjamin, brazier. 1669 (ANNO DOM: I669) ½d. 5.77; R|BS. BW 271 but ANNO|DOM:|I669. Baldwin [ex Gilbert]
3263b	1.83	28.2	Br	0°	Same dies. [?Nott]

WATTON

The reading is WATTON

| 3264a | 0.94 | 14.5 | M | 0° | *Hey,* Christopher, mercer. nd. 5.14 Mercers; H|CM. BW 276. Nott [?Baldwin ex Gilbert] |
| 3264b | 0.91 | 14.1 | M | 180° | Same dies. [?Nott] |

WELLS NEXT THE SEA

The reading is WELLES throughout, with IN NORFOLKE on 3265, 3268, IN NORFOLK[E] ON 3266-7

3265	0.59	9.0	M	180°	*Mansuar,* Richard. nd. 5.14 Mercers; R M. BW 277 but NORFOLKE. [Baldwin ex Gilbert]
3266a	0.86	13.2	Br	180°	*Mansuar,* Richard. nd. 5.14 Mercers; R M. BW 277. [?Nott]. Same obv. die as 3267
3266b	0.70	10.8	Br	90°	Same dies. Nott [?Baldwin ex Gilbert]
3267	1.15	17.8	M	90°	*Mansuar,* Richard. nd. 5.14 Mercers; R M. BW 277. Nott [?Baldwin ex Gilbert]. Same obv. die as 3266

WELLS NEXT THE SEA (*cont.*)

	Weight			Die	
	g	gr		axis	
3268a	0.82	12.6	Br	0°	*Mansuar,* Richard. nd. 5.14 Mercers; R M. BW 277 but NORFOLKE. [?Baldwin]
3268b	0.69	10.6	Br	0°	Same dies. Nott [?Baldwin ex Gilbert]
	(pierced)				

WILTON [*subsequently* HOCKWOLD CUM WILTON]

The reading is WILTON on both

3269	1.13	17.5	Br	90°	*Clark,* Thomas. 1664. 3.44.3; T C. BW 278. Baldwin. Attributed to Thomas Clark(e) fl. 1664-1706 (BW 278 n.;Frankel 1983, p. 41) *?H—, G— see* 'WILTON' (Uncertain I) *Newman,* William *see* WILTON (Wilts.)
3270a	1.08	16.6	Br	180°	*Wace,* Francis. 1658. 5.42.30; 5.14 Drapers. BW 281. Nott [?Baldwin ex Gilbert]. Attribution from documentation of Francis Wace, 1655-78 (BW 281 n.; Frankel 1983, p. 41), and presence of four worn specimens in Norwich Castle Museum
3270b	0.60	9.2	M	180°	Same dies. [?Nott]

WYMONDHAM

The reading is WINDHAM on both, with IN NORFOLK on 3272; cf. *Wimondham (comonly called Windham)* 1588 (Smith 1879, p. 28), *Windham* Adams 1680, and pronunciation (winndam)

| 3271 | 0.81 | 12.6 | Br | 0° | *Burrell,* John. nd. 5.14 Drapers; B|IE. BW 282. Nott [?Baldwin ex Gilbert]. Attributed to 'Mr John Burrell' 1664 (Frankel 1983, p. 28) |
| 3272 | 1.22 | 18.9 | Br | 0° | *Lock,* Anthony. nd. 5.14 Grocers; A L. BW 283. Nott [?Baldwin ex Gilbert] |

YARMOUTH, Great

See also Southtown in Suffolk. For 'North Yarmouth' below cf. SOVTH YARMOVTH on tokens 2045-6 of Yarmouth, Isle of Wight. The reading is YEARMOVTH on 3325, 3352-3; YARMOTH on 3326 (NORTH YARMOTH), 3327; YARMVTH on 3337-8; NORTH YARMOVG- on 3315; and YARMOVTH on the remainder (GREAT YARMOVTH on 3273-98, 3324, 3329-30, 3332-3, 3344, NORTH YARMOVTH on 3303, 3331, 3334-5, 3347-8, 3358-9, GRET YARMOVTH on 3322-3, and GRE^TYARMOVTH on 3346). Note on 3273-98: The arms of Great Yarmouth are *Party per pale gules and azure three demi-lions passant guardant or conjoined to the bodies of as many herrings argent* (Fox-Davies 1915, p. 872)

3273a	2.80	43.2	Br	0°	*Yarmouth,* Borough. 1667 [¼d.], for the use of the poor (POORE). 5.14 Yarmouth; 5.14 Yarmouth. BW 284. Nott [?Baldwin ex Gilbert]. Denomination for 3273-98 from the assembly approval, 6 June 1667, of 'what the overseers have done in getting a stamp for farthings, for payment of the poor' (Snelling 1766, appendix no. VI)
3273b	2.57	39.7	M	0°	Same dies. [?Baldwin]
3273c	1.92	29.7	M	0°	Same dies. [?Baldwin]
	(chipped, corroded)				
3274a	2.95	45.6	Br	0°	*Yarmouth,* Borough. 1667 [¼d.], for the use of the poor. 5.14 Yarmouth; 5.14 Yarmouth. BW 285. [?Baldwin]. Same rev. die as 3275
3274b	2.74	42.3	Br	0°	Same dies. [?Baldwin]
3274c	2.68	41.3	Br	0°	Same dies. [Baldwin ex Gilbert]
3274d	2.28	35.2	Br	0°	Same dies. [?Baldwin]
3275a	2.78	42.9	Br	0°	*Yarmouth...* 1667... [Same description as 3274]. [?Baldwin]. Same rev. die as 3274. Struck from clashed dies, as evident on the obverse
3275b	2.41	37.2	Br	0°	Same (clashed) dies. [Baldwin ex Gilbert]
3276a	2.72	41.9	Br	0°	*Yarmouth...* 1667... [Same description as 3274]. [Baldwin ex Gilbert]. Same obv. die as 3277
3276b	2.20	34.0	Br	0°	Same dies. [?Baldwin]
3276c	1.85	28.6	Br	0°	Same dies. [?Baldwin]
3277	2.70	41.7	Br	0°	*Yarmouth...* 1667... [Same description as 3274]. [Baldwin ex Gilbert]. Same obv. die as 3276
3278a	2.57	39.7	Br	180°	*Yarmouth...* 1667... [Same description as 3274]. [Baldwin ex Gilbert]. Same obv. die as 3279
3278b	2.27	35.0	Br	180°	Same dies. [?Baldwin]
3279a	3.18	49.1	Br	180°	*Yarmouth...* 1667... [Same description as 3274]. [?Baldwin]. Same obv. die as 3278; same rev. die as 3280
3279b	2.79	43.1	Br	180°	Same dies. [?Baldwin]
3279c	2.46	38.0	Br	180°	Same dies. [?Baldwin]

[*continued overleaf*]

PLATE 12

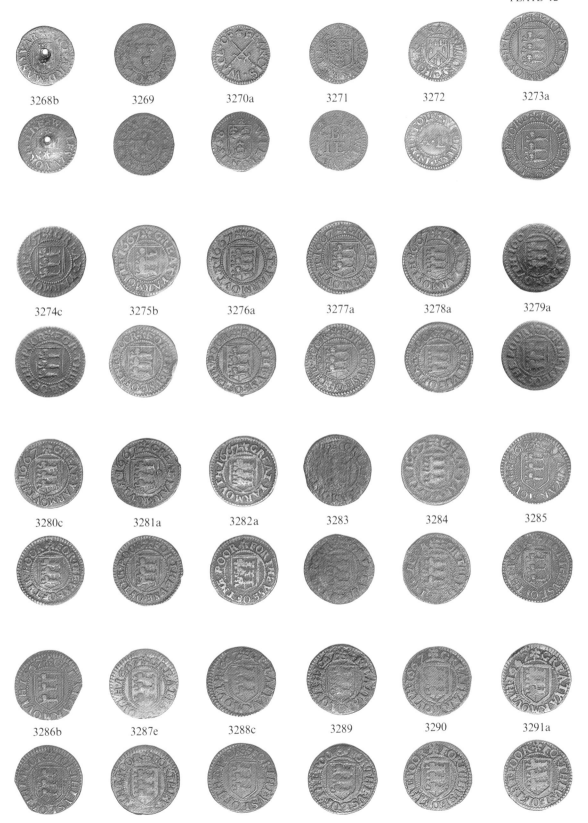

3268b   3269   3270a   3271   3272   3273a

3274c   3275b   3276a   3277a   3278a   3279a

3280c   3281a   3282a   3283   3284   3285

3286b   3287e   3288c   3289   3290   3291a

Plate 12 (*cont.*)

	Weight			Die	
	g	gr		axis	
3280a	2.82	43.6	Br	180°	*Yarmouth. . .* 1667. . . [Same description as 3274]. [?Baldwin]. Same rev. die as 3279
3280b	2.71	41.9	Br	180°	Same dies. [?Baldwin]
3280c	2.46	37.9	Br	180°	Same dies. [Baldwin ex Gilbert]
3281a	2.77	42.7	Br	180°	*Yarmouth. . .* 1667. . . [Same description as 3274]. [Baldwin ex Gilbert]
3281b	2.72	42.0	Br	180°	Same dies. [?Baldwin]
3281c	2.54	39.2	Br	180°	Same dies. [?Baldwin]
3282a	3.59	55.4	Br	180°	*Yarmouth. . .* 1667. . . [Same description as 3274]. [?Baldwin]
3282b	2.77	42.7	Br	180°	Same dies. [?Baldwin]
3283	2.07	31.9	Br	90°	*Yarmouth. . .* 1667. . . [Same description as 3274]. [?Baldwin]
3284	3.61	55.8	Br	180°	*Yarmouth. . .* 1667. . . [Same description as 3274]. [?Baldwin]
3285	2.59	40.0	Br	180°	*Yarmouth. . .* 1667. . . [Same description as 3274]. [?Baldwin]
3286a	2.74	42.3	Br	0°	*Yarmouth. . .* 1667. . . [Same description as 3274]. Nott [?Baldwin ex Gilbert]. Same obv. die as 3287
3286b	2.61	40.3	Br	0°	Same dies. [Baldwin]
3286c	2.26	34.9	Br	0°	Same dies. [?Baldwin]
3287a	2.94	45.4	Br	0°	*Yarmouth. . .* 1667. . . [Same description as 3274]. [?Baldwin]. Same obv. die as 3286
3287b	2.82	43.5	Br	0°	Same dies. [?Baldwin]
3287c	2.62	40.4	Br	0°	Same dies. [?Baldwin]
3287d	2.44	37.6	Br	0°	Same dies. [?Baldwin]
3287e	2.36	36.4	Br	0°	Same dies. [Baldwin]
3288a	2.72	41.9	Br	180°	*Yarmouth. . .* 1667. . . [Same description as 3274]. [?Baldwin]. Same obv. die as 3289
3288b	2.50	38.6	Br	180°	Same dies. [?Baldwin]
3288c	2.39	36.9	Br	180°	Same dies. [Baldwin ex Gilbert]
3289	2.74	42.2	Br	180°	*Yarmouth. . .* 1667. . . [Same description as 3274]. [?Baldwin]. Same obv. die as 3288
3290	1.93	29.8	Br	180°	*Yarmouth. . .* 1667. . . [Same description as 3274]. [?Baldwin]
3291a	2.67	41.3	Br	180°	*Yarmouth. . .* 1667. . . [Same description as 3274]. [?Baldwin]
3291b	2.25	34.8	Br	180°	Same dies. [?Baldwin]

	Weight			Die	
	g	*gr*		*axis*	
3292a	2.99	46.1	Br	180°	*Yarmouth,* Borough. 1669 [¼d.], for the use of the poor. 5.14 Yarmouth; 5.14 Yarmouth. BW 286 but initial mark a pierced sexfoil (both sides). [Baldwin]
3292b	2.38	36.7	Br	180°	Same dies. Baldwin [ex Gilbert]
3292c	1.91	29.4	Br	180°	Same dies. [?Baldwin]
	(chipped)				
3292d	1.09	16.9	Br	180°	Same dies. [?Baldwin]
3293a	3.17	49.0	Br	180°	*Yarmouth,* Borough. 1669 [¼d.], for the use of the poor. 5.14 Yarmouth; 5.14 Yarmouth. BW 286 but initial mark a pierced sexfoil (both sides). [?Baldwin]
3293b	2.47	38.2	Br	180°	Same dies. [Baldwin ex Gilbert]
3294a	3.27	50.4	Br	180°	*Yarmouth,* Borough. 1669 [¼d.], for the use of the poor. 5.14 Yarmouth; 5.14 Yarmouth. BW 286. Baldwin. Diameter 19.5 mm
3294b	3.01	46.4	Br	180°	Same dies. [?Baldwin]. Diameter 18.5 mm
3294c	2.27	35.1	Br	180°	Same dies. [?Baldwin]. Diameter 18.5 mm
	(chipped)				
3294d	1.67	25.7	Br	180°	Same dies. [?Baldwin]. Diameter 18.5-19 mm
3294e	1.62	25.0	Br	180°	Same dies. [?Baldwin]. Diameter 18 mm
3295	3.76	58.1	Br	180°	*Yarmouth. . .* 1669. . . [Same description as 3294]. [Baldwin ex Gilbert]. Same rev. die as 3296-7
3296	2.50	38.6	Br	180°	*Yarmouth. . .* 1669. . . [Same description as 3294]. [?Baldwin]. Same rev. die as 3295, 3297
3297	1.42	21.9	Br	180°	*Yarmouth. . .* 1669. . . [Same description as 3294]. [?Nott]. Same obv. die as 3298; same rev. die as 3295-6
3298a	2.32	35.7	Br	180°	*Yarmouth. . .* 1669. . . [Same description as 3294]. [Baldwin ex Gilbert]. Same obv. die as 3297
3298b	1.64	25.3	Br	180°	Same dies. [?Baldwin]
3299a	1.19	18.4	M	0°	*Ames,* John. 1652. 3.3.13; A|II. BW 289. Clark 1977. Diameter 16-17 mm. Same rev. die as 3300. For attribution cf. 'John Amis' 1664 (Frankel 1983, p. 126)
	(chipped)				
3299b	1.15	17.7	M	180°	Same dies. [?Baldwin]. Diameter 15.5-16 mm
3299c	1.09	16.8	M	180°	Same dies. Nott [?Baldwin ex Gilbert]. Diameter 16-16.5 mm
3299d	1.00	15.5	M	180°	Same dies. [?Baldwin]. Diameter 16 mm
3299e	1.00	15.4	M	180°	Same dies. [?Nott]. Diameter 16 mm
3299f	0.99	15.2	M	180°	Same dies. No provenance. Diameter 16 mm
	(chipped)				
3300a	1.09	16.8	M	180°	*Ames,* John. 1652. 3.3.13; A|II. BW 288. [?Nott]. Same obv. die as 3301; same rev. die as 3299
3300b	1.02	15.8	M	180°	Same dies. [Baldwin ex Gilbert]
3301a	1.09	16.9	M	180°	*Ames,* John. 1652. 3.3.13; A|II. BW 288. Nott. Same obv. die as 3300; same rev. die as 3302
3301b	0.98	15.1	M	180°	Same dies. [Baldwin]
3302a	1.07	16.5	M	180°	*Ames,* John. 1652. 3.3.13; A|II. BW 287. Baldwin. Same rev. die as 3301
3302b	1.02	15.7	M	180°	Same dies. [?Nott]
3303a	1.08	16.7	M	0°	*Arnold,* John. nd. 4.9.5; A|IM. BW 291. Nott [?Baldwin]
3303b	1.08	16.7	Br	180°	Same dies. [?Nott]
					Ball, Francis *see Bell,* Francis
3304a	1.23	19.0	Cu	90°	*Barker,* Benjamin. 1662. Date; B B. BW 292. [Baldwin ex Gilbert]
3304b	1.10	17.0	Cu	0°	Same dies. [?Nott]
3305	0.85	13.1	Cu	270°	*Barker,* Benjamin. 1662. Date; B B. BW 292. Nott [?Baldwin ex Gilbert]
3306	1.20	18.5	Cu	0°	*Barker,* Benjamin. 1662. Date; B B. BW 293. Baldwin [ex Gilbert]
3307	0.66	10.2	Br	90°	*Batch,* William. nd. 4.10.1; W B. BW 294-6. Baldwin [ex Gilbert]
3308a	0.88	13.6	Br	0°	*Batch,* William. nd. 4.10.1; W B. BW 294-6. Nott [?Baldwin ex Gilbert]
3308b	0.78	12.0	Br	0°	Same dies. [?Nott]
3309a	1.19	18.4	M	180°	*Bateman,* William. 1656. 5.76.79 (W B); 5.76.80 (W B). BW 298. Nott. Same obv. die as 3310. William Bateman, merchant, 1664 (Rutledge 1979, no. 584)
3309b	0.85	13.0	M	180°	Same dies. [?Nott]
3310a	1.16	17.9	M	180°	*Bateman,* William. 1656. 5.76.79 (W B); 5.76.80 (W B). BW 297. Baldwin. Same obv. die as 3309. Diameter 15.5-16.5 mm
3310b	1.03	15.8	M	180°	Same dies. [?Nott]. Diameter 16-17 mm
3310c	0.94	14.4	M	180°	Same dies. [?Baldwin]. Diameter 15 mm
	(worn)				
3311a	1.16	18.0	M	270°	*Bateman,* William. 1667. 5.76.79 (W B); 5.62.2 (W B). BW 299. Nott [?Baldwin ex Gilbert]. Same rev. die as 3312
3311b	0.76	11.8	M	270°	Same dies. [?Nott]

[*continued overleaf*]

PLATE 13

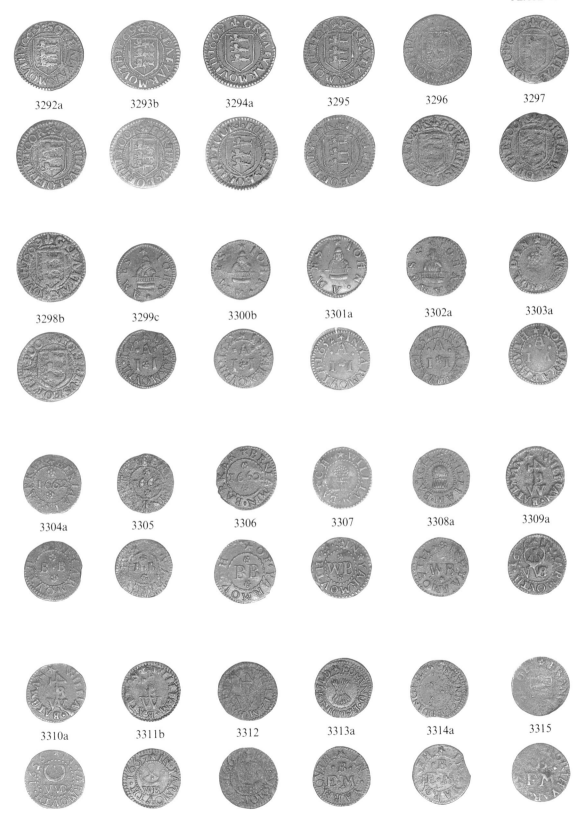

3292a 3293b 3294a 3295 3296 3297

3298b 3299c 3300b 3301a 3302a 3303a

3304a 3305 3306 3307 3308a 3309a

3310a 3311b 3312 3313a 3314a 3315

Plate 13 (*cont.*)

	Weight			Die	
	g	*gr*		*axis*	
3312	1.15	17.8	M	90°	*Bateman*, William. 1667. 5.76.79 (W B); 5.62.2 (W B). BW 299. [Baldwin]. Same rev. die as 3311
3313a	1.17	18.0	Br	180°	*Beddingfild*, Edmund. nd. 5.40.9; B|EM. BW 300. Nott [?Baldwin ex Gilbert]. Same rev. die as 3314
3313b	1.14	17.6	Br	180°	Same dies. [?Baldwin]
3314a	1.62	25.0	Br	90°	*Beddingfild*, Edmund. nd. 5.40.9; B|EM. BW 300. [?Nott]. Same rev. die as 3313
3314b	1.33	20.5	Br	90°	Same dies. [Baldwin ex Gilbert]
3315	0.70	10.8	Br	180°	*Bell* (- -LL), Francis. nd. 5.17.20 (·FRANCIS ← -LL ·OF around); B|FM (.B.|F M; –NORTH YARMOVG- . . . around). BW —; *Sharman 1984, p. 23; Dickinson 291A. Nott

	Weight			Die	
	g	gr		axis	
3316a	1.22	18.8	Br	180°	*Bradford*, Thomas. 1655. 2.4.11; T B. BW 302. Nott [?Baldwin ex Gilbert]
3316b	1.16	17.9	Br	180°	Same dies. [?Nott]
3317a	1.21	18.7	Br	180°	*Bretton* (BRATIN), William, baker. nd. 4.10.1; B|WR. BW 303. [?Baldwin]. Form of surname from 3318
3317b	1.07	16.5	Br	180°	Same dies. Nott [?Baldwin ex Gilbert]
3317c	1.01	15.5	Br	180°	Same dies. [?Baldwin]
3317d	0.53	8.2	Br	180°	Same dies. [?Nott]
	(chipped)				
3318	1.22	18.8	M	180°	*Bretton,* William, baker. nd. 4.10.1; B|WR. BW 304. Nott [?Baldwin ex Gilbert]
3319	1.13	17.4	M	180°	*Condley,* John, merchant (MARCHANT). nd. 5.76.81 (C); C|IM. BW 305. Nott [?Baldwin ex Gilbert]. Same rev. die as 3320
3320a	1.27	19.6	Cu	180°	*Condley,* John, merchant (MARCHANT). nd. 5.76.81 (C); C|IM. BW 305. [Baldwin ex Gilbert]. Same rev. die as 3319
3320b	1.20	18.4	Cu	180°	Same dies. [Nott]
3321a	1.23	18.9	Br	0°	*Cooper,* Joseph, merchant (MARCHANT). 1656. C|IF; date. BW 307. [Nott]. For attribution cf. Joseph Cowper, apprenticed 1614 (Rutledge 1979, no. 192)
3321b	1.21	18.7	M	180°	Same dies. [Baldwin]
3321c	1.05	16.2	M	180°	Same dies. Nott [?Baldwin ex Gilbert]
3321d	1.01	15.6	M	180°	Same dies. [?Baldwin]
3322a	1.28	19.8	M	180°	*Cozens,* Christo—, grocer. nd. 5.14 Grocers; C|CA. BW 308. Nott [?Baldwin ex Gilbert]. Same rev. die as 3323-4
3322b	1.03	15.9	M	180°	Same dies. [Nott]
3323a	1.04	16.0	M	90°	*Cozens,* Christo—, grocer. nd. 5.14 Grocers; C|CA. BW 308. Nott [?Baldwin ex Gilbert]. Same rev. die as 3322, 3324
3323b	0.89	13.7	M	180°	Same dies. [?Baldwin]
3324a	1.54	23.8	Cu	180°	*Cozens,* Christ—, grocer. nd. 5.14 Grocers; C|CA. BW 311. Nott [?Baldwin ex Gilbert]. Same rev. die as 3322-3
3324b	1.20	18.4	Cu	180°	Same dies. [Nott]
	(chipped)				
3324c	0.88	13.6	Cu	180°	Same dies. [?Baldwin]
3324d	0.67	10.4	Cu	180°	Same dies. [Nott]
	(chipped)				
3325	0.94	14.5	M	180°	*Crafford,* Richard. [16]59. 5.8.1; C|RD. BW 312 but obv. the Royal Exchange; Thompson 1993, p. 78. Nott [?Baldwin ex Gilbert]
3326	0.88	13.5	Cu	180°	*Crane,* Thomas. 1665. 3.99.1; C|TI. BW 313. Nott [?Baldwin ex Gilbert]
3327a	1.16	17.9	Cu	0°	*Curtis,* John, baker. 1662. 3.4.2; I C|date. BW 314. [Nott]. Rev. legend starts at 6 o'clock. For attribution cf. 'John Curtis sen' 1664 (Frankel 1983, p. 127)
3327b	0.94	14.5	Cu	0°	Same dies. Baldwin
3328	1.05	16.2	Cu	0°	*Dawson,* Thomas. 1667. 3.6.58; D|TM. BW 315. Nott [?Baldwin ex Gilbert]
3329a	0.97	14.9	Cu	0°	*Emperor,* John. 1664. I E; date. BW 316. Nott [?Baldwin ex Gilbert]. Diameter 16 mm
3329b	0.81	12.5	Br	0°	Same dies. Baldwin. Diameter 17.5 mm
3329c	0.69	10.7	Cu	0°	Same dies. [?Baldwin]. Diameter 15.5 mm
3330	1.58	24.3	Cu	0°	*Emperor,* John. 1664. I E; date. BW 318. Nott [?Baldwin ex Gilbert]
3331	1.00	15.4	Br	270°	*Flaxman,* Richard. [16]57. 3.35.9?; F|RM. BW 319. Nott [?Baldwin ex Gilbert]
	(chipped)				
3332a	1.29	19.8	M	180°	*Godfray,* Thomas. nd. 3.64.4; T G. BW 320 but GREAT ·. Nott [?Baldwin ex Gilbert]
3332b	1.13	17.4	Br	180°	Same dies. [?Baldwin]
3332c	1.06	16.4	Br	180°	Same dies. [?Baldwin]
3333	1.03	15.8	M	180°	*Godfray,* Thomas. nd. 3.64.4; T G. BW 320 but GREAT ·. Baldwin [or Nott]. Obv. legend starts at 6 o'clock
					Harvey, William *see* SOUTHTOWN (Suffolk)
3334	1.03	16.0	Br	180°	*Hering,* Thomas (THOVMAS). nd. 5.81.13; T H. BW 323. Nott [?Baldwin ex Gilbert]. Same rev. die as 3335. Thomas Herring, apprentice pulley maker, 1624 (Rutledge 1979, no. 292)
3335a	0.93	14.4	Br	180°	*Hering,* Thomas. nd. 5.81.13; T H. BW 322. Nott [?Baldwin ex Gilbert]. Same rev. die as 3334
3335b	0.86	13.2	Br	180°	Same dies. [Nott]
3336	1.00	15.4	Br	180°	*Hooke,* John. nd. 5.82.1; H|II. BW 324. Nott [?Baldwin ex Gilbert]

[*continued overleaf*]

PLATE 14

| 3316a | 3317b | 3318 | 3319 | 3320a | 3321c |

| 3322a | 3323a | 3324a | 3325 | 3326 | 3327b |

| 3328 | 3329a | 3330 | 3331 | 3332 | 3333 |

| 3334 | 3335a | 3336 | 3337a | 3338a | 3339 |

Plate 14 (*cont.*)

	Weight			Die	
	g	*gr*		*axis*	
3337a	1.21	18.7	M	180°	*Lincolne,* William. 1652. 5.14 Grocers; L|WI. BW 325. Nott [?Baldwin ex Gilbert]. Same rev. die as 3338. For attribution cf. 'Mr Lincolne' 1664 (Frankel 1983, p. 115)
3337b	1.08	16.6	M	180°	Same dies. Nott
3338a	1.18	18.1	M	180°	*Lincolne,* William. 1652. 5.14 Grocers; L|WI. BW 325. Nott. Same rev. die as 3337
3338b	1.10	16.9	M	180°	Same dies. Nott [?Baldwin ex Gilbert]
3339	1.14	17.5	M	180°	*Murril,* Rebekah (REBEKKA). nd. 5.14 Bakers; R M. BW 329. Nott [?Baldwin ex Gilbert]. Attributed to 'Widd Murrell' 1664 (Frankel 1983, p. 124)

	Weight			Die	
	g	gr		axis	
3340	1.14	17.6	Br	0°	*Neave,* Jonas. 1659. 5.38.20; N|IE. BW 330. Nott [?Baldwin ex Gilbert]. For attribution cf. 'Mr Neave' 1664 (Frankel 1983, p. 114)
3341	0.92	14.1	Br	180°	*Neave,* Jonas. 1661. 3.109.17; N|IE. BW 331 but obv. re-described. Nott [?Baldwin ex Gilbert]
3342	1.12	17.3	M	180°	*Owner,* Edward, grocer. nd. 5.14 Grocers; E O. BW 332-3. [?Baldwin]. Same rev. die as 3343
3343a	1.30	20.0	M	180°	*Owner,* Edward, grocer. nd. 5.14 Grocers; E O. BW 332-3. Nott. Same rev. die as 3342
3343b	1.20	18.5	M	180°	Same dies. Nott [?Baldwin ex Gilbert]
3344a	1.60	24.7	M	0°	*Peterson,* Edward. nd. 2.1; P|EM. BW 334. Seaby 1961. Associated with Norwich record of Ed'rus Peterson, vintner, free 1634 (Tillett 1882, p. 40)
3344b	1.24	19.2	M	0°	Same dies. [Baldwin ex Gilbert]
3344c	0.91	14.0	M	0°	Same dies. [Nott]
3344d	0.88	13.6	M	0°	Same dies. [Nott]
	(chipped)				
3345	1.55	23.9	Cu	180°	*Richmund,* Thomas. 1654. T R; date. BW 336 but RICHMVND. Nott [?Baldwin ex Gilbert]
3346	0.81	12.5	Br	0°	*Shipdham,* Francis (FRANC^S). nd. 3.109.1; F S. BW 337 but FRANC^S, GRE^TYARMOVTH. Baldwin
3347a	1.08	16.6	Br	180°	*Spilman,* George. nd. 3.1.8; S|GE. BW 338. [Nott]. Issuer perhaps George Spilman, merchant, 1648 and 1668 (Norfolk 1910, pp. 80, 100)
	(pierced)				
3347b	0.99	15.2	Br	180°	Same dies. Nott [?Baldwin ex Gilbert]
3347c	0.86	13.3	Br	180°	Same dies. [?Baldwin]
3348a	1.08	16.7	Cu	0°	*Tilles,* Michael (MICHALL). 1666. 5.14 Grocers; T|MA. BW 339. Nott [?Baldwin ex Gilbert]
3348b	1.02	15.8	Cu	0°	Same dies. [Nott]
	(chipped)				
3348c	0.99	15.3	Cu	0°	Same dies. [?Nott]
3349a	1.51	23.3	M	180°	*Tracey,* Stephen. nd. 3.11; T|SA. BW 340. Nott [?Baldwin ex Gilbert]. Same rev. die as 3350
3349b	1.03	16.0	M	180°	Same dies. [Nott]
3349c	0.76	11.7	M	180°	Same dies. [?Baldwin]
3350a	1.19	18.4	M	90°	*Tracey,* Stephen. nd. 3.11; T|SA. BW 341. [Nott]. Same rev. die as 3349. Obv. legend starts at 3 o'clock
3350b	1.14	17.5	M	90°	Same dies. Nott [?Baldwin ex Gilbert]
3350c	1.01	15.6	M	90°	Same dies. [?Nott]
3351a	1.20	18.5	Br	180°	*Trotter,* Clement. 1653. 5.13.15; T|CS. BW 343. [Nott]
3351b	1.08	16.7	Br	180°	Same dies. Nott [?Baldwin ex Gilbert]
3352a	1.24	19.1	M	180°	*Waller,* Benjamin. 1658. Date; W|BA. BW 344-5. Nott [?Baldwin ex Gilbert]. Same rev. die as 3353. Benjamin Waller, merchant, 1687 (Norfolk 1910, p. 122)
3352b	0.96	14.8	M	180°	Same dies. [?Baldwin]
3352c	0.86	13.2	M	180°	Same dies. [Nott]
3353a	1.19	18.4	M	0°	*Waller,* Benjamin. 1658. Date; W|BA. BW 344-5. Nott. Same rev. die as 3352
3353b	1.04	16.1	M	0°	Same dies. [Baldwin ex Gilbert]
3354a	1.12	17.3	M	180°	*Wallton,* Benjamin. 1654. 5.38.1; W|BA. BW 346 but WALLTON. [Nott]. Same obv. die as 3355. Diameter 16.5 mm
3354b	1.07	16.5	M	180°	Same dies. Nott [?Baldwin]. Diameter 15.5-16 mm
3354c	0.96	14.8	M	180°	Same dies. [Nott]. Diameter 15.5 mm
3354d	0.86	13.3	M	180°	Same dies. [?Baldwin]. Diameter 15 mm
3355a	1.27	19.6	Cu	270°	*Wallton,* Benjamin. 1666. 5.38.1; W|BA. BW 347 but WALLTON. [Nott]. Same obv. die as 3354
3355b	0.83	12.9	Cu	180°	Same dies. Nott [?Baldwin]
3356	0.78	12.0	Cu	0°	*Waters,* Roger. nd. R W. BW 348. Baldwin. Cf. Roger Wa(l)ters, glover, 1622-40 (Norfolk 1910, pp. 61, 73; Rutledge 1979, no. 357)
3357a	1.47	22.7	M	180°	*Waters,* Thomas. 1656. 3.7.1; W|TE. BW 349. Nott [?Baldwin ex Gilbert]. For attribution cf. Thomas Waters 1663, 1664 (Rutledge 1979, no. 537; Frankel 1983, p. 115)
3357b	1.12	17.3	M	180°	Same dies. [Nott]
3358a	1.40	21.6	Br	90°	*Woodrooffe,* Gabriel (GABRIELL). nd. 5.14 Grocers; G W. BW 351. [Spink]. Same rev. die as 3359
3358b	1.06	16.4	Br	180°	Same dies. [Nott]
	(chipped)				
3358c	0.97	15.0	Br	0°	Same dies. Nott [?Baldwin ex Gilbert]
3358d	0.89	13.8	Br	270°	Same dies. [?Baldwin] -1972

[*continued overleaf*]

PLATE 15

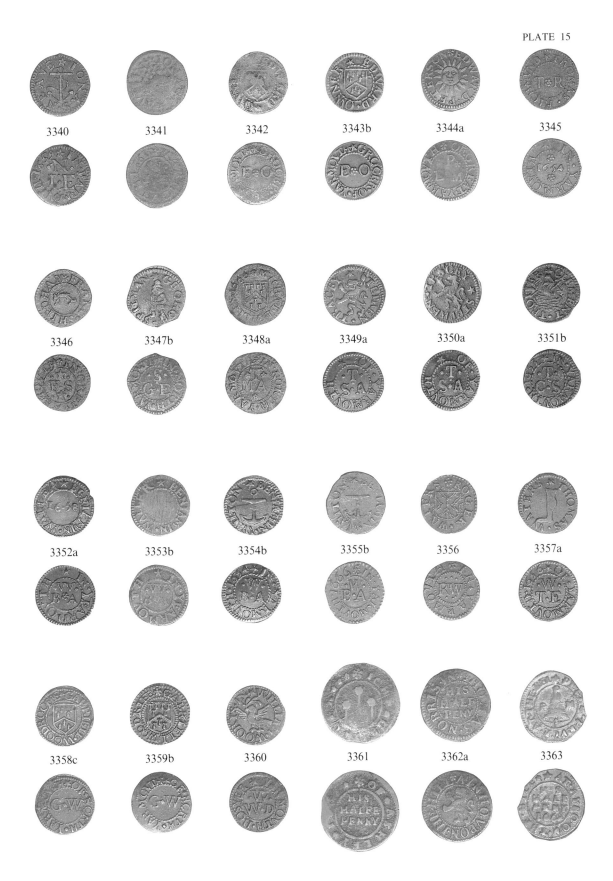

3340   3341   3342   3343b   3344a   3345

3346   3347b   3348a   3349a   3350a   3351b

3352a   3353b   3354b   3355b   3356   3357a

3358c   3359b   3360   3361   3362a   3363

Plate 15 (*cont.*)

	Weight			*Die*	
	g	*gr*		*axis*	
3359a	1.19	18.4	Br	0°	*Woodrooffe* (WOODRIFE), Gabriel (GABRIELL). nd. 5.14 Grocers; G W. BW 350. [Nott]. Same rev. die as 3358, whence form of surname
3359b	0.80	12.3	Br	0°	Same dies. Baldwin -1972 [ex Gilbert]
3360	0.99	15.3	M	180°	*Woorts,* William, hosier (HOSYER). nd. 3.108.10; W|WD. BW 352. Nott [?Baldwin ex Gilbert]

NORTHAMPTONSHIRE including the Soke of Peterborough

The county occurs as NORTHAM:SH on 3387; NORTHAMPTON SHER on 3397-8. Peterborough was transferred to the Soke of Peterborough Administrative County in 1889; to Hunts. and Peterborough in 1965; and to Cambridgeshire in 1974

ASHLEY

The reading is ASHLEY

| 3361 | 1.42 | 22.0 | Br | 270° | *Granger,* John. 1668 ½d. 4.1.12; 5.77. BW 1 but obv. description revised. Deane [1977 ex ? ex Carthew]. Attributed to John Granger d. 1670 (Wells, p. 20) |

AYNHO

The reading is AYNHO VPON THE HILL on 3362, AYNO ON THE HILL on 3363, cf. *Ayno on the Hill* Adams 1680

| 3362a | 1.97 | 30.5 | M | 270° | *Norris,* Thomas. nd ½d. 5.77; 3.11. BW 2 but AYNHO. Nott [ex Seaby] |
| 3362b | 1.03 | 15.9 | M | 180° | Same dies. [Baldwin] |

Named signs

| 3363 | 2.11 | 32.6 | Sn | 0° | *Bell* (AT THE BEL): Pruce, Peter. 1668 ½d. 5.70.2 (P|PM); 5.77. BW 3; Wells 3, but rev. die different from fig. 2. Baldwin. Specific Gravity 8.36: could be a tin-lead alloy of approximate composition tin 75% + lead 25%; optical microscopy x80 shows a dendritic structure, found only on cast objects: a cast counterfeit (E.G.V. Newman, Monnaies Numismatic Consultants Ltd., 11.8.92) |
| | (chipped) | | | | |

BANBURY *see* Oxfordshire

BOWDEN, Little (Northants. *subsequently* Leicestershire)

Bronson, Richard *see* 2814 (Leics.: Bowden, Great)

BOZEAT

The reading is BOZEAT

	Weight		Die		
	g	gr	axis		
3364	0.58	9.0	Br	0°	*Glover,* William. 1668 ½d. W G; 5.77. BW 6. Baldwin

BRACKLEY

The reading is BRACKLEY on 3365-8, 3370; BRACKLY on 3369

3365a	1.24	19.1	M	180°	*Attow* [i.e. *Atton*], Bartholomew, draper. nd. 5.70.1; B A. BW 7 but ATTOW [*sic*]. Baldwin. Bartholomew Atton, b. Buckingham 1631, fl. Brackley 1655-1700; the sign may refer to his grandfather's bell-foundry (Wells, pp. 26-8). See also 295 (William Atton)
3365b	1.02	15.7	M	180°	Same dies. [Nott]
3366	0.91	14.0	Br	180°	*Rand* or *Rands* (RAND), Conway (CONAWAY). nd. 3.11; C R. BW 9 but RAND. Spink 1975
3367	1.66	25.7	Br	90°	*Rand* or *Rands* (RANDS), Conway (CONNOWAY). 1671 ½d. 5.64.1; 5.77 (C R). BW 8. Baldwin. Issuer mayor of Brackley 1670 (Wells, p. 28)
3368a	1.42	21.9	Br	0°	*Stoakes,* John. 1670 ½d. 4.15.4; 5.77 (I S). BW 11. Nott. Struck from clashed dies
3368b	1.37	21.1	Br	0°	Same (clashed) dies. [Baldwin]
3369	2.05 (pierced)	31.7	Br	270°	*Wilkins,* Robert. nd ½d. 3.5.105; W|RE. BW 12. Baldwin. Robert Wilkins, gent., 1686 (Wells, p. 30)

Named signs

3370a	2.35	36.2	Br	90°	*Sun Inn* (AT THE SVN): Skilden, Mary. 1665 ½d. 2.1; 5.77. BW 10 but PENNY. Nott. Widow Skelden; bequeathed the Sun Inn (Wells, p. 29)
3370b	1.89	29.2	Br	90°	Same dies. [Baldwin or Seaby]

BRAMPTON, Church

Smith, Thomas *see* BRAMPTON (Suffolk)

BRIGSTOCK

The reading is BRIDGSTOCK, cf. *Brydgstock* 1614 (EPNS 1933, p. 158)

3371	0.77 (chipped)	11.9	Cu	0°	*Allen,* Tho—, chandler. nd. 5.14 Grocers; T A. BW 14 but THO:, CHANDL[ER]. Baldwin

BRIXWORTH

Isham, Gardener *see* IXWORTH (Suffolk)

BULWICK

The reading is BVLWICK

3372	1.18	18.2	M	0°	*Watts,* William. 1669 ½d. 5.77 (W|WM); 3.102.1. BW 15. Nott

CORBY

Risby, William *see* Uncertain II

DAVENTRY

The reading is DAINTREE on 3374, DAYNTREE on 3373, cf. *Daventre al. Deyntre* 1564, *Daintree* 1620, 1657 (EPNS 1933, p. 19)

3373	0.95	14.7	Br	90°	*Arnold,* Edward. 1667. 5.14 Grocers; E A. BW 17. Clark 1978
3374a	1.01	15.5	Br	0°	*Farmor,* Richard. nd. 5.14 Grocers; 3.1.30. BW 19-20 but RICHAR[D], figure grasping tree; Wells 19. Baldwin. The 1595 seal of Daventry bears the figure of a man (a Dane) holding an axe in one hand, and in the other one of the branches of a tree (Lewis 1845, ii. 15; Scott-Giles 1953, p. 295)
3374b	0.81	12.4	Br	0°	Same dies. Nott

DODDINGTON, Great

Johnson, John *see* 'DODDINGTON' (Uncertain I)

[*continued overleaf*]

PLATE 16

3364   3365a   3366   3367   3368a   3369

3370   3371   3372   3373   3374a   3375a

3376   3377   3378   3379b   3380   3381

3382   3383a   3384   3385b   3386   3387

Plate 16 (*cont.*)

ELTON (Northants. *and* Hunts.) *see* Huntingdonshire

FINEDON [*subsequently* Wellingborough parish (part)]

The reading is THINDON, cf. *Thyndon als' finedon* (Saxton 1576), *Thindon al. Thingdon al. Finedon* 1685 (EPNS 1933, p. 181)

	- Weight			Die	
	g	gr		axis	
3375a	1.41	21.8	Br	0°	*Bagerley,* America. 1669 ½d. 4.1.3; 5.77. BW 152. Nott. America Baggerley 'grosser' 1697 (Wells, p. 148).
3375b	1.13	17.5	Br	0°	Same dies. [Baldwin]

GEDDINGTON

The reading is GEDINGTON on both

3376	0.61	9.5	Br	180°	*Rowlett,* Jonathan (IONATH[N]). 1657. I R; date. BW 26 but IONATH[N]. Deane 1977 [ex ? ex Baldwin]
3377	1.01	15.6	Br	0°	*Rowlett,* Jonathan (IONATH:). 1664. I R; date. BW 27 but IONATH:. Baldwin

GRENDON

The reading is GRENDON

3378	1.36	20.9	Cu	180°	*Gawtherne,* Thomas. nd. G|TE; 5.14 Cordwainers. BW 29. Deane 1977 [ex ? ex Carthew]

HADDON, West

The reading is WEST HADDON

3379a	1.95	30.2	M	180°	*Almey,* Elisha. nd ½d. 5.14 Grocers; 5.77. BW 31. [Nott]
3379b	1.95	30.1	M	180°	Same dies. Spink 1971

HARRINGWORTH

The reading is HARINWORTH on both

Named signs

3380	2.18	33.6	M	0°	*Pack Saddle* (THE PACK SADEL): Bearly, Tho—, carrier (A CAROR). nd. ½d. 5.77 (B|TA); 5.79.33. BW 33 but THO:. Spink 1975. Same obv. die as 3381
3381	2.20	33.9	Cu	270°	*Pack Saddle* (THE PACK SADLE): Bearly, Tho—, carrier (A CARIER). nd ½d. 5.77 (B|TA); 5.79.33. BW 32 but THO:, CARIER. Baldwin. Same obv. die as 3380. Thomas Bearlie's 1669 will proved 1670 (Wells, p. 149)

HARTWELL (Roade parish)

The reading is HARTWELL

3382	2.01	31.0	Br	90°	*Church,* William. 1666 ½d. 5.65.1; C|WA|date. BW 34. Deane 1977 [ex ? ex Carthew].
	(pierced)				Attributed to William Church senior, buried Hartwell 11 Feb. 1687[-8] (Wells, p. 55; Wells 1931/3)

HIGHAM FERRERS

The reading is HIGHAM FERERS on 3384; HIGHAM FERRERS on 3385; HYGHAM FERRIS on 3383, cf. *Higham Ferris* Adams 1680

3383a	1.88	29.0	Br	270°	*Chetle,* John. 1667 ½d. 5.32.9; 5.77. BW 35 but HYGHAM; BW Addenda. Baldwin
3383b	0.86	13.3	Br	90°	Same dies. [Nott]
3384	1.75	27.1	Cu	0°	*Negus,* Gilbert. 1669 ½d. 5.37.16; 5.77 (N|GE). BW 39. Baldwin
3385a	2.50	38.6	M	180°	*Worthington,* Twyford. 1656. 3.54.3; date. BW 41 but HIGHAM:FERRERS; Wells 42. [Nott]. Issuer 'gent' 1655; Mayor 1656 (Wells, p. 58). The crest of Worthington, of Lancs. and elsewhere, was *A goat passant argent holding in the mouth an oak branch vert fructed or* (Burke 1884, p. 1136)
3385b	2.27	35.0	M	270°	Same dies. Nott [?Baldwin]
3385c	2.19	33.8	M	0°	Same dies. Nott

'IXWORTH' [*i.e.* BRIXWORTH]

Isham, Gardener *see* IXWORTH (Suffolk)

KETTERING

The reading is KEATRING on 3386; KET:|TERING NORTHAM:SH on 3387; KETTERING on 3388

	Weight			Die	
	g	*gr*		*axis*	
3386	1.12	17.3	Cu	90°	*Fox,* John. 1664. 5.14 Grocers; I F. BW 44. Deane 1977 [ex ? ex Carthew or Baldwin]
3387	1.27	19.6	Br	90°	*Ladds,* John. 1657. Date (· · ·|I657| · · ·; · IOHN · LADDS · OF · KET: around); L|IA (· L · |I · A; · TERING · NORTHAM:SH around). BW —; Dickinson 45A. Spink 1976. Date on obv. die subsequently altered to I664 (Wells, fig. 32)

KETTERING (*cont.*)

	Weight			Die	
	g	gr		axis	
3388a	1.12	17.3	Br	180°	*Webb,* Thomas, mercer. nd. 5.14 Mercers; T W. BW 46. [Baldwin]. Tho. Webb 'gent.' 1717 (Wells, p. 63)
3388b	0.80	12.3	Br	90°	Same dies. Nott

KILSBY

The reading is KILSBEY

3389	1.42	21.9	Br	180°	*Burgis,* John, mercer. 1670 ½d. 5.77; B|IM. BW 47. Baldwin

KINGS CLIFFE

The reading is CLIFE on 3394; KINGS CLIFFE on 3390; KINGSCLIFF on the remainder

3390a	1.63	25.1	M	0°	*Kings Cliffe,* Parish. nd Kings Cliffe ½d., changed (CHAINGED) by the (Y^E) Overseers. 5.60.1; 4.13.1. BW 48. [Nott ex Seaby]
3390b	0.91	14.1	M	0°	Same dies. Baldwin
3391	0.97	15.0	Br	90°	*Browne,* Jane. 1660. Date; I B. BW 50 but KINGSCLIFF. Deane 1977 [ex ? ex Baldwin]
3392	1.99	30.7	Br	0°	*Browne,* Jane. 1660 ½d. I B; 5.77. BW 51 but BROWNE, KINGSCLIFF. Deane 1977 [ex ? ex Carthew]
3393a	1.56	24.1	Br	0°	*Browne,* Jane. 1660 ½d. I B; 5.77. BW 49 but KINGSCLIFF. Nott. Diameter 20.5-21 mm
3393b	1.35	20.9	Br	0°	Same dies. [Baldwin]. Diameter 19.5 mm
3394	1.18	18.2	Br	270°	*Law,* Thomas. 1665+1659. Date; T L. BW 55. Nott [?Baldwin]. Thomas Law, grocer (Wells, pp. 65-6)

KINGS SUTTON

The reading is KINGS SVTTON

3395a	2.42	37.3	M	270°	*Chandler,* Edmund. 1666 ½d. 5.77; 4.15.5 (C|EE). BW 151 but rev. three cloves, E.E.C. I666. Nott
3395b	2.17	33.5	Br	270°	Same dies. [Baldwin]
3395c	1.42	21.9	M	0°	Same dies. [?Baldwin]

LAMPORT

Browning, John *see* 4074 (Somerset: Langport)

LOWICK

The reading is LVFWICK ALIS LOWICK, cf. *Luffwick al. Lowick* 1604 (EPNS 1933, p. 186), *Lufwick* (Adams 1680)

3396	2.26	34.9	Br	90°	*Sulch,* Lewis (LEWES). 1666 ½d. 3.53.1; 5.77. BW 59 but LEWES, LVFWICK, HALFE|PENNY. Nott [?Baldwin]

MOULTON

The reading is MOVLTON NORTHAMPTON SHER on both

3397	0.98	15.1	Br	270°	*Peryn,* John. nd 5.65.1; I P. BW 62-3 but NORTHAMPTON · SHER; Wells 64. Baldwin
3398	1.20	18.5	Cu	0°	*Peryn,* John. nd 5.65.1; I P. BW 62-3 but NORTHAMPTON · SHER; Wells 65. [Nott]. See also 3786a

NORTHAMPTON

The reading is NORTHAMPTON on 3403, 3405-15; NORTHAMTON on 3404; NORTHHAMTON on 3401-2; NORTHHATON [*sic*] on 3399-3400

3399a	1.18	18.2	Br	180°	*Northampton,* Borough (S.R. [*i.e.* ?Selby and Rands, chamberlains]). [1653 ¼d.]. 5.5.1; 3.40.1. BW 74 but NORTHHATON; Wells 66. Nott. 'The Chamberlins. . . shall forthwith. . . disburse fortie shillings for farthin tokens to be stamped with the town arms upon them', 24 March 1652/3; the chamberlains were William Selby and Richard Rands (Wells, p. 74)
3399b	1.11	17.1	Br	180°	Same dies. Nott
3399c	1.10	17.0	Br	180°	Same dies. [Baldwin]
3399d	1.06	16.4	Br	180°	Same dies. [?Baldwin]
3399e	0.96	14.8	Br	180°	Same dies. Spink 1973

[*continued overleaf*]

PLATE 17

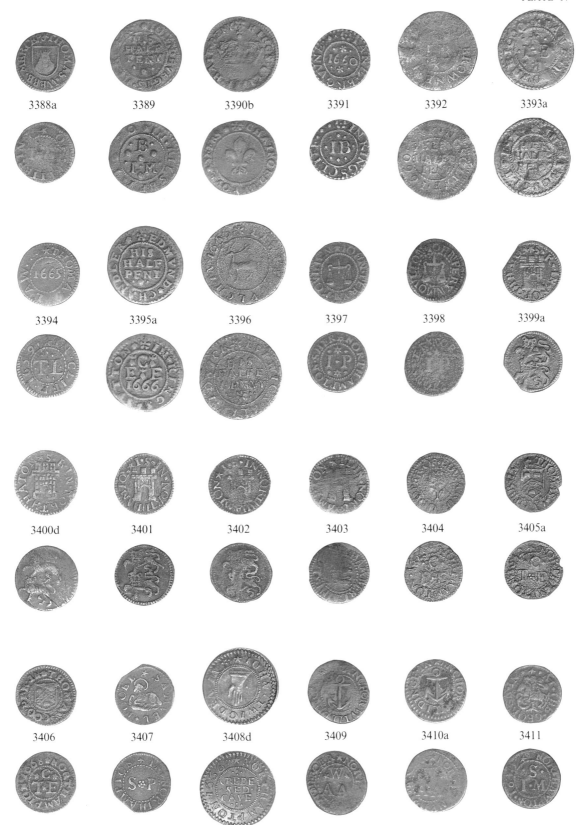

3388a   3389   3390b   3391   3392   3393a

3394   3395a   3396   3397   3398   3399a

3400d   3401   3402   3403   3404   3405a

3406   3407   3408d   3409   3410a   3411

Plate 17 (*cont.*)

	Weight			Die	
	g	gr		axis	
3400a	1.18	18.3	Br	90°	*Northampton,* Borough (S.R. [*i.e.* ?Selby and Rands, chamberlains]). [1653 ¼d. *i.e.* ?1662 ½d.]. 5.5.1; 3.40.1. BW 74 but NORTHHATON; Wells 68. [?Baldwin]. For Selby and Rands, original date and denomination, see 3399. 'Henceforth the farthings. . . shall freely pass and go currant and be esteemed and taken for halfepence apeece', 27 Apr. 1655. 'The chamberlaines doe forthwith procure the brasse halfepence which were the paste yeare called in, to be melted againe & new stamped with some marke upon them to distinguish them from the former stampe', 2 May 1662 (Wells, pp. 75-6)
3400b	1.11	17.2	Br	0°	Same dies. [?Baldwin]
3400c	1.04	16.1	Br	0°	Same dies. Nott [?Baldwin]
3400d	0.91	14.1	Br	0°	Same dies. [Coins & Antiquities]
3401	1.04	16.1	Br	180°	*Northampton,* Borough (I.S. [*i.e.* John Stevens, chamberlain]). [1657 ½d.]. 5.5.1; 3.40.1. BW 75 but NORTHHAMTON; Wells 70, but rev. die different from fig. 46. Baldwin. 'Mr John Stevens, one of the Chamberlaines, doe provide a new stampe for brasse halfepence', 12 Nov. 1657 (Wells, p. 75)
3402	1.05	16.2	Br	180°	*Northampton,* Borough (I.S. [*i.e.* John Stevens, chamberlain]). [1657 ½d.]. 5.5.1; 3.40.1. BW 75 but NORTHHAMTON; Wells 71. Spink 1976. For John Stevens, date, and denomination, see 3401; he was chamberlain 1657-8 and 1658-9
3403	0.82	12.7	Br	180°	*Northampton,* Borough (I.T. [*i.e.* John Twigden], chamberlain (CHAMBERLAINE)). 1660 [½d.]. 5.5.1; 3.40.1. BW 84 but I[no stop]T. Deane 1977 [ex ? ex Carthew]. John Twigden, chamberlain 1659-60 (Wells, p. 75); see also 3408.
3404	1.20	18.5	M	180°	*Cooper,* Edward. 1654. 4.11.19; C|EE. BW 67 but NORTHAMTON, obv. device an artichoke; Wells, fig. 50. Deane 1977 [ex ? ex Carthew]. 'Edward Cooper linendraper et mercer' 1654 (Wells, p. 78)
3405a	0.95 (chipped)	14.7	M	180°	*Cooper,* Thomas. 1652. 5.14 Ironmongers; C|TE. BW 68. Nott. Mr Thomas Cooper, ironmonger (Wells, pp. 79-80)
3405b	0.76 (chipped)	11.7	M	180°	Same dies. [Baldwin]
3406	1.19	18.4	Cu	180°	*Cooper,* Thomas. 1668. 5.14 Ironmongers; C|TE. BW 69. Nott. For issuer see 3405
3407	0.99	15.3	Br	180°	*Pooel,* Samuel. nd. 3.56.1; S P. BW 73. Deane 1977 [ex ? ex Carthew]. Mr Samuel Poole, chandler (Wells, p. 84)
3408a	1.70	26.2	Br	90°	*Twigden,* John. 1666, 'Crede sed cave'. 3.6.2; 5.77. BW 85 but ❖|CREDE|·SED·|CAVE| ❖. Brand [or Baldwin]. Mr John Twigden, glover (Wells, p. 87); see also 3403. Obv. perhaps in earlier state with no lozenge to right of glove. Diameter 19 mm
3408b	1.11	17.1	Br	0°	Same dies. [?Baldwin]. State of dies uncertain. Diameter 18-18.5 mm
3408c	0.84	12.9	Br	90°	Same dies. [Nott]. Lozenge to right of glove; dies unrusted. Diameter 18.5 mm
3408d	1.95	30.1	Ar	0°	Same dies. [Seaby 1968 ex Selwood, see *SCMB* (1968), 364]. Struck in silver; cf. Wells 1915, pp. 4-5. Lozenge to right of glove; rust before date and below CAVE, as in Wetton 1969, pl. 5. Diameter 20 mm
3409	1.76	27.2	Cu	270°	*Willdinge,* Anchor, mercer. nd. 5.38.1; W|AA. BW 87; Wells 86. [Baldwin]. Issuer free 1661; 'Anker Wilden mercer et trunkmaker' 1667 (Wells, p. 88). Same rev. die as 3410
3410a	0.98	15.0	M	90°	*Willdinge,* Anchor, mercer. nd. 5.38.1; W|AA. BW 86; Wells 85. Nott [?Baldwin]. Same rev. die as 3409. Will of Anchor Wylding proved 1667 (Wells, p. 157)
3410b	0.77 (chipped)	11.8	M	0°	Same dies. [?Baldwin]
3410c	0.72	11.1	M	180°	Same dies. Nott

Named signs

3411	0.98	15.0	M	180°	*George* (AT THE): ?S—, I/J—. 1650. 3.2.8; S|IM. BW 83. Baldwin. Attributed to John Smith, innholder; wife Margaret (Wells, pp. 84-5)

Named signs (*cont.*)

	Weight			Die	
	g	gr		axis	
3412	1.46	22.6	Br	0°	*One Pigeon* (AT Y^E): Alcout, Richard. 1667 ½d. 3.108.2 (A|RM); 5.77. BW 65. Deane [1977 ex ? ex Carthew]

NORTHAMPTON. 'Bird Street'

The reading is BIRD STREETE IN NORTHAMPTON on 3413, IN BIRD STREETE NORTHAMPTON on 3414. Perhaps for Bearward Street, *le Berewood strete* 1540 (EPNS 1933, p. 7), rather than Boyne's suggested corruption of Bridge Street (1858, p. 360)?

3413a	2.04	31.5	M	0°	*?S—, I/J—*. 1651. 5.65.1; S|ID. BW 80 but Rev. = I.D.S. [Baldwin]
3413b	1.11	17.1	M	180°	Same dies. Nott
3414	1.32	20.4	M	180°	*?S—, I/J—*. 1651. 5.65.1; S|ID. BW 81 but IN · BIRD · STREETE = Scales, Rev. = I.D.S. Baldwin

NORTHAMPTON. Drapery

The reading is IN THE DRAPERE NORTHAMPTON, cf. *The Drapery* Speed 1610

3415	1.15	17.8	M	180°	*Labram,* John. nd 5.64.1; L|IS. BW 71. Clark 1977. John Labram, mercer (Wells, pp. 83, 155)

OUNDLE

The reading is OVNDELL on 3420-1, 3429; OWNDELL on 3419; OWNDLE on 3418, 3424; OVNDLE on the remainder

3416a	2.44	37.7	M	0°	*Oundle,* Town. nd Oundle ½d., to be changed by the feoffees (Y^E FEEFEES). 3.67.1; 3.114.1. BW 88 but TO:, rev. a dragon. Nott. For the Feoffees of the Town Estates see *VCH Northants.* iii. 100-1. The Feoffees and Overseers met at the Talbot Inn (Wells, p. 90)
3416b	1.60	24.7	M	0°	Same dies. [Baldwin]
3417a	2.32	35.8	M	0°	*Oundle,* Town. 1669 Oundle ½d., for the use of the poor. 3.67.1; 3.67.1. BW 89. [Baldwin]. For the talbots see 3416
3417b	2.09	32.3	M	0°	Same dies. [Nott ex Daniels]
3418	1.26	19.4	Br	180°	*Audley,* John, tobacconist. 1669 ½d. 5.77; 5.64.66. BW 90 but I · 6 · 6 · 9, rev. description revised. Spink 1976
3419	0.81	12.5	Br	0°	*Austin,* Matthew (MATHEW). nd. 4.13.1; M A. BW 91; Wells 90. Nott [ex Seaby]. Matthew Austin 'grocer' 1698 (Wells, p. 157)
3420	1.39	21.5	M	180°	*Brow[n]ing, Nath—*, chandler. 1659. 3.55.5; N B|date. BW 92. Nott
3421	1.21 (chipped)	18.7	Br	0°	*Eaton,* John. nd. 5.14 Grocers; I E. BW 94. Nott
3422	0.61	9.4	Br	90°	*Filbrigg,* Will—, linen-draper. 1658. 5.15.23; W F|date. BW 95 but WILL:; Wells 95. Nott [?Baldwin]. William Filbrigge 'gent' 1687 (Wells, pp. 94, 157). The arms of Felbrigge, co. Norfolk, were *Or a lion rampant gules*; crest *Out of a ducal coronet gules a plume of ostrich feathers ermine* (Burke 1884, p. 344)
3423	1.20	18.5	Br	0°	*Hauton,* Lawrence (LAWRANCE). 1664. 3.3.13; L H. BW 96 but LAWRANCE; Wells, fig. 69. Nott
3424	0.75	11.5	Br	180°	*Hunt,* Matthew (MATHEW). 1657. M H; date. BW 98. Nott [?Baldwin]
3425	0.48	7.4	Br	300°	*James,* William, chandler. 1663. 4.15.4; W I|date. BW 99. Spink 1971. Legends start at 8 o'clock on both sides
3426a	1.13	17.4	Br	0°	*Mauley,* Daniel, chandler (CHANDLE^R). 1657. 5.14.89 (DM); 3.108.10. BW 100 but CHANDLE^R. Nott
3426b	0.99 (pierced)	15.3	Br	0°	Same dies. [Baldwin]
3427	0.98 (pierced)	15.1	Br	180°	*Pashler,* John, chandler. 1668. Date; 3.108.10. BW 101. Nott [?Baldwin]
3428	0.98	15.1	M	180°	*Stevenson,* Rich—, chandler. nd. 5.14 Grocers; R S. BW 102; Wells 104 but dies different from fig. 74. Deane 1977 [ex ? ex Carthew]
3429	1.19	18.3	Br	0°	*Terrewest* (TERREW-ST), William (WILL^M). nd. 5.14 Merchant Taylors; T|WK. BW 103 but WILL^{M}TERREW-ST; BW Addenda. Baldwin. The missing letter in the surname takes the form of F on this specimen, but may have been E in the ideal state; the preceding E is defective. William *Terrewest, Terrywist* 1653-79 (Wells, pp. 97-8)

[*continued overleaf*]

PLATE 18

3412 3413b 3414 3415 3416b 3417b

3418 3419 3420 3421 3422 3423

3424 3425 3426a 3427 3428 3429

3430c 3431 3432b 3433 3434a 3435

Plate 18 (*cont.*)

PETERBOROUGH (Soke of Peterborough)

The reading is PEETERBOROVGH on 3443, 3446, -BOVROWGH on 3450, -BROVGH on 3439, 3445; PETER BOROVGH on 3447; PETERBOROW on 3441, -BOROWGH on 3449, -BORROW on 3442; *Peterbrough* on 3430, PETERBROVGH on 3451; *Peterburg* on 3441-2, *-burgh* on 3433-4; PETERBOROVGH on the remainder. Note on 3430-4: The arms of the Dean of Peterborough, used by the City (the Dean and Chapter being Lords of the Manor), are *Gules two swords in saltire between four crosses pattée argent* (Fox-Davies 1915, p. 602)

	Weight			Die	
	g	gr		axis	
3430a	2.93	45.2	Br	180°	*Peterborough*, City (Overseers of the Poor). 1669 ½d. 5.42.32; 5.77.1. BW 104 but *Ouerseers*, I669, obv. and rev. transposed. Baldwin. £10 to be laid out for the public halfpenny, 11 Feb. 1668[-9] (Mellows 1937, p. 172; there are differences of substance in Wells, p. 101). Same obv. die as 3431
3430b	2.89	44.5	Br	180°	Same dies. [?Baldwin]
3430c	2.35	36.3	Br	180°	Same dies. [Nott]
	(chipped)				
3430d	0.91	14.0	Br	180°	Same dies. [?Baldwin]
	(chipped)				
3431	2.13	32.9	Br	0°	*Peterborough*, City. 1670 Peterborough (*Peterburg*) ½d., to be changed by the Town Bailiff (*towne Bailife*). 5.42.32; 5.77.1. BW 107 but *towne Bailife, Peterburg*, obv. and rev. transposed. Baldwin [or Nott]. £20 to be laid out for town halfpence, 10 May 1670 (Mellows 1937, p. 176; there are differences in Wells, pp. 102-3). Same obv. die as 3430
3432a	2.00	30.9	Br	0°	*Peterborough*, City. 1670 Peterborough (*Peterburg*) ½d., to be changed by the Town Bailiff (*towne Bailife*). 5.42.32; 5.77.1. BW 107 but *towne Bailife, Peterburg*, obv. and rev. transposed; Wells 110. [?Baldwin]
3432b	1.59	24.6	Br	0°	Same dies. [Seaby 1957+]
3433	2.29	35.3	Br	0°	*Peterborough*, City. 1670 Peterborough (*Peterburgh*) ½d., to be changed by the Town Bailiff (*towne Bailife*). 5.42.32; 5.77.1. BW 106 but obv. and rev. transposed; Wells 108, fig. 79. Baldwin. Same obv. die as 3434
3434a	3.22	49.7	Br	180°	*Peterborough*, City. 1670[-2?] Peterborough (*Peterburgh*) ½d., to be changed by the Town Bailiff (*towne Bailife*). 5.42.32; 5.77.1. BW 106 but obv. and rev. transposed; Wells 109. Coins & Antiquities 1977. Same obv. die as 3433. Dies rusted; perhaps struck in pursuance of order that £20 be laid out for more halfpence, 12 Jan. 1672 [N.S.] (Mellows 1937, p. 181; there are differences in Wells, p. 103)
3434b	2.13	32.9	Br	0°	Same dies. [?Baldwin]
	(chipped)				
3434c	1.96	30.3	Br	0°	Same dies. [?Baldwin]
3435	0.79	12.1	Br	0°	*Andrewes*, Robert. nd. 5.14 Bakers; R A. BW 108 but PETERBOROVGH. Deane 1977 [ex ? ex Carthew]. Reading completed from Wells, fig. 77

PETERBOROUGH (*cont.*)

	Weight			Die	
	g	*gr*		*axis*	
3436a	1.40	21.7	Br	90°	B[urton], R[ichard]. nd. 5.85.2 (R B); 5.77 (FEARE GOD HONOR THE KING). BW 109 but A^T; Wells 112. Longman 1958, lot 452. For identification of issuer see 3437
3436b	0.98	15.1	Br	90°	Same dies. [Baldwin]
3437	2.94	45.4	Br	180°	*Burton*, Richard. 1668 ½d. 5.85.1; 5.77. BW 111 but obv. device a closed book, clasped; Wells 1924, col. 412. Nott. Description completed from a specimen available to the authors
3438	1.23 (chipped)	18.9	M	180°	*Butler*, John. 1664. 5.14 Grocers; B|IE. BW 112 but PETERBOROVGH. Deane 1977 [ex ? ex Carthew]
3439	0.66	10.2	Br	0°	*Caryer*, Robert (ROBART). nd. 3.108.30; R C. BW 113 but PEETERBROVGH; Wells 117. Nott. Robert Caryer 'gent' 1673 (Wells, p. 161). The arms of Caryer of Canterbury, granted 1612, were *Azure a pelican argent vulning herself gules between eight fleurs de lis argent* (Papworth 1874, p. 317)
3440	0.96	14.7	Br	180°	*Cawthorne*, John. nd. 5.14 Bakers; I C. BW 115. Baldwin
3441	1.82	28.1	Br	270°	*Danyell*, Robert. 1668 ½d. 5.14.1 Grocers (R D); 5.77. BW 116. Nott
3442	0.35	5.4	Br	0°	*Dillingham*, Tho—. nd. T D; 5.82.9. BW 118; Wells 121. Nott
3443	1.07	16.5	Br	180°	*French*, John, draper. nd. 5.14 Drapers; F|IF. BW 119. Nott
3444a	1.01	15.6	Br	0°	*Hamerton*, George. 1667 ½d. 5.14.1 Grocers (H|GM); 5.77. BW 122 but PETERBOROVGH · I667.Nott
3444b	0.85	13.1	Br	0°	Same dies. [?Nott]
3445a	1.06	16.3	M	0°	*Kempe*, Margaret (MARGRET). 1664. Date; M K. BW 127; Wells 128. Nott [ex Seaby]. Second R of PEETERBROVGH over O or D
3445b	1.01	15.6	M	0°	Same dies. [?Baldwin]
3446	1.29	19.9	Br	90°	*Manisty*, Joan (IONE). 1668 ½d. 5.77; I M. BW 130. Nott. Double-struck on rev. Joane Manestie 'widdow' 1673 (Wells, p. 163)
3447	0.79	12.2	Br	0°	*Shinn* (SHINNE), Tho[mas], [?sen.]. nd. 5.14 Grocers; T S. BW 135 but THO:; Wells 137. Deane [1977 ex ? ex Carthew or Baldwin]. Form of surname for 3447-8 as in Reaney 1976. Mr Thomas Shinne the elder buried 1664 (Wells, p. 113)
3448	1.00	15.5	Br	0°	*Shinn*, Thomas, [jun.]. 1667 ½d. 5.14 Grocers; 5.77. BW 134. Deane 1977 [ex ? ex Carthew]. Form of surname for 3447-8 as in Reaney 1976
3449	1.35	20.8	Br	180°	*Slye*, Geo—. nd. 5.14 Bakers; G S. BW 136 but GEO:. Clark [1978]. Will of George Sly, baker, proved 1657 (Wells, p. 164)
3450a	1.30	20.0	Br	90°	*Taler*, James. 1669 ½d. 5.77; 5.14 Cordwainers. BW 137. [Baldwin]
3450b	1.07	16.6	Br	90°	Same dies. Nott
3451	1.89	29.2	Cu	0°	*Tompson*, Richard. 1668 ½d. 5.77; R T. BW 138. Nott
3452	0.52	8.0	Br	0°	*Wells*, William. nd. 5.14 Grocers; W W. BW 139; Wells 142. Baldwin

POTTERSPURY

The reading is POTTERSPERRY, cf. *Potters Perry* 1675 (EPNS 1933, p. 105)

3453	1.64	25.4	Br	0°	*Saul*, Thomas. 1668 ½d. 3.92.2; 5.77. BW 141 but POTTERSPERRY. Clark 1977

ROCKINGHAM

The reading is ROCKINGHAM

3454	1.14	17.6	M	270°	*Peake*, Samuel (SAMVELL). 1668 ½d. 5.14 Grocers; 5.77. BW 142 but SAMVELL · PEAKE, I668, HALF. Baldwin. Samuell Peake 'mercer' 1680 (Wells, p. 165)

ROTHWELL

The reading is ROELL on 3455-7, ROWEL on 3459, ROWELL on 3458, cf. *Rothwell or Rowel* Morden 1695

3455	1.46	22.5	Br	0°	*Bebee*, Thomas, baker. nd ½d. 4.10.1; 5.77. BW 143. Nott
3456	0.99	15.3	Br	90°	*Collier*, John. 1658. 1.31.8; C|IM. BW 144 but a chevron between three cloves. Clark 1977
3457	1.16	17.9	Br	270°	*Dodson*, William. 1666 ½d. 5.14 Mercers; W D. BW 145. Baldwin
3458	1.16	17.9	Br	180°	*Ponder*, John. 1655. 5.32.9; P|ID. BW 147 but I655. Baldwin
3459	1.76	27.2	M	90°	*Ponder*, John. 1664 ½d. (A HALF PENNY, *ob'*). P|ID; 5.77.1. BW 146 but *ob* with mark of abbreviation on the *b*. Baldwin. Reading confirmed from a specimen available to the authors. John Ponder 'chawndler' 1665 (Wells, p. 122)

PLATE 19

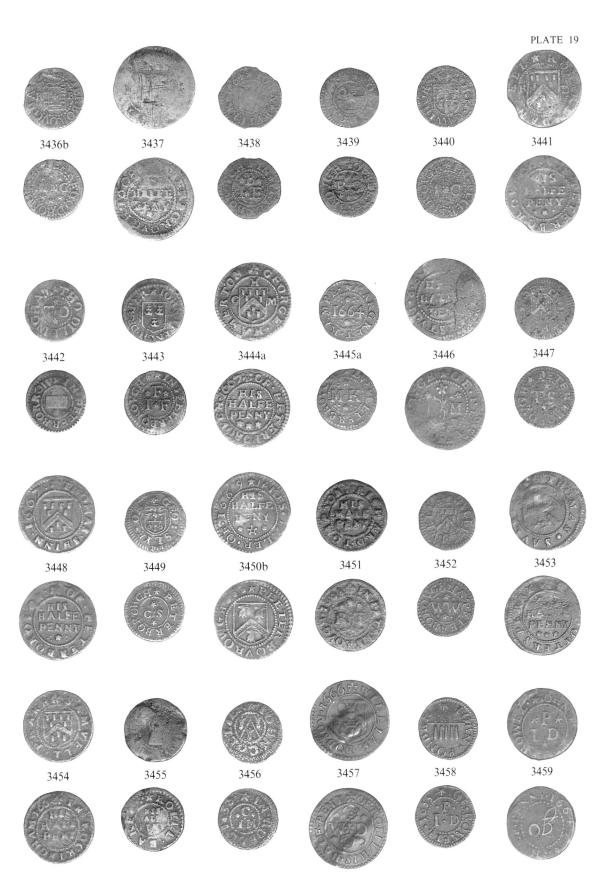

3436b   3437   3438   3439   3440   3441

3442   3443   3444a   3445a   3446   3447

3448   3449   3450b   3451   3452   3453

3454   3455   3456   3457   3458   3459

RUSHDEN

The reading is RVSDEN

	Weight		Die		
	g	*gr*	*axis*		
3460	1.93	29.8	Br	180°	*Carter,* George. 1666 ½d. 3.2.9; C|GE. BW 148. Baldwin. Attributed to George Carter, fl. Rushden 1669 (Wells, p. 122)

SUTTON, Kings *see* KINGS SUTTON

THINGDEN *see* FINEDON

THRAPSTON

The reading is THRAPSTON on 3463; THRAPSTONE on 3462; THROPSTON on 3461, cf. *Thropston* 1605 (EPNS 1933, p. 220)

3461	0.75	11.5	Br	180°	*Hunt,* John. nd. 3.3.13; I H. BW 154. Deane 1977 [ex ? ex Baldwin]. Attributed to John Hunt, fl. Thrapston 1660 (Wells, p. 124)
3462	0.76	11.8	Br	180°	*Palmer,* Edmond, bak[e]r. [16]68. 5.14 Bakers; E P. BW 155 but THRAPSTONE · 68. Deane 1977 [ex ? ex Carthew]
3463	1.29	19.8	Br	0°	*Willmot,* William. 1666. 3.102.1; W W. BW 156. Baldwin

TOWCESTER

The reading is TONCEŞTER [*sic*] on 3467-8 (TONCEŞTER on 3468); TOSSETER on 3473, TOWSETER on 3464, cf. *Towcester vulg. Tosseter* 1675 (EPNS 1933, p. 94); *Towcester* on 3472, and TOWCESTER on the remainder

3464	1.77	27.3	M	270°	*Bell,* William, dyer. nd [?1663] ½d. 5.14 Dyers; 5.77. BW 158 but DYER; Wells 158. Nott. The YER of DYER cancels 663, and the vertical of the D perhaps a figure I
3465	2.56	39.4	M	270°	*Bell,* William, dyer. nd ½d. 5.14 Dyers; 5.77. BW 157 but DYER; Wells 157. [Baldwin]. Reading completed from a specimen available to the authors
3466	1.80	27.8	M	0°	*Bell,* William, dyer. nd ½d. 5.14 Dyers; 5.77. BW 157 but DYER; Wells 1915, 157a. Nott
3467	0.85	13.1	M	180°	*Clarke,* Thomas. nd. 5.59.3; C|TA. BW 160 but TONCEŞTER [*sic*]; Wells 161 or 163; BW Yorks. 66. Seaby [1974 ex Glendining 6.3.74 lot 285 ex Hird]
3468	0.72	11.0	Cu	240°	*Clarke* (C̦-ARKE), Thomas. nd. 5.59.3; C|TA. *BW 160 (CLARKE) but TONCEŞTER [*sic*]; Wells 164; *BW Yorks. 66. Nott
3469	1.24 (pierced)	19.1	Br	270°	*Clarke,* Thomas. 1669 ½d. 5.14 Drapers; 5.77. BW 159. Nott. 'Thomas Clarke, draper' 1677 (Wells, p. 127)
3470	1.60	24.7	Br	0°	*Gore,* Charles. 1663 ½d. 5.15.24; 5.77. BW 163. Nott. Charles Gore 'mercer' 1682, 'woollen draper' 1684 (Wells, pp. 129, 169). The arms of Gore, of Leicestershire, were *Argent three bulls' heads couped proper;* crest *A bull's head couped* (Wells, p. 129)
3471a	1.74	26.8	Br	0°	*Harris,* Thomas. 1668 ½d. 5.64.182 (H|TM); 5.77. BW 164. Nott
3471b	1.51	23.3	Br	0°	Same dies. [Baldwin]
3472	2.21 (chipped)	34.0	Br	0°	*Herron,* Patrick (*Pattricke*). nd ½d. 5.77.1; 5.14.90 (P H). BW 165 but *His|Halfpeny|* · P · H · |Arms. Nott. Patrick Heron 'mercer' (Wells, p. 131)
3473	1.19	18.4	Br	180°	*Kingston,* John, mercer. nd. 5.14 Grocers; K|IG. BW 168. Deane 1977 [ex ? ex Carthew]
3474	0.82	12.7	Br	0°	*Kingston,* John. 1666. 5.65.1; I K|date. BW 167. Nott
3475a	2.26	34.9	Cu	180°	*Waple,* George. 1667 ½d. 5.14 Mercers; 5.77. BW 169. Nott. George Waples 'mercer' (Wells, p. 133)
3475b	2.11	32.5	M	0°	Same dies. [Baldwin]

WANSFORD (Soke of Peterborough, Thornhaugh parish)

The reading is WANSFORD

3476	1.00 (chipped)	15.4	Br	180°	*Boseman,* George. 1663. 5.64.4; G B. BW 173 but I6[Sugar-loaf]63; Wells 173 but dies different from fig. 111. Baldwin

WEEDON BECK [*subsequently* WEEDON BEC]

The reading is WEEDEN throughout

3477	1.19	18.3	Br	180°	*Marriott,* Thomas. 1657. 5.14 Grocers; M|TF. BW 170. Deane 1977 [ex ? ex Carthew]. Attributed to Thomas Marriott, d. Weedon Beck 1658 (Wells, p. 136)

[*continued overleaf*]

PLATE 20

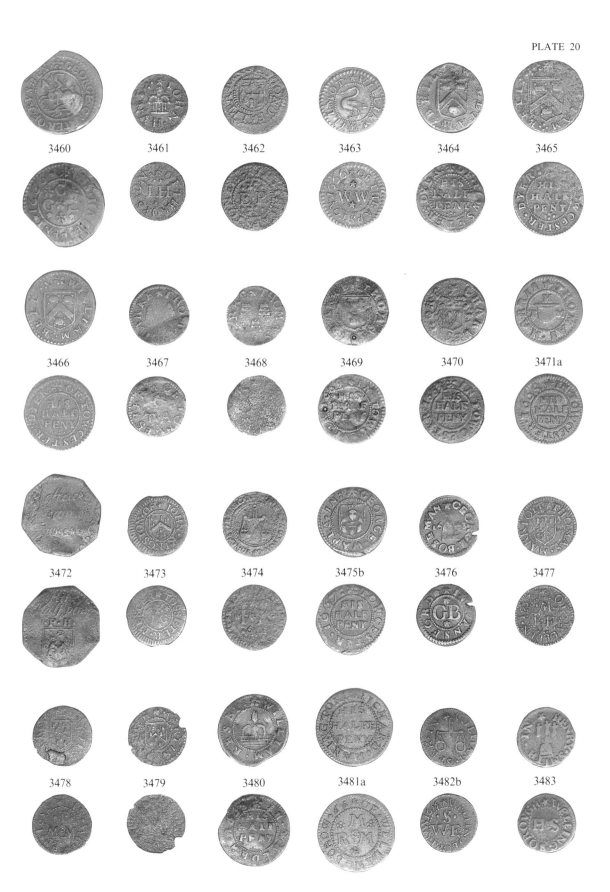

| 3460 | 3461 | 3462 | 3463 | 3464 | 3465 |

| 3466 | 3467 | 3468 | 3469 | 3470 | 3471a |

| 3472 | 3473 | 3474 | 3475b | 3476 | 3477 |

| 3478 | 3479 | 3480 | 3481a | 3482b | 3483 |

Plate 20 (*cont.*)

	Weight			Die
	g	gr		axis
3478	1.05	16.2	Br	0°	*Packer* (-ACKER), Martin. 1652. 5.14 Grocers (·MARTIN...ACKER around); P|MM (·P·|M·M;·IN·WEEDEN·I652around)*BW Addenda; *Wells 175 (not as fig. 113, which illustrates 176). Baldwin. The C of [P]ACKER perhaps cancels R, if not the effect of corrosion. Same rev. die as 3479
3479	0.60	9.3	Br	180°	*Packer* (PARKER), Martin. 1652. 5.14 Grocers; P|MM. BW 171; Wells 177. Spink 1975. Same rev. die as 3478. Martin *Packer* or *Pacur*, fl. Weedon Beck 1621-79 (Wells, pp. 137-8)
	(chipped)				

WELDON, Great

The reading is WELDEN

3480	1.51	23.3	Br	270°	*Resby,* William. 1668 ½d. 3.3.13; 5.77. BW 172. Baldwin. William Reesby or Reisby, tallow-chandler, 1693 (Wells, pp. 139, 170)

WELLINGBOROUGH

The reading is WELLING BOROVGH on 3483; WELLINGBOROVGH on 3484-5, -BOROW on 3481, -BORROW on 3482. See also FINEDON

3481a	2.30	35.4	Br	180°	*Manington,* Richard. [16]65 ½d. 5.77; M|RM. BW 175. Baldwin
3481b	1.74	26.9	Br	270°	Same dies. [Nott]
	(pierced)				
3482a	1.09	16.7	Br	180°	*Seer,* William. 1655. 5.65.1; S|WE. BW 176, Wells 182, but [no stop]I655. [Nott ex Daniels]
3482b	1.05	16.2	Br	0°	Same dies. Baldwin
3482c	0.88	13.5	Br	180°	Same dies. [Baldwin]
3483	1.21	18.6	Br	0°	*Smith,* Henry. nd. 5.70.5; H S. BW 177, Wells 185, but WELLING·BOROVGH. Nott

WELLINGBOROUGH (*cont.*)

	Weight			Die	
	g	*gr*		*axis*	
3484a	0.87	13.4	M	0°	*Smith,* Henry. nd. 5.70.5; H S. BW 177; Wells 184. [?Baldwin]
3484b	0.76	11.7	M	0°	Same dies. [Baldwin]
	(pierced)				
3485	1.25	19.3	Cu	180°	*Worthington,* John. 1668 ½d. 2.1; 2.2.6. BW 178 but HIS·HALF·PENY = a crescent moon. Baldwin (envelope), Nott (record)

NORTHUMBERLAND

NEWCASTLE UPON TYNE

The reading is NEWCASTLE on 3490, 3492-3, and NEW|CASTLE VPON TYNE on 3491; NEWCASTELL on 3486 (NEW|CAST|ELL), 3488-9; NEWCASTILE on 3487

3486a	1.05	16.2	Br	90°	*Barker,* Charles [and] *Fulthorp,* Gabriel (GABRILL). nd. 5.14 Mercers; 5.77. BW 1 but GABRILL. No provenance. Charles Barker and Gabriel Fullthorp, apprentices of Alderman Milbank, both free of the Mercers' Company 1660 (Boyne 1858, p. 366)
3486b	0.77	11.8	Br	90°	Same dies. Spink 1968 [ex Hird]
3487	1.05	16.2	Br	180°	*Dobson,* Anthony. nd. A D; A D. BW 3 but NEWCASTILE. Spink 1968 [ex Hird]
3488	1.12	17.3	Br	180°	*Dobson,* Anthony. nd. A D (·|A·D|·; ·ANTHONY·DOBSON around); 3.5.105 (·IN·NEWCASTELL· around). BW —; Hird 3 var.; Dickinson 3 [*recte* 3A]. Spink 1968 [ex Hird]
3489	0.73	11.2	Br	180°	*Gaustell,* John. nd. 3.58.1; G|II. BW 4 but NEWCASTELL. Spink 1968 [ex Hird]. Attributed to 'Mr John Garstall', Newcastle upon Tyne 1665 (Welford 1911, p. 72)
3490	1.53	23.7	Br	180°	*Hutchinson,* William. 166-. 5.5.1; 5.76.82 (W, H). *BW 5 (I660). Spink 1968 [ex Hird]. Issuer a Merchant-Adventurer (Boyne 1858, p. 366)
3491	1.63	25.1	Cu	0°	*London,* Will—. nd. 5.14.91; W L. BW 6 but WILL:, obv. device revised. Spink 1968 [ex Hird], illus. Hird 1951, pl. iv, 7. William London, bookseller, fl. Newcastle 1653-60 (Plomer 1907, pp. 119-20)
3492	0.67	10.4	Br	180°	*Slinger,* Henry. 1664. Date; H S. BW 7. Spink 1968 [ex Hird]. Attributed to 'Mr Henry Slinger', Newcastle upon Tyne 1665 (Welford 1911, p. 70)
3493	1.33	20.4	Br	90°	*Thomas,* John. 1659. 3.4.21; T|IM. BW 10. Spink 1968 [ex Hird]. Attributed to 'Mr John Thomas', Newcastle upon Tyne 1665 (Welford 1911, p. 72). Transposition of obv. and rev. would put the date in the correct order, but would be otherwise most unusual

NOTTINGHAMSHIRE

BINGHAM

The reading is *bingham*

3494	1.12	17.3	M	90°	*Banbury,* Edward. nd ½d. E B; 5.77.1. BW 1 but *bingham*:; Preston-Morley 1. Seaby 1971 [ex Glendining 22.9.71 ex Lowe]. Date *c.*1666 (Preston-Morley, p. 41)

BLYTH (Notts. *and* Yorks., W.R.)

The reading is BLYTH

3495	1.93	29.8	Cu	0°	*Carier,* Henry, mercer. nd. 3.78; C|HR. BW 4; Preston-Morley 5, pl. 7 (this specimen). Baldwin

COLLINGHAM, North

The reading is COLLINGHAM

3496a	2.04	31.5	Br	0°	*Ridge,* Thomas, mercer. 1664 ½d. 5.14 Grocers; 3.5.98 (T R). BW 6; Preston-Morley 7. Nott. Attribution to North Collingham from Hearth Tax records, 1663-74 (Preston-Morley, p. 45; Webster 1988, p. 19)
3496b	1.64	25.3	Cu	180°	Same dies. [?Baldwin]

COSSALL (Wollaton parish)

Digby, John *see* 1145 (Essex: Coggeshall)
Sadler, Richard *see* COLESHILL (Warks.)

[*continued overleaf*]

PLATE 21

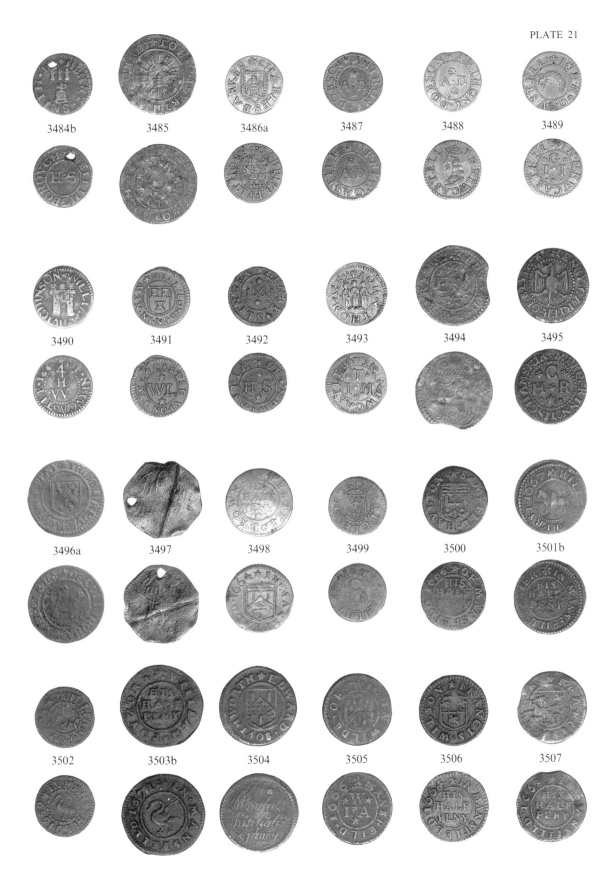

3484b   3485   3486a   3487   3488   3489

3490   3491   3492   3493   3494   3495

3496a   3497   3498   3499   3500   3501b

3502   3503b   3504   3505   3506   3507

Plate 21 (*cont.*)

LANEHAM

The reading is *Laneham*

	Weight			Die	
	g	gr		axis	
3497	0.86	13.3	Br	90°	*Adlington,* Mary. nd ½d. 5.77.1; 5.77.1. BW 10; Preston-Morley 11, pl. 8. Nott
	(pierced, chipped)				

MANSFIELD

The reading is MANSFIELD on 3506-7; *Mansfeild* on 3504, and MANSFEILD on the remainder

3498	1.15	17.7	Br	90°	*Browne,* Peter (PEETER). 1664 ½d. 5.77; 5.14 Blacksmiths. BW 11; Preston-Morley 12. Baldwin
3499	0.95	14.6	Br	180°	*Clegge,* Robert. 1659. 5.14 Apothecaries; C|RA. BW 12; Preston-Morley 13. Seaby 1971 [ex Glendining 22.9.71 ex Lowe]
3500	1.67	25.8	Br	0°	*Haulton,* Samuel (SAMVELL). 1664 ½d. 5.14 Bakers; 5.77. BW 13; Preston-Morley 14. Nott
3501a	2.06	31.7	Cu	0°	*Hurst,* William, carrier (CARIER). 1667 ½d. 3.60.7; 5.77. BW 15; Preston-Morley 17. [?Baldwin]
	(pierced)				
3501b	1.55	23.9	Cu	0°	Same dies. Nott
3501c	1.38	21.3	Cu	0°	Same dies. [Baldwin]
3502	0.72	11.1	Br	0°	*Poyzor,* William. 1659. P|WK; 3.102.11. BW 16; Preston-Morley 18. Seaby 1971 [ex Glendining 22.9.71 ex Lowe]. Legends start at 10 o'clock on both sides
3503a	2.00	30.9	Br	0°	*Poyzor,* William. 1671 ½d. 5.77; 3.102.11. BW 17; Preston-Morley 19. [?Baldwin]
	(pierced)				
3503b	1.59	24.5	Br	0°	Same dies. Nott
3504	2.60	40.1	Cu	90°	*Southworth,* Edward. nd ½d. 5.14 Ironmongers; 5.77.1. BW 20; Preston-Morley 20, pl. 6. Baldwin. Date *c.*1667 (Preston-Morley, p. 42)
3505	1.89	29.2	Cu	180°	*Wilde,* John. 1666. 5.14 Grocers; W|IA. BW 22; Preston-Morley 22. Nott
3506	2.00	30.9	Cu	300°	*Wilson,* Francis. 1664 ½d. 5.14 Tallow Chandlers; 5.77. BW 23; Preston-Morley 24, pl. 2 (this specimen). Nott
3507	1.80	27.8	Cu	90°	*Wilson,* Francis. 1668 ½d. 5.14 Tallow Chandlers; 5.77. BW 25; Preston-Morley 26, pl. 4. Clark 1977

MANSFIELD (*cont.*)

	Weight			Die	
	g	gr		axis	
3508	3.37	52.0	Cu	90°	*Wood*, Robert. 1667 [i.e. 1668/9] ½d. 5.61.7; 5.77. BW 26 but ROBERT·WOOD; Preston-Morley 28, pl. 5 (this specimen). Nott. For the later date see Preston-Morley, p. 26

NEWARK UPON TRENT

The reading is NEWARKE on 3510, 3515-16, 3520-1, and *Newarke* on 3511, 3513, 3517; NEWARK on 3509, 3512, 3514, 3518, 3522; NEWORKE on 3519

3509	1.89	29.1	Cu	180°	*Alvey,* Matthew (MATHEW), mercer. 1664 ½d. 5.14 Grocers; 3.5.98 (M A). BW 29; Preston-Morley 30, pl. 3. Nott
3510	1.53	23.5	Br	180°	*Burnett,* Christo—, saddler (SADLER). [16]68 ½d. 5.14 Saddlers; 5.77 (C B). BW 30 but CHRISTO:; Preston-Morley 31. Nott
3511	1.58	24.3	Br	270°	*Cam,* Henry, apothecary. 1666 ½d. 5.14 Apothecaries; 5.77.1 (H G). BW 31 but ·H·G· [*sic*]; Preston-Morley 32. Seaby 1971 [ex Glendining 22.9.71 ex Lowe]
	(chipped)				
3512a	2.09	32.3	Cu	90°	*Clarke,* Joshua, mercer. 1666 ½d. 5.14 Grocers; 3.5.98 (I C). BW 32; Preston-Morley 33. Nott
3512b	1.89	29.1	Cu	0°	Same dies. [Baldwin]
3513	1.94	29.9	Br	90°	*Cooling,* Denis, 'an apothecary'. 1666 ½d. 5.14 Apothecaries; 5.76.83 (D C). BW 33 but *halfe peny*; Preston-Morley 35, pl. 3. Seaby 1971 [ex Glendining 22.9.71 ex Lowe]
3514	1.81	27.9	Br	0°	*Glover,* Will—, chandler. 1664 ½d. 5.14 Tallow Chandlers; G|WA. BW 36 but WILL:; Preston-Morley 38, pl. 3. Nott
3515	2.14	33.1	Br	0°	*Lambe,* Henry. 1667 ½d., 'No (NOE) want where these are'. 5.77; 5.77. BW 39; Preston-Morley 42. Baldwin
3516a	1.96	30.2	Cu	0°	*Newham,* Matthew (MATHEW). 1657. 5.14 Mercers; M N. BW 40; Preston-Morley 43. Baldwin. Issuer was mayor 1656 (Preston-Morley, p. 48)
3516b	1.34	20.7	Cu	0°	Same dies. [Nott]
3517	1.33	20.5	Br	90°	*Shipman,* Richard, mercer. nd ½d. 3.5.96; 5.77.1. BW 41 but MERCER, *penny*; Preston-Morley 45, pl. 3 (this specimen). Spink [1971]. Date *c.*1666 (Preston-Morley, p. 42)
3518	1.67	25.8	Br	180°	*Whitton,* William, ironmonger (IRON MONGER). 1668 ½d. 5.14 Ironmongers; 5.77. BW 43; Preston-Morley 47. Nott
	(chipped)				
3519	1.12	17.2	Br	180°	*Wilson* (WILLSON), Robert, mercer. nd. 5.14 Mercers; W|RE. BW 48 but NEWORKE; Preston-Morley 52 (on pl. 1 '51' and '52' should be transposed). Nott. Form of surname from 3520. Date *c.*1657 (Preston-Morley, p. 42)
3520	1.13	17.4	Br	0°	*Wilson,* Robert, mercer. 1667 ½d. 5.14 Mercers; 5.77. BW 49; Preston-Morley 53. Nott
3521	2.07	31.9	Br	90°	*Wilson,* William, mercer. nd ½d. 5.77.1; 3.5.98 (W W). BW 50; Preston-Morley 54. Nott. Issuer 'gentleman'; one specimen overstruck on a token dated 1666 (Preston-Morley, pp. 48, 59 n. 62)

Named signs

3522	1.69	26.0	Br	270°	*Golden* [*?Horseshoe*] (AT Y^E): Goddard, Tho—, blacksmith. 1669 ½d. 5.77; 5.68.10. BW 37 but THO:; Preston-Morley 40. Brand

NOTTINGHAM

The reading is NOTTINGHAM on 3525, 3528-38, 3541-8, 3550, and *Nottingham* on 3523-4, 3540, 3552; NOTINGHAM on 3526-7, 3549, 3551; NOTTINGAME on 3539. Note on 3523-4: The arms of Nottingham are *Gules rising from the base of the shield a ragged cross of wood proper between three open crowns of gold the lowest encircling the bottom limb of the cross* (Scott-Giles 1953, p. 304)

3523a	3.99	61.5	Cu	180°	*Nottingham,* [Borough]. 1669 ½d., changed (*Chainged*) by the (y^e) chamberlains. 5.14.52; 5.77.1. BW 51 but *halfe · penny|Chainged · by · y^e, 1669*, obv. and rev. transposed; Preston-Morley 56. Nott. For the Common Council order see Nottingham 1900, v. 315; Preston-Morley, p. 48, prints *the* for *this Corporacion*
3523b	3.89	60.0	Cu	180°	Same dies. [?Baldwin]
3523c	3.66	56.4	Cu	180°	Same dies. Nott
3523d	3.29	50.8	Cu	180°	Same dies. Nott
3523e	2.57	39.7	Cu	180°	Same dies. Nott
3524	3.51	54.2	Cu	0°	*Nottingham,* [Borough]. 1669 ½d., changed (*Chainged*) by the (y^e) chamberlains. 5.14.52; 5.77.1. BW 51 but *halfe · penny|Chainged · by · y^e, 1669*, obv. and rev. transposed; Preston-Morley 57. Baldwin 1961
3525	1.74	26.8	Cu	0°	*Berridge,* John, apothecary. nd. 5.14 Apothecaries; I B. BW 52; Preston-Morley 59, pl. 4 (this specimen). Nott. Date *c.*1667 (Preston-Morley, p. 43)

[*continued overleaf*]

PLATE 22

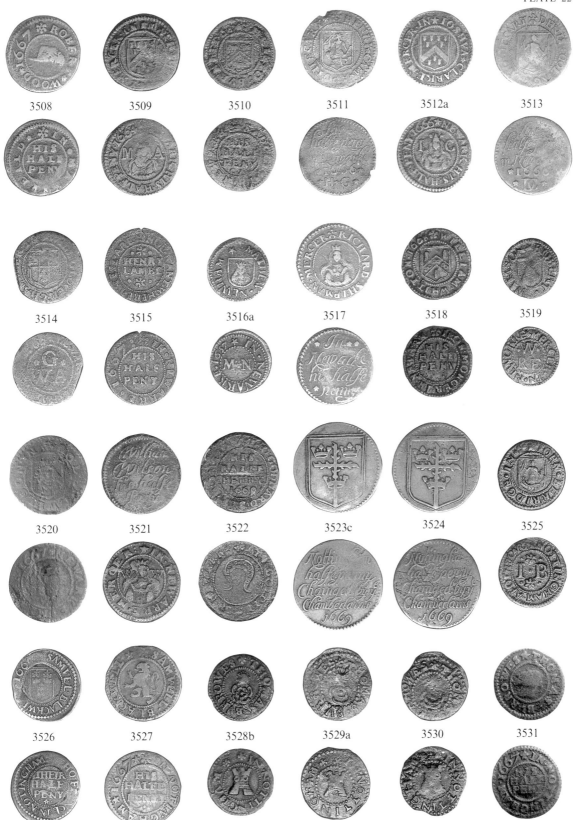

3508   3509   3510   3511   3512a   3513

3514   3515   3516a   3517   3518   3519

3520   3521   3522   3523c   3524   3525

3526   3527   3528b   3529a   3530   3531

Plate 22 (*cont.*)

	Weight			Die	
	g	gr		axis	
3526	1.73	26.6	Cu	0°	*Blackwell* (BLACKWE- -), Samuel [and] *France,* Thomas. 1666 ½d. 5.14 Drapers; 5.77. *BW 69 (BLACKWELL) but obv. and rev. transposed, Drapers' Arms, THO:, NOTINGHAM = THEIR|HALF|PENY|···; *Preston-Morley 61, pl. 3 (this specimen). Baldwin. Copper with central plug of brass (not brass with central plug of copper, as indicated by Preston-Morley, p. 33). Reading of rev. confirmed from Preston-Morley 60, pl. 3; France's forename extended on the authority of BW 70
3527	2.75	42.5	Br	0°	*Blackwell,* Samuel (SAMVELL). 1667 ½d. 3.11; 5.77. BW 56; Preston-Morley 63. Nott
3528a	2.70	41.6	Cu	180°	*Burrowes,* Thomas. nd. 4.12.6; 5.5.1. BW 58, Preston-Morley 66, but obv. description revised. [?Nott]. Date *c.*1663 (Preston-Morley, p. 43). Overstruck. Diameter 20-21 mm
3528b	1.54	23.7	Cu	0°	Same dies. Nott. Diameter 17.5 mm
3529a	2.28	35.2	Cu	30°	*Burrowes,* Thomas. nd. 4.12.6; 5.5.1. BW 59, Preston-Morley 68, but obv. description revised. Baldwin 1961
3529b	1.70 (pierced)	26.2	Cu	90°	Same dies. [Nott]
3530	2.02	31.2	Cu	210°	*Burrowes* (BARROWES), Thomas. nd. 4.12.6; 5.5.1. BW 60, Preston-Morley 70, but obv. description revised. Nott
3531	1.66	25.6	Cu	90°	*Burrowes,* Thomas. 1667 ½d. 3.65.1; 5.77. BW 62; Preston-Morley 71. Nott

	Weight			Die	
	g	gr		axis	
3532	1.88	29.0	Cu	0°	*Cockinge,* Tho—, chandler. nd. 3.108.20; T C. BW 64 but THO:; Preston-Morley 72, pl. 2. Spink 1975. Date *c.*1663 (Preston-Morley, p. 43)
3533	1.11	17.1	Cu	0°	*Cramton,* Robert. nd ½d. 5.14 Apothecaries; 5.77. BW 65; Preston-Morley 73. Seaby 1971 [ex Glendining 22.9.71 ex Lowe]. Date *c.*1664 (Preston-Morley, p. 43)
3534a	2.05	31.6	Cu	30°	*Dodsley,* Thomas. nd. 4.10.1; D|TS. BW 67; Preston-Morley 75, pl. 8 (this specimen). Seaby [1971 ex Glendining 22.9.71 ex Lowe]
3534b	1.48	22.8	Cu	330°	Same dies. [?Nott]
3534c	1.40	21.6	Cu	90°	Same dies. Nott
3535a	2.13	32.9	Br	270°	*Ellison,* Joshua. 1666 ½d. 5.77.1; 3.54.15. BW 68 but obv. = *His|Halfe|Penny*; Preston-Morley 77, pl. 5. Spink [1975] or Nott
3535b	1.73	26.7	Br	180°	Same dies. [Spink, *NCirc* Sep. 1976, 7641]
3536a	2.27	35.0	Cu	90°	*Farnworth,* Hugh. nd. 4.10.1; F|HI. BW 72; Preston-Morley 81, pl. 8 (this specimen). Seaby [1971 ex Glendining 22.9.71 ex Lowe]
3536b	2.00	30.9	Cu	150°	Same dies. Nott
					France, Thomas see *Blackwell,* Samuel and *France,* Thomas
3537	2.87	44.3	Cu	270°	*Garner,* Sam—, apothecary. nd. 3.10.13; S G. BW 74 but SAM:; Preston-Morley 83, pl. 7, but Y of APOTHECARY not considered to be superscript (cf. p. 34). Spink 1975
3538	2.27	35.0	Cu	180°	*Garner,* Stephen (STEVEN), apothecary. nd. 3.63.10; S G. BW 75 but rhinoceros upon a torse, as a crest; Preston-Morley 85. Brand
3539	1.75	27.1	Br	0°	*Greaton,* Thomas, brewer. nd ½d. 5.77; 5.64.40. BW 76; Preston-Morley 86, pl. 1. Spink [1975]. Date *c.*1661 (Preston-Morley, p. 43, and Challis 1989, p. 187)
3540	2.11	32.6	Cu	0°	*Hart,* John, chandler. nd ½d., 'Take these that will (WIL) I'll change (ILE CHAING) them still (STI^L)'. 5.77.1; 3.9.4 (H|IE). BW 83 but *Chandler.in, his.halfe*; Preston-Morley 93. Nott
3541	2.45	37.8	M	0°	*Hodges,* Joh—. nd ½d. 5.14 Ironmongers; H|IE. BW 87 but IOH:; Preston-Morley 97. Nott. Date *c.*1660 (Preston-Morley, p. 43)
3542	1.81	27.9	Br	0°	*Houitt,* John. 1667 ½d. 3.102.1; 5.77. BW 88; Preston-Morley 98 but surname improved on 'Hovitt' (p. 8). Spink 1975. Overstruck on another halfpenny token which has the Grocers' Arms as the main type
3543	1.93	29.8	M	0°	*Innocent,* Joseph. 1667 ½d. 5.14 Apothecaries; 5.77. BW 89; Preston-Morley 99. Nott
3544	1.18	18.2	Br	180°	*N[ewcombe],* W[illiam], 'meal (MEALE) and salt'. 1667 ½d. 3.10.2 (W N); 5.77. BW 91; Preston-Morley 101, pl. 5. Nott. For identification of issuer see Preston-Morley, pp. 34 and 49, where he is connected with an inn in Angel Yard
3545	1.96	30.2	Cu	180°	*Parker,* John. nd. 3.10.12; P|IM. BW 93; Preston-Morley 103. Clark 1977. Rev. legend starts at 6 o'clock. Date *c.*1659 (Preston-Morley, p. 44)
3546	2.15	33.1	Cu	0°	*Rotheram,* Robert. 1667 ½d. 5.14 Salters; 5.77. BW 95 but ROTHERAM; Preston-Morley 105. Nott
3547	1.38 (pierced)	21.3	Br	270°	*Toplady,* Thomas, draper. 1671. 5.14 Drapers; T|TS|date. BW 101; Preston-Morley 112. Seaby 1971 [ex Glendining 22.9.71 ex Lowe]
3548	1.88	28.9	Br	0°	*Turpin,* Richard, chandler. nd. 3.108.21; R T. BW 104; Preston-Morley 115. Nott. For the error perceived by Preston-Morley in the description of the device (p. 35) see classification no. 3.108.21
3549	1.96	30.2	Br	0°	*Wright,* Edward, milliner. [16]67 ½d. 4.13.1; 5.77. BW 107; Preston-Morley 118, pl. 5 (this specimen). Clark 1977
3550a	2.19	33.8	Cu	180°	*Wright,* Joseph. nd. 5.70.13; I W. BW 108; Preston-Morley 119. Seaby 1971 [ex Glendining 22.9.71 ex Lowe]. Date *c.*1663 (Preston-Morley, p. 44)
3550b	1.50	23.1	Cu	180°	Same dies. [Spink]

NOTTINGHAM. Trent Bridge neighbourhood

Garner, Stephen (STE·), tollman *see* FORGERIES

NOTTINGHAM. WeekdayCross

Occurs as *Wekeday markett,* probably so named in contrast to *Setterday Merket,* the former Great Market-place (EPNS 1940, p. 22). The reading is AT THE WEEKE:\|day\|Cross of\|Nottingham on 3552, cf. *The Wekedey Crosse* 1541; AT THE WEEKE:\|DERROSS [*sic*] OF NOTINGHAM on 3551

| 3551 | 2.44 | 37.7 | Cu | 0° | *Blunt,* John, baker. nd ½d. 3.2.1; 5.77. BW 54 but WEEKE:; Preston-Morley 64 but DERROSS. Nott. Same obv. die as 3552. Date *c.*1667 (Preston-Morley, p. 43) |

[*continued overleaf*]

PLATE 23

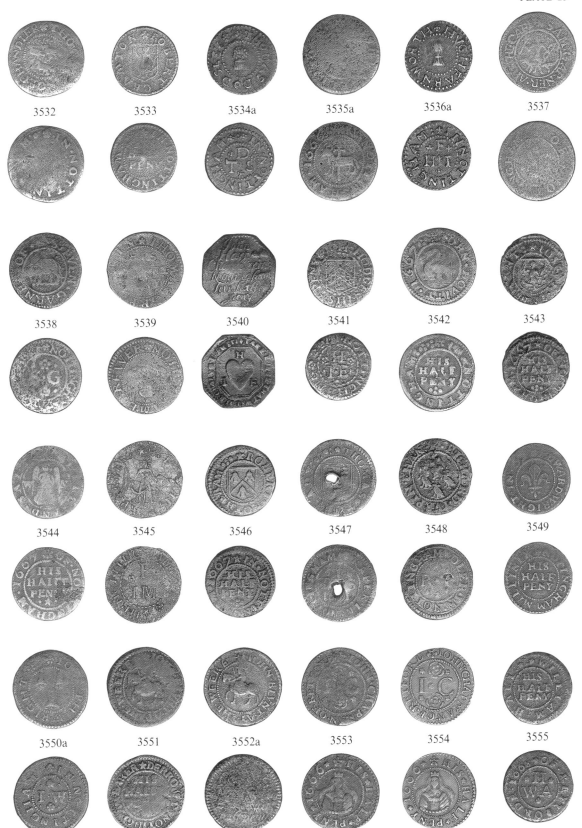

3532 3533 3534a 3535a 3536a 3537

3538 3539 3540 3541 3542 3543

3544 3545 3546 3547 3548 3549

3550a 3551 3552a 3553 3554 3555

Plate 23 (*cont.*)

	Weight			Die	
	g	gr		axis	
3552a	2.64	40.8	Cu	0°	*Blunt,* John, baker. nd ½d. 3.2.1; 5.77.1. BW 55 but WEEKE:, *Cross.of, Baker.his, half.peny*; Preston-Morley 65, pl. 4. Nott. Same obv. die as 3551. Date *c.*1667 (Preston-Morley, p. 43). Diameter 20.5-21 mm
3552b	1.46 (chipped)	22.6	Cu	0°	Same dies. [?Baldwin]. Diameter 19.5 mm

RETFORD, East

The reading is RETFORD on 3553-4, 3556; REDFORDE on 3557, cf. *Redford(e)* 1086-1675 (EPNS 1940, p. 58); RETTFORDE on 3555. Unless further evidence is specified, attributions are to this Retford as the only market-town of the name (Adams 1680)

3553	2.19	33.8	Cu	0°	*Chapman,* John. 1666 ½d. I C; 3.5.96. BW 112 but CHAPMAN; Preston-Morley 125, pl. 3 (this specimen). Baldwin. Same rev. die as 3554
3554	1.67	25.8	Cu	180°	*Chapman,* John. 1666 ½d. I C; 3.5.96. BW 112 but CHAPMAN; Preston-Morley 126, pl. 4 (this specimen). Spink 1973. Same rev. die as 3553
3555	1.98	30.5	Br	0°	*Hall,* William. 1668 ½d. 5.77. H|WA. BW 113; Preston-Morley 127. Seaby 1971 [ex Glendining 22.9.71 ex Lowe]

RETFORD, East (*cont.*)

	Weight			Die	
	g	gr		axis	
3556	1.49	23.0	Cu	270°	*Moody,* William, baker. 1666. 5.14 Bakers; M|WA. BW 114; Preston-Morley 128. Nott. Attribution confirmed by Hearth Tax assessment, 1663 (Preston-Morley, p. 47)
3557	1.87	28.8	Br	90°	*Scroopp,* William. 1669 ½d. 5.77 (· HIS · |HALFE|PENY|···; · WILLIAM · SCROOPP ❖ around); 5.14.92 (· OF · REDFORDE · I669 around). BW —; *Preston-Morley 129, pl. 6 (obv. of this specimen); Dickinson 114A. Nott [ex Carthew], reading REDBORNE with the 'Haberdashers' arms, and attributed to Redbourn, Herts.; attribution to this Retford confirmed by Hearth Tax assessment, 1663 (Preston-Morley, pp. 30, 47)

SOUTHWELL

The reading is SOVTH\|WELL

| 3558 | 0.99 | 15.2 | Cu | 0° | *Silvester,* Gregory [and] *Leaver,* William. 1664. 5.77; G S\|W L. BW 116; Preston-Morley 131, pl. 3. Nott |

TUXFORD

The reading is TVXFORD

| 3559 | 1.44 | 22.3 | Br | 0° | *Strutt,* Fran— (m.), mercer. 1669 ½d. 5.14 Grocers; 5.14.2 Mercers. BW 118 but FRAN:; Preston-Morley 134. Spink 1971 |

WORKSOP

The reading is WORKSOP on both

| 3560 | 2.61 | 40.3 | Cu | 270° | *Flecher,* Joseph. nd ½d. 5.14 Apothecaries; F\|IK. BW 119; Preston-Morley 135. Baldwin. Date *c.*1663 (Preston-Morley, p. 44) |
| 3561 | 1.23 | 18.9 | M | 90° | *Rutter,* Rich—. 1664 ½d. 5.14 Mercers; R\|RA. BW 121 but RICH:, PEN[Y]; Preston-Morley 138. Brand |

OXFORDSHIRE

The county occurs as COM[T]OXFOR[D] on 3610; COVNTY OF OXFORD on 3813; THE COVNTY OXON on 3844; Y[E]COVNTY OF OXON on 3814; OXFORD SHEIRE on 3594, 3639, SHIERE on 3608, SHIR on 3789; OXFORDSHEIRE on 3595, 3597; OXFORDSH[R] on 3636

ADDERBURY

The reading is ADDERBERY on 3562; ATTERBVRY on 3563

| 3562 | 1.22 | 18.8 | M | 180° | *Hunt,* Henry. 1656. 5.60.1; H\|HE. BW 2; Milne 2. Nott. Henry Hunt, chandler, 1664 (Milne, p. 31) |

Named signs

| 3563a | 2.30 | 35.5 | Br | 0° | *Red Lion* (AT THE RED LYON): Austin, Tho—. 1669 ½d. 3.11; 5.77 (A\|TM). BW 1 but THO:, AT · THE · RED, ATTERBVRY; BW Uncertain 14 but THO:, T.M.A.; Milne 1. Baldwin. For attribution see Milne, p. 31 |
| 3563b | 1.06 | 16.3 | Br | 0° | Same dies. Nott |

BAMPTON

The reading is BAMTON on 3566; BAMTON THE BVSH on 3564, BAMPTON OF THE BVSH on 3565, cf. *Bampton in the Bush* 1797 etc., from the surrounding region of common scrub across which there were no roads up to 1750 (EPNS 1954, p. 304)

3564a	1.65	25.5	Br	180°	*Bassett,* Simon. 1669 ½d. 5.77 (B|SE); 3.91.2. BW 3 but BASSETT, I669; Milne 3. Nott. Simon Bassett, fellmonger, 1681 (Milne, p. 31)
3564b	1.36	20.9	Br	180°	Same dies. [?Baldwin]
	(chipped)				
3565a	1.54	23.8	Br	150°	*Lardner,* Walter. nd ½d. 3.3.13; 5.77 (L|WM). BW 4 but BAMPTON; Milne 4. [?Baldwin]. Walter Lardner (d. 1702/3?), chandler (Milne, p. 31)
3565b	1.47	22.7	Br	330°	Same dies. Nott
3566a	1.18	18.3	M	180°	*Tull,* John. 1656. 5.14 Mercers; T|IR. BW 5; Milne 5. [?Baldwin]
3566b	0.67	10.3	M	180°	Same dies. Brand [or Nott]
3566c	0.61	9.4	Br	0°	Same dies. [?Baldwin]

[*continued overleaf*]

PLATE 24

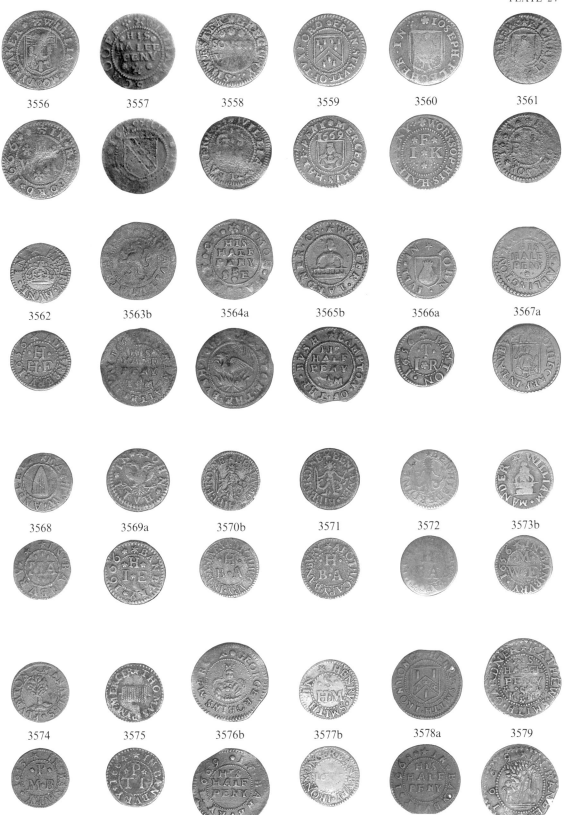

3556   3557   3558   3559   3560   3561

3562   3563b   3564a   3565b   3566a   3567a

3568   3569a   3570b   3571   3572   3573b

3574   3575   3576b   3577b   3578a   3579

Plate 24 (*cont.*)

BANBURY (Oxon. *and* Northamptonshire)

The reading is BANBERIE on 3588; BANBERY on 3579; BANBVRYE on 3580; BANBVRY on the remainder

	Weight		Die	
	g	gr	axis	
3567a	2.50	38.6	Cu	0°	*Allington*, John, apothecary. 1666 ½d. 5.77; 5.14.1 Apothecaries (I A). BW 6; Milne 6. Nott
3567b	2.27	35.0	Cu	0°	Same dies. [Baldwin]
3567c	1.67	25.8	Cu	0°	Same dies. [?Baldwin]
3568	1.01	15.6	Br	90°	*Ansley*, Matthew (MATHEW). nd. 5.64.1; M A. BW 7; Milne 7. Nott
3569a	1.53	23.7	Cu	270°	*Hall*, John. 1666. 3.95.1; H|IE. BW 9; Milne 9. Nott. John Hall, mercer, 1666 (Milne, p. 32)
3569b	1.16	17.8	Br	0°	Same dies. [?Baldwin]
3570a	1.13	17.4	Br	180°	*Hibberdine*, Benjamin (BENIAMEN), apothecary. nd. 3.10.12; H|BA. BW 10; Milne 10. [?Baldwin]. Benjamin Hibberdine d. 1662/3 (Milne, p. 32). Same obv. die as 3571
3570b	1.05	16.2	Br	180°	Same dies. Nott
3571	1.03	15.9	Br	0°	*Hibberdine*, Benjamin (BENIAMEN), apothecary. nd. 3.10.12 (· BENIAMEN · HIBBERDINE around); H|BA (· H · |B · A; · APOTHECARY · BANBVRY around). BW —, cf. 10; Milne 11. [?Baldwin]. Same obv. die as 3570. Also in the collection: a Nott ticket reading 'W.10.A.|Not in W[illiamson]|R.R.R.' [*i.e.* extremely rare], in envelope inscribed 'W.10A, missing', probably indicating a second specimen
3572	0.88	13.6	Br	0°	*Hibberdine*, Benjamin (BEN:), apothecary. nd. 3.10.12; H|BA. BW 11 but BEN:, BANBVRY; Milne 12 but HIBBERDINE:. Nott. Forename completed from 3570-1.
3573a	1.41 (pierced)	21.7	Br	180°	*Mander*, William. 1656. 3.3.13; M|WE. BW 12; Milne 13. [Baldwin]. William Maunder, tallowchandler (Gibson 1977, p. 315)
3573b	1.05	16.2	Br	180°	Same dies. Nott
3574	1.05	16.1	Br	180°	*Plumton*, Manasses (MANASLES). 1653. 4.1.1; P|MB. BW 14 but a tree; Milne 16; Dickinson 14A. Nott
3575	0.88	13.6	Br	180°	*Pym*, Thomas, mercer. 1664. 5.82.30; P|TI. BW 15; Milne 18. Nott
3576a	1.96	30.3	Cu	270°	*Robins*, George, mercer. 1669 ½d. 3.5.96; 5.77. BW 16; Milne 19. [?Baldwin]
3576b	1.52	23.5	Cu	270°	Same dies. Brand [or Nott]
3577a	1.14	17.5	Br	0°	*Smith*, Henry, ironmonger. 1656. S|HM; date. BW 20; Milne 21. Baldwin. Overstruck on a token of William Bissy of Milton next Sittingbourne (BW Kent 429), axis 0°. Confirmed from a die duplicate with the same axis available to the authors
3577b	1.10	17.0	Br	0°	Same dies. Nott
3578a	1.17 (pierced)	18.0	Cu	180°	*Smith*, Henry, ironmong[e]r. 1668 ½d. 5.14 Ironmongers; 5.77. BW 19; Milne 22. Baldwin [or Nott]
3578b	1.10	16.9	Br	180°	Same dies. [Baldwin]
3578c	1.06 (chipped)	16.4	Br	180°	Same dies. [?Baldwin]
3579	1.62 (edge filed)	25.0	Cu	180°	*Smith*, Matthew (MATHEW), gard[e]ner. 1669 ½d. 5.77 (S|MM); 4.2.1. BW 21; Milne 23. Nott

BANBURY (*cont.*)

	Weight			Die	
	g	gr		axis	
3580	0.90	13.9	Br	180°	*Vivers,* John. 1652. 5.14 Mercers; V|IE. BW 24; Milne 26. Nott
3581	1.63	25.2	Br	270°	*Vivers,* Nathaniel. 1668 ½d. 4.2.1; 5.77. BW 25; Milne 27. Nott
3582a	1.22	18.9	M	180°	*Wagstafe,* James. 1651. 4.13.1; W|IM. BW 26; Milne 28. [?Baldwin]. James Wagstaffe, mercer, innkeeper of the Flower-de-Luce (Gibson 1977, p. 325). Same rev. die as 3583
3582b	0.87	13.4	M	180°	Same dies. [?Nott]
3583a	1.42	21.9	M	0°	*Wagstafe,* James. 1651. 4.13.1; W|IM. BW 26; Milne 29 but different obv. die from 28 (cf. p. 24). Nott. Same rev. die as 3582
3583b	1.22	18.8	M	180°	Same dies. [?Baldwin]
3583c	0.98	15.1	M	0°	Same dies. [Baldwin]
3584a	1.01	15.6	Br	180°	*Wagstaffe,* John. nd. 5.14 Mercers; W|IA. BW 27; Milne 30. Nott. Legends start at 10 o'clock on both sides
3584b	0.71	10.9	Br	0°	Same dies. [?Baldwin]
3585	1.94	29.9	Br	0°	*Wagstaffe,* William. nd ½d. 4.13.1; W|WM. BW 28; Milne 31. Nott
3586	0.92	14.2	Br	270°	*Wheatly,* Nathaniel (NATHANIELL). 1664. 5.14 Mercers; W|NM. BW 32; Milne 33. Nott. Nathaniel Wheatly, mercer, 1707 (Milne, p. 33)

Named signs

3587a	2.37	36.6	Cu	180°	*Reindeer* (AT THE RAINDEAR): Sutton, Thomas. 1666 ½d. 3.53.2 (S|TS); 5.77. BW 23 but THE; Milne 25. [Baldwin]. Thomas Sutton, vintner, 1685 (Milne, pp. 32-3)
3587b	2.02	31.2	Cu	270°	Same dies. [?Baldwin]
3587c	1.85	28.6	M	180°	Same dies. [?Nott]
3587d	1.47	22.6	Cu	180°	Same dies. Brand [or ? ex Baldwin 1918]
3588	0.90	13.8	Br	180°	*Unicorn* (AT THE VNICORNE): S[tokes], W[illiam]. 1650. 3.61.1; S|WI. BW 18 but BANBERIE; Milne 20. Nott. William Stokes (d. 1658), innholder, of the Unicorn (Gibson 1977, p. 322)

BARFORD ST JOHN (Adderbury parish) / BARFORD ST MICHAEL

Knight, John *see* 3599 (Burford)

BICESTER

The reading is BISSETER on 3591, BISSITOR on 3592-3, cf. *Bysseter* 1517, *Bisseter* 1676 (EPNS 1954, p. 198); BISTER on the remainder, with IN OXFORDSHEIRE on 3595, 3597, IN OXFORD SHEIRE on 3594, cf. *Bister* 1685 (EPNS 1954, p. 198) and current pronunciation

3589a	1.30	20.0	Br	180°	*Borrows,* John, ironmonger (IRON|MONGER). nd. I B; I B. BW 37; Milne 34. Nott
3589b	1.19	18.3	Br	180°	Same dies. [?Baldwin]
3590a	1.09	16.9	Br	180°	*Burges,* Thomas. 1665. 5.14 Pewterers; B|TM. BW 38; Milne 35. [?Baldwin]. E of BISTER cancels O
3590b	0.77	11.8	Br	270°	Same dies. Nott
3590c	0.42 (chipped)	6.5	Br	180°	Same dies. [?Baldwin]
3591a	0.91	14.0	M	0°	*Burrowes,* Gabriel (GABRIELL), ironmonger. nd. 5.14 Ironmongers; G B. BW 39 but GABRIELL · BVRROWES, Ironmongers' Arms; Milne 36. [?Baldwin]. Diameter 16 mm
3591b	0.64	9.9	Br	270°	Same dies. Nott. Diameter 17-17.5 mm
3592a	1.08 (chipped)	16.6	M	180°	*Clements,* Thomas, draper. nd. 5.14 Drapers; T C. BW 41; Milne 38. [?Baldwin]. Thomas Clements, 'mercer', d. 1664 (Milne, p. 34). Same rev. die as 3593
3592b	1.05	16.3	M	180°	Same dies. Nott
3592c	0.76	11.8	M	180°	Same dies. [?Baldwin]
3592d	0.66	10.1	M	180°	Same dies. [Baldwin]
3593	1.21	18.7	M	180°	*Clements* (CLEMENE), Thomas, draper. nd. 5.14 Grocers; T C. BW 40; Milne 37. Nott. Form of surname from, and same rev. die as, 3592, q.v.
3594a	1.76 (chipped)	27.2	Br	0°	*Hudson,* Will—. 1669 ½d. 5.45.20; 5.77 (H|WS). BW 42 but WILL:, OXFORD · SHEIRE; Milne 39. [?Baldwin]. William Hudson, butcher, 1691 (Milne, p. 34)
3594b	1.33	20.5	Br	180°	Same dies. Nott
3595a	1.11	17.1	Br	0°	*Stevens,* Will—. 1669 ½d. 5.60.36; 5.77 (S|WE). BW 43 but WILL:, W.E.S.; Milne 40 but · S ·|W · E;Dickinson,pl.3.[?Baldwin]
3595b	1.10	16.9	Br	0°	Same dies. [?Baldwin]
3595c	1.02	15.7	Br	0°	Same dies. Nott

[*continued overleaf*]

PLATE 25

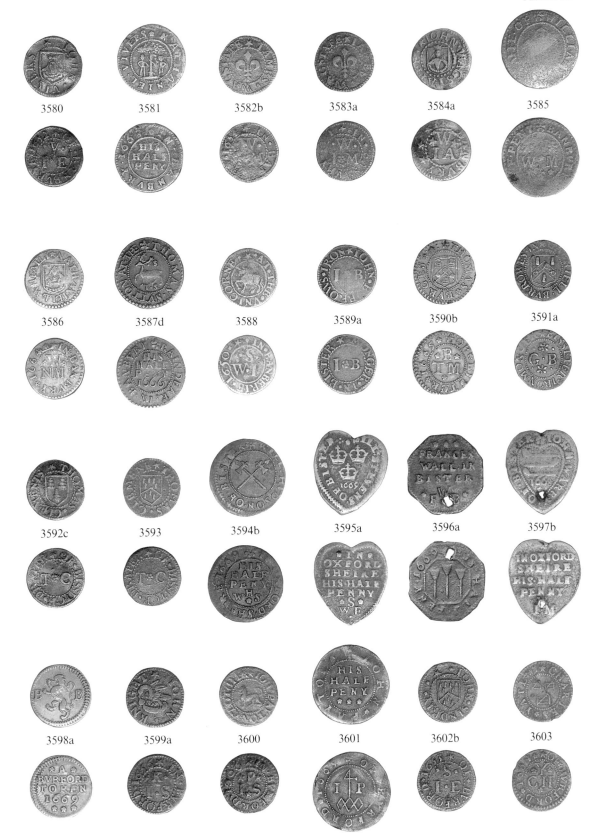

3580   3581   3582b   3583a   3584a   3585

3586   3587d   3588   3589a   3590b   3591a

3592c   3593   3594b   3595a   3596a   3597b

3598a   3599a   3600   3601   3602b   3603

Plate 25 (*cont.*)

	Weight			Die	
	g	gr		axis	
3596a	1.77	27.2	Br	180°	*Wall,* Francis (FRANCES). 1669 ½d. 5.77 (W|FB); 5.34.12. BW 44 but
	(pierced, chipped)				FRANCES|WALL.IN|BISTER| · W · |F.B, HALF · PENY, 3 peels; Milne 41. [?Baldwin]
3596b	1.49	23.0	Br	180°	Same dies. Nott
3596c	1.34	20.6	Br	180°	Same dies. [?Baldwin]
3597a	2.44	37.7	Br	0°	*Warry,* John. 1668 ½d. 5.84.32; 5.77 (W|IM). BW 45; Milne 42. Nott
3597b	1.93	29.8	Br	0°	Same dies. [?Baldwin]
	(pierced)				

BURFORD

The reading is BVRFORT on 3607; BVRFORD on the remainder

3598a	1.38	21.2	Br	0°	*Burford,* Borough. 1669 Burford token. 3.32 (B B); 5.77. BW 46 but B [Lion] B, obv. and rev. transposed; Milne 43. [Baldwin]. The common seal of the ancient Corporation bears a lion rampant guardant facing to sinister (!) and the legend SIGILL' COMMVNE BVRGENSIVM DE BVREFORD (Lewis 1845, i. 420; Gretton 1920, pp. xiv-xv, pl. facing p. 295)
3598b	1.28	19.8	Br	0°	Same dies. [Spink]
3598c	1.20	18.6	Br	0°	Same dies. Nott
3598d	0.93	14.4	Br	0°	Same dies. [?Baldwin]
3599a	1.08	16.7	Br	180°	*Knight,* John. 1656. 3.82.1; K|IS. BW 35 but I656; Milne 47. Nott [ex Seaby]. John Knight, mercer, 1657 (Milne, p. 35)
3599b	1.01	15.6	Br	180°	Same dies. Baldwin
3599c	1.00	15.4	Br	180°	Same dies. [Nott]
3600	0.74	11.4	Cu	0°	*Payton,* John (IOH:) [sen.], clothier (CLOTHYER). 1666. 3.67.1; P|IS. BW 51 but IOH:; Milne 51. Nott. John Payton senior, clothier, of the Talbot in Witney Street, 1660; wife Susanna, 1680 (Milne, p. 35)
3601	1.14	17.6	Br	0°	*Payton,* John [?jun.]. 1669 ½d. 5.77; 5.81.14 (I P). BW 50; Milne 52. Nott. John Payton, junior, fl. 1662-80; clothier (Milne, p. 35)
3602a	1.01	15.6	M	180°	*Sindriy,* John. 1653. 5.14 Grocers; S|IE. BW 52; Milne 53. [?Baldwin]. John 'Sindrey' 1652-65 (Milne, p. 35)
3602b	1.00	15.4	M	180°	Same dies. Nott
3603	0.86	13.3	Cu	270°	*Yate,* Charles. 1664. 5.17.32; Y|CH. BW 54; Milne 55. Nott

BURFORD (*cont.*)

Named signs

	Weight g	gr		Die axis	
3604a	1.04	16.0	M	180°	*Bear* (AT THE BEARE): Mathewes, Thomas. nd. 3.49.5; M|TE. BW 48; Milne —, cf. 48 (same rev. die). [?Baldwin]. Thomas Mathews, innholder, 1657 (Milne, p. 35)
3604b	0.96	14.8	M	180°	Same dies. [Baldwin]
3605	1.44	22.2	M	180°	*Bear* (AT THE BEARE): Mathewes, Thomas. nd. 3.49.5; M|TE. BW 48; Milne 49. Nott
3606a	1.04	16.1	Br	180°	*George* (AT THE): V[eysey], R[ichard]. 1652. 3.2.8; V|RA. BW 53 but BVRFORD · I652; Milne 54. Nott. Richard Veysey, tenant of the George, 1652 (Milne, p. 35)
3606b	0.71 (worn)	10.9	Br	180°	Same dies. Baldwin
3607	0.95	14.7	M	180°	*Three Sugar-loaves* (AT THE 3 SHVGER LOVES): C[astle], E[dmond]. 1653. 5.64.16; E C. BW 47; Milne 45. Nott. Edmond Castle fl. Burford 1636 (Milne, p. 34)

CHINNOR

The reading is CHENER IN OXFORD SHIERE on 3608; CHINNER on 3609

3608a	0.81	12.5	M	180°	*Beckly,* Tho—. nd. 3.44.3; B|TS. BW 55; Milne 57. Nott [?Baldwin]. Thomas Beckley, weaver (Chinnor 1982, pp. 6-7). Diameter 15.5 mm
3608b	0.62	9.6	M	0°	Same dies. Baldwin. Diameter 16.5-17 mm
3609a	1.31	20.2	Br	0°	*Goldfinch,* Wil[l]iam. 1662. 5.14.93; G|WE. BW 56 but WILIAM; Milne 58. [?Baldwin]. William Goldfinch, schoolmaster and scrivener (Chinnor 1982, pp. 7-9)
3609b	0.94	14.4	Br	180°	Same dies. Nott
3609c	0.73	11.3	Br	90°	Same dies. [?Baldwin]

CHIPPING NORTON

The reading is CHIPPING NORTON on 3613, 3615-19, 3621; CHIPIN NORTO[N]COM[T]OXFOR[D] on 3610; CHIPINGNORTON on 3622; CHIPPINGNORTON on 3611-12, 3614, 3620; CHIPPINORTON on 3623-4

3610	0.79	12.2	Br	90°	*Cornish,* Joh[n]. nd. 5.14 Oxford 2; C|IK. BW 58 but NORTO[N]COM[T]OXFOR[D]; Milne 60. Nott. Forename completed from Milne, p. 36
3611a	1.27	19.6	Cu	0°	*Cornish,* Michael (MICHAELL). nd. 5.15.25; C|ME. BW 59 but CHIPPINGNORTON; Milne 62. Nott. Michael Cornish, 'mercer' 1680, also 'draper' (Milne, p. 36)
3611b	0.83	12.8	Cu	0°	Same dies. [?Baldwin]
3612a	1.10	16.9	Br	180°	*Davis,* Joseph. nd. 5.82.1; D|IE. BW 60 but CHIPPINGNORTON; Milne 63. Nott
3612b	0.82	12.7	Br	180°	Same dies. [?Baldwin]
3613	1.23	19.0	Cu	270°	*Dix,* David. 1664 ½d. 5.77; D|DS. BW 63; Milne 66. Nott
3614	1.05	16.2	M	180°	*Farmer,* Samuel. nd. 3.10.12; F|SE. BW 64 but CHIPPINGNORTON; Milne 67. Nott. Samuel Farmer, apothecary, 1683 (Milne, p. 36; Whittet 1986a, p. 112)
3615	0.93	14.4	M	180°	*Fawler,* Henry. nd. 3.92.1; F|HH. BW 66; Milne 68. [?Baldwin]. Same rev. die as 3616
3616a	1.24	19.2	M	180°	*Fawler,* Henry. nd. 3.92.1; F|HH. BW 66; Milne 69. Nott. Same rev. die as 3615
3616b	0.96	14.8	M	180°	Same dies. [?Baldwin]
	(chipped)				
3617a	2.17	33.5	Cu	0°	*Fawler,* Henry. 1669 ½d. 3.92.2; 5.77 (F|HH). BW 65; Milne 70. Nott. Diameter 20.5 mm
3617b	1.31	20.3	Cu	0°	Same dies. [?Baldwin] -1972. Diameter 21 mm
3617c	0.91 (chipped)	14.0	Cu	0°	Same dies. Spink [1972]. Overstruck on. . .MAT. . ., rev. . . .ARE. . . Diameter 21.5-22.5 mm
3618a	0.93	14.3	Cu	0°	*Groves,* Richard. 1659. 3.1.18; G|RE. BW 68; Milne 71. [?Baldwin]. Richard Groves, grocer, 1672 (Milne, p. 36). Legends both sides start at 10 o'clock
3618b	0.67	10.3	Cu	180°	Same dies. Nott
3619a	1.11	17.1	Cu	0°	*Groves,* Richard. 1663. 3.1.18; G|RE. BW 69 but a woman; Milne 73 but a woman. Nott. See 3618. Obv. legend starts at 10 o'clock. Diameter 16-17 mm
3619b	0.56	8.7	Cu	180°	Same dies. [?Baldwin]. Diameter 15.5 mm
3620a	0.90	13.8	Cu	90°	*Rowlright,* Edmond. nd. R|ED; 3.11. BW 71 but ROWLRIGHT, CHIPPINGNORTON; Milne 74. Nott. Edmond Fuller alias Rowlright, 1662 (Milne, p. 37)
3620b	0.62	9.6	Cu	90°	Same dies. Nott
3621a	1.87 (edge filed)	28.9	Br	0°	*R[owlright],* E[dmond]. 1668 ½d. 5.84.25 (R|ED); 5.77. BW 70 but R|ED below device; Milne 75. [?Baldwin]
3621b	1.84	28.5	Br	0°	Same dies. Nott
3621c	0.78	12.0	Br	0°	Same dies. Nott

[*continued overleaf*]

PLATE 26

3604a   3605   3606a   3607   3608a   3609b

3610   3611a   3612a   3613   3614   3615

3616a   3617a   3618b   3619a   3620a   3621b

3622   3623   3624d   3625   3626b   3627

Plate 26 (*cont.*)

	Weight			Die	
	g	gr		axis	
3622	2.12	32.8	Br	0°	*Wisdome,* Philip (PHILLIPP). 1670 ½d. 5.77; W|PK. BW 72 but CHIPINGNORTON; Milne 77. Nott. Philip Wisdom, upholsterer, 1709 (Milne, p. 37)

Named signs
3623	0.99	15.3	Br	180°	[*White Hart*] (AT Y^E): Diston, William. 1666. 3.53.20; D	WM. BW 62; Milne 65. Nott. Sign name from 3624
3624a	2.14	33.0	Cu	0°	*White* [*Hart*] (AT Y^EWHIT): Diston, William. 1666 ½d. 3.53.22; D	WM. BW 61; Milne 64. Baldwin. Sign name completed from BW 62 n. and Milne, p. 36
3624b	1.89	29.1	Cu	0°	Same dies. Baldwin
3624c	1.76	27.1	Cu	180°	Same dies. Baldwin
	(pierced)				
3624d	1.70	26.3	Cu	90°	Same dies. Nott

CORNWELL

Worth, Thomas *see* 560 (Cornwall: Penryn)

CROPREDY (Oxon. *and* Warwickshire)

The reading is CROPREADY. See also Wardington

| 3625 | 0.72 | 11.1 | Cu | 90° | *King,* Margaret (MARGRET). 1664. 5.14 Grocers; M K. BW 75; Milne 78. Nott |

CULHAM (Oxon. *and* Berkshire)

The reading is CVLVM, cf. *Cullum* 1675 (Ogilby 1675, pl. 14)

Harwell, Matthew *see* FULHAM (Middx). Ferry neighbourhood

Named signs
| 3626a | 1.45 | 22.4 | Br | 180° | *Horseshoe* (AT THE HORS SHOOE): Wells, John. nd. 5.68.1; I W. BW 77 but SHOOE; Milne 79. Nott |
| 3626b | 1.08 | 16.6 | Br | 0° | Same dies. Nott |

DEDDINGTON

The reading is DADINGTON on 3629-31, cf. *Dadington . . .* to 1526 (EPNS 1954, p. 256); DEDDINGTON on 3627-8
3627a	2.15	33.2	Br	0°	*Belcher,* Samuel (SAMVELL). 1668 ½d. 5.14 Apothecaries; 5.77 (B	SB). BW 78; Milne 80. Nott. All three Norweb specimens have a small cut in the edge at about 12 o'clock
3627b	1.78	27.4	Br	0°	Same dies. Nott
3627c	1.69	26.0	Br	0°	Same dies. Nott

DEDDINGTON *(cont.)*

	Weight			Die	
	g	gr		axis	
3628a	2.08	32.1	Cu	180°	*Elkington,* John. 1667 ½d. 3.62.1; 5.77. BW 79; Milne 81. Nott. John Elkington, 'innkeeper'
	(pierced)				1688, 'cordwainer' 1693 (Milne, p. 37)
3628b	2.03	31.3	M	180°	Same dies. Nott
3628c	1.72	26.6	M	180°	Same dies. Nott
3629	0.40	6.2	Br	180°	*Makepace,* Ann, mercer. nd. 3.82.1; A M. BW 81; Milne 83. Nott [?Baldwin]. Attributed to
					Deddington as the only market-town similarly named (Adams 1680)
3630	0.83	12.8	Br	180°	*Nutt,* Thomas, mercer. 1653. T N; date. BW 82; Milne 84. Nott

Named signs

3631	1.84	28.5	Br	90°	*Unicorn* (AT Y^E|VNICORNE): Elkinton, Michael. 1668 ½d. 5.77; 3.61.1. BW 80 but Y^E,
	(chipped)				DADINGTON; Milne 82. Nott

DORCHESTER

The reading is DORCHESTER on 3632, 3635. The place is unnamed on 3633-4

3632a	0.92	14.1	Br	180°	*Brock,* William. nd. 5.14 Grocers; W B. BW 83 but rev. = W • B; BW Dorset 61; Milne 87. [Spink
					1971]. William Brock, mercer, 1686 (Milne, p. 38). Diameter 17 mm
3632b	0.87	13.4	Br	180°	Same dies. Nott. Diameter 17 mm
3632c	0.58	8.9	Br	270°	Same dies. Spink [1975]. Diameter 15-15.5 mm
3632d	0.52	8.0	Br	270°	Same dies. Nott. Diameter 15 mm
3632e	0.37	5.8	Br	270°	Same dies. Nott [?Baldwin]. Diameter 15 mm
	(chipped)				
3633a	1.28	19.8	M	180°	*Brock,* William and *Couldry,* Robert. nd, 'for William Brock and Robert Couldry'. B|WM; R C.
					BW 84; BW Uncertain 29; Milne —. [Baldwin]. Attribution from Dorchester provenances of
					Ashmolean specimens (Milne, p. 26), and from issuer of 3632. Same obv. die as 3634. Diameter
					16 mm
3633b	1.12	17.3	M	0°	Same dies. Nott. Diameter 17 mm
3633c	0.93	14.3	M	180°	Same dies. [?Nott]. Diameter 15.5 mm
	(pierced)				
3633d	0.91	14.0	Br	180°	Same dies. Nott. Diameter 16 mm
3633e	0.74	11.4	M	0°	Same dies. Nott. Diameter 15.5 mm
3634a	1.06	16.4	M	180°	*Brock,* William and *Couldry,* Robert. nd, 'for William Brock and Robert Couldry'. B|WM; R C.
					BW 84; BW Uncertain 29; Milne 86. [Brand]. Same obv. die as 3633
3634b	0.98	15.1	M	180°	Same dies. Nott
3634c	0.90	13.9	M	180°	Same dies. [?Baldwin]
3634d	0.83	12.8	M	180°	Same dies. Nott
	(chipped)				
3634e	0.78	12.0	M	180°	Same dies. [?Baldwin]

Named signs

3635	1.09	16.8	Br	180°	*Crown* (AT Y^E): Applegat, Thomas. [16]69 ½d. 5.60.1; 5.77 (A|TE). BW Dorset 60; Milne 85;
					Dickinson 82A. Nott [ex ?Seaby]. Attributed to Dorchester co. Oxon. by Willis, *c.*1740, and
					to Thomas Applegate fl. 1662-72 (Milne, pp. 26, 30, 38)

DUNS TEW

The reading is DVNSTV on both, with OXFORDSH^R on 3636, cf. *Dunsto* Ogilby 1675, pl. 82

3636a	0.81	12.5	Cu	135°	*Barret,* Thomas (THO:), carrier (CARRER). nd. 5.64.180; B|TM. BW 86 but THO:,
	(chipped)				OXFORDSH^R; Milne 89. [?Baldwin]. Forename completed from 3637
3636b	0.53	8.2	Br	135°	Same dies. Nott
3637	1.11	17.1	Br	270°	*Barret,* Thomas, carrier. 1669 ½d. 5.64.180; 5.77. BW 85 but BARRET, DVNSTV; BW Beds.
					35 but DVNSTV; Milne —, cf. p. 26. Nott

ENSTONE

The reading is ANSTON, cf. *Anestan c.*1260 (EPNS 1954, p. 347)

3638a	1.11	17.1	Br	270°	*Newman,* Thomas. 1669 ½d. 3.67.1; 5.77. BW Uncertain 19 but NEWMAN, ANSTON; Milne
					—; Dickinson 86A. Seaby [1974 ex Glendining 6.3.74 lot 285 ex Hird]. Attribution from 1970
					find of eighteen specimens two miles away in Kiddington with Asterleigh (Short 1972)
3638b	0.74	11.4	Br	270°	Same dies. Baldwin

[continued overleaf]

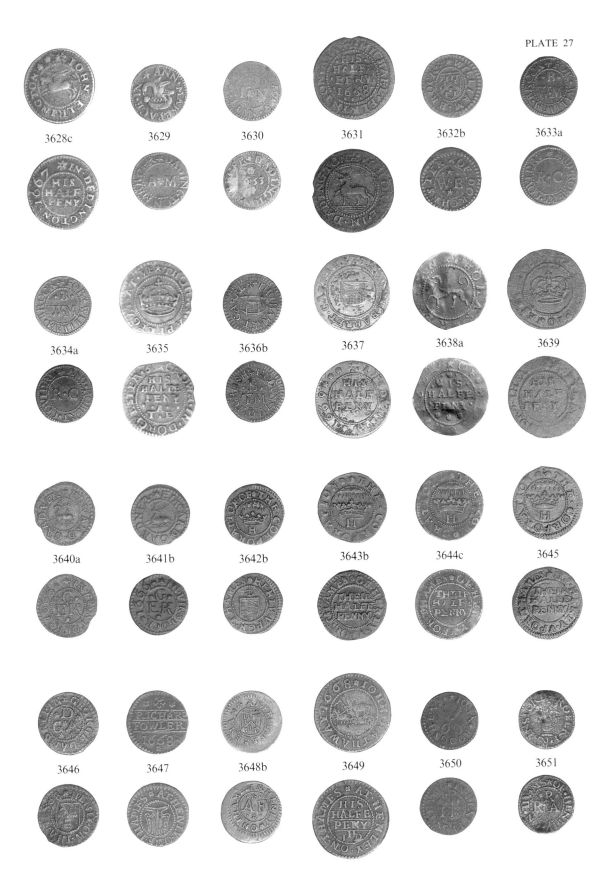

PLATE 27

3628c 3629 3630 3631 3632b 3633a

3634a 3635 3636b 3637 3638a 3639

3640a 3641b 3642b 3643b 3644c 3645

3646 3647 3648b 3649 3650 3651

Plate 27 (*cont.*)

EWELME

The reading is EWELME IN OXFORD SHEIRE

	Weight			Die	
	g	gr		axis	
3639	0.97	14.9	Br	270°	*Jones,* William. 1669 ½d. 5.60.1; 5.77. BW 87 but OXFORD · SHEIRE; Milne 90. Nott

FINSTOCK (Charlbury parish)

The reading is FINSTOCK on both

3640a	0.79	12.2	Cu	0°	*Gardner,* Edward. 1666. 3.53.20; G|EK. BW 88; Milne 91. [?Baldwin]
	(chipped)				
3640b	0.72	11.2	Cu	0°	Same dies. [?Baldwin]
	(chipped)				
3641a	0.88	13.6	M	0°	*Gardner,* Edward. 1666. 3.53.20; G|EK. BW 88; Milne 92. [?Baldwin]
3641b	0.74	11.4	M	180°	Same dies. Nott
	(chipped)				
3641c	0.66	10.2	M	180°	Same dies. [Baldwin]

GREAT TEW *see* TEW, Great

HENLEY ON THAMES

The place is unnamed on 3654. The reading is HENLEY ON THAMES on 3649-50; HENLIY ON THAMS on 3651; HENLY on the remainder, with ON THAMES on 3646, 3648, 3653, ON THAMS on 3657, ONE THAMES on 3647, 3656, VPON THAMES on 3642-5, 3655. Note on 3642-5: The seal of Henley bore the letter H ducally crowned, in chief rain issuing from clouds (Vis. Oxon. 1566-1634, p. 284)

3642a	0.76	11.7	Br	270°	*Henley on Thames,* Borough (CORPORATION). [1669 ¼d.]. 5.76(H).1; 5.15.26. BW 92; Milne 96. Nott. Date and denomination from Gill 1881, p. 164
3642b	0.71	11.0	Br	270°	Same dies. [?Baldwin]
3642c	0.58	8.9	Br	270°	Same dies. [?Baldwin]
3642d	0.57	8.8	Br	270°	Same dies. [Baldwin]
3643a	0.89	13.7	Br	180°	*Henley on Thames,* Borough (CORPORATION). [1669] ½d. 5.76(H).1; 5.77. BW 91; Milne 95. [?Baldwin]. Date from Gill 1881, p. 164. Same obv. die as 3644
	(chipped)				
3643b	0.72	11.1	Br	0°	Same dies. Nott
3644a	1.05	16.3	Br	270°	*Henley on Thames,* Borough (CORPORATION). [1669] ½d. 5.76(H).1; 5.77. BW 91; Milne 94. [Baldwin]. Same obv. die as 3643 (q.v. for date); same rev. die as 3645
3644b	0.90	14.0	Br	270°	Same dies. [?Baldwin]
3644c	0.75	11.6	Br	270°	Same dies. Nott. Obv. in later state with cloud flawed into inner circle, whence sequence of 3643-4
3645	1.61	24.8	Br	0°	*Henley on Thames,* Borough (CORPORATION). [1669] ½d. 5.76(H).1; 5.77. BW 91; Milne —. [?Baldwin]. Same rev. die as 3644
3646	0.84	13.0	Br	0°	*Damsell,* George. [16]68. D|GA; 5.14 Drapers. BW 94; Milne 98. Nott. George Damsell, gent. 1652, senior 1662-5 (Milne, p. 39)
3647	1.04	16.1	Br	60°	*Fowler,* Richard. 1668. 5.77; 3.1.92. BW 95 but RICHAR^D, rev. a corset; Milne 99. Nott. Issuer ?Richard Fowler of Caversham, bodice-maker, 1677, wife Joan (Milne, p. 39); but see also 1778-81
3648a	1.14	17.6	Br	270°	*Freeman,* Ambrose (AMBROS). nd. 5.14 Grocers; A F. BW 96; Milne 100. [?Baldwin]. Issuer ?Ambrose Freeman senior, mercer, d. 1669/70; ?Mr Ambrose Freeman, gent., fl. 1652-65 (Milne, p. 39). Cinquefoil in rev. legend not considered an initial mark (cf. Milne, p. 27)
3648b	0.95	14.6	Br	0°	Same dies. [?Baldwin]
3648c	0.89	13.7	Br	0°	Same dies. Nott
3649	1.61	24.9	Br	0°	*Hathaway,* John. 1668 ½d. 5.53.4; 5.77 (H|ID). BW 97 but PENY|rule|H|ID; Milne 102. Nott. John Gibbs or Hathaway, 1662; coachman, 1671 (Milne, p. 39)
3650	0.78	12.0	Cu	180°	*Hodgshens,* John. nd. 5.43.20; H|IK. BW 98; Milne 103. Nott
3651	0.98	15.1	Br	180°	*Rainsford,* Robert. nd. 4.11.20; R|RA. BW 99; Milne 104. Nott. Robert Rainsford, barber-surgeon, fl. 1642-90 (Milne, pp. 39-40; Whittet 1986a, p. 112)

HENLEY ON THAMES (*cont.*)

	Weight			Die	
	g	*gr*		*axis*	
3652a	2.26	34.9	Br	0°	*Robinson,* William, fishmonger. 1668 ½d. 3.109.1; 5.77 (W R). BW 100; Milne 105. Nott. William Robinson, Bailiff in 1668-9 (Milne, p. 40)
3652b	1.88	29.0	Br	0°	Same dies. [?Baldwin]
3653	1.42	21.9	Br	0°	*Smith,* Seth. nd. 5.14 Oxford 2; S|SI. BW 101; Milne 106. Nott. Seth Smith, chandler, 1680 (Milne, p. 40)
3654	2.30	35.5	Pb	0°	*Stevens,* Edward. nd. 5.14 Barber-Surgeons; ES (·|ES|·; ··EDWARD·STEVENS·around). BW —, cf. 102; Milne —; Dickinson 102A. [?Baldwin], ex Sotheby 25 July 1918 (not identified). Attributed to Faringdon, Berks., by Milne 1946, p. 18; to Henley, by West 1976, p. 271, cf. 3655. Edward Stevens, barber-surgeon, d. 1663 (Milne, p. 40)
3655a	1.37	21.2	Br	0°	*Stevens* (STEAVENS), Edward. nd. 5.14 Barber-Surgeons; E S. BW 102; Milne 107. Nott. Form of surname from Milne, p. 40, and 3654 (q.v.)
3655b	1.34	20.7	Br	0°	Same dies. [Baldwin]
3656a	1.18	18.2	Br	0°	*Sury,* Robert. nd. 3.53.20; S|RE. BW 103; Milne 108. [Nott]
3656b	1.08	16.6	Br	180°	Same dies. [?Baldwin]
3656c	0.81	12.4	Br	180°	Same dies. Baldwin. Overstruck on. . . –OHN. . . and read as 'Robert Short'
3656d	0.65	10.1	Br	180°	Same dies. Baldwin
3657	0.94	14.5	Br	180°	*Wickins,* Thomas. nd. 5.32.13; W|TF. BW 104; Milne 109. Nott. Thomas Wickins junior, tallow-chandler, 1651 (Milne, p. 40)

HOOK NORTON

The reading is HOOKENORTON throughout

3658a	1.15	17.8	Br	90°	*Beale,* James, mercer. nd. 5.82.30; B|IM. BW 105 but IAMES, HOOKENORTON; Milne 110 but HOOKENORTON·MERCER. [?Baldwin]
3658b	0.85	13.1	Br	90°	Same dies. Nott
3659a	2.17	33.4	Br	270°	*Beale,* James, mercer. 1668 ½d. 5.82.31 (B|IM); 5.77. BW 106 but HOOKENORTON; Milne 111. Nott [?Baldwin]. Diameter 20-20.5 mm
3659b	1.33	20.6	Br	0°	Same dies. Nott. Diameter 21-21.5 mm
3660a	2.33	35.9	Cu	0°	*Parcks,* Richard, ironmonger (IREMONGER). 1666 ½d. 5.77; P|RE. BW 107 but HOOKENORTON; Milne 112. [?Baldwin]. Diameter 20.5-21 mm
3660b	2.08	32.1	Cu	0°	Same dies. [?Baldwin]. Diameter 18.5 mm
3660c	1.90	29.3	Cu	0°	Same dies. Brand [or Nott]. Diameter 19 mm
3660d	1.90	29.3	Cu	0°	Same dies. [?Baldwin]. Diameter 18.5 mm
3660e	1.86	28.7	Cu	0°	Same dies. [Baldwin]. Diameter 18.5-19 mm
	(pierced)				

LEIGH, North

The reading is NORTHLY on both

3661a	3.49	53.9	Br	0°	*Mason,* William and *Mason,* Ann. nd ½d. 3.9.7 (M|WA) (·WILLIAM·AND·ANN· around); 5.77 (⊣ THEIR|HALF|PENY; ·MASON·IN·NORTHLY around). BW —, cf. 110; Milne 116; Dickinson 110A. Nott. William Mason 'yeoman' 1676 (Milne, p. 41). Same rev. die as 3662. Diameter 20.5-21 mm
3661b	1.76	27.1	Br	0°	Same dies. [Baldwin]. Diameter 19 mm
3662a	1.78	27.5	Br	0°	*Mason,* William and *Mason,* Ann. nd ½d. 3.9.6 (M|WA); 5.77. BW 110; Milne 115. [?Baldwin]. Same rev. die as 3661. Diameter 20.5 mm
3662b	1.18	18.2	Br	0°	Same dies. [Baldwin]. Diameter 18.5 mm
3662c	1.07	16.6	Br	0°	Same dies. [?Baldwin]. Diameter 19-19.5 mm
	(chipped)				
3662d	0.94	14.6	Br	0°	Same dies. [?Baldwin]. Diameter 19 mm

NETTLEBED

The reading is NETTLE BED on both

Named signs

3663	1.01	15.6	Br	90°	*Bull* (AT Y^E): Gasquon, David (DAVIDE). nd ½d. 5.77; 3.52.6. BW 108 but PENY, NETTLE·BED; Milne 113. Nott
3664a	1.92	29.6	Br	90°	*White Hart* (AT Y^EWHIT): Holding, Timothy. 1669 ½d. 3.53.20; 5.77. BW 109 but NETTLE·BED; Milne 114. Nott
3664b	1.24	19.1	Br	270°	Same dies. [?Baldwin]

[*continued overleaf*]

PLATE 28

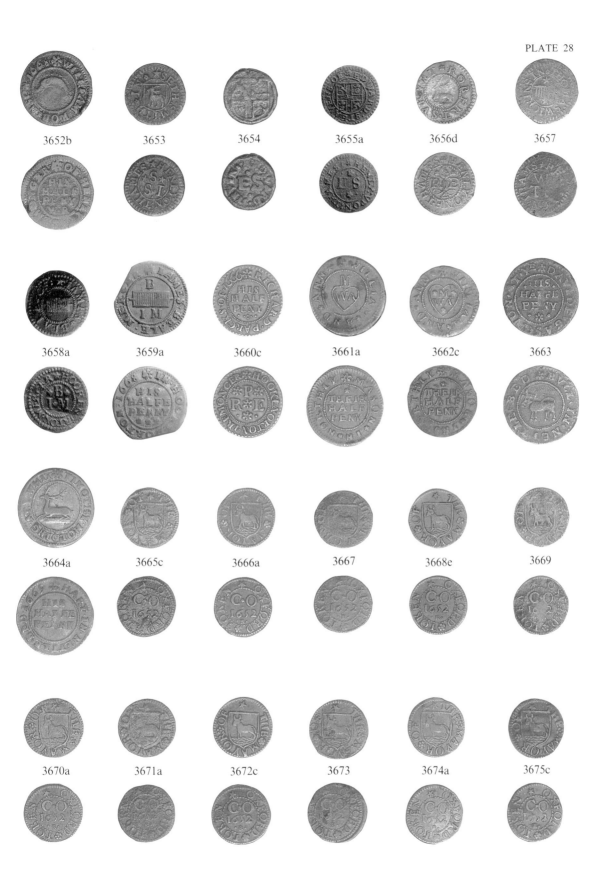

3652b   3653   3654   3655a   3656d   3657

3658a   3659a   3660c   3661a   3662c   3663

3664a   3665c   3666a   3667   3668e   3669

3670a   3671a   3672c   3673   3674a   3675c

Plate 28 (*cont.*)

NEWINGTON

Short, Lawrence *see* 'NEWINGTON' (Uncertain I)

NORTH LEIGH *see* LEIGH, North

OXFORD

The reading is OXFORD on 3665-75, 3677-9, 3681, 3688, 3694-5, 3703-5, 3712, 3720-2, 3730-2, 3736-7, 3741-2, 3744-6; *Oxon* on 3702; OXON on the remainder. Note on 3665-75: *Ox passing ford of water* is the device on a 13-cent. seal of the city of Oxford (Chesshyre 1992, p. 212). For the dating 1652-7 see Hobson 1933, pp. 437-40. For the attribution of the R signature below the date to David Ramage in place of Thomas Rawlins, see Milne, p. xiv

3665a	0.87	13.5	M	180°	*Oxford,* City (the Mayor). 1652[-7] token. 5.14 Oxford; C O|date|R. BW 111-12; Leeds 1. [?Baldwin]. Same rev. die as 3666
3665b	0.87	13.4	M	180°	Same dies. [?Baldwin]
3665c	0.84	12.9	M	180°	Same dies. [?Baldwin]
3665d	0.78	12.0	M	180°	Same dies. [?Baldwin]
3666a	1.15	17.7	M	180°	*Oxford,* City (the Mayor). 1652[-7] token. 5.14 Oxford; C O|date|R. BW 111-12; Leeds 2. [Baldwin]. Same rev. die as 3665
3666b	1.04	16.0	M	180°	Same dies. [?Baldwin]
3667	0.72	11.2	M	180°	*Oxford,* City (the Mayor). 1652[-7] token. 5.14 Oxford; C O|date|R. BW 111-12; Leeds 9. Baldwin
3668a	1.42	21.9	M	180°	*Oxford,* City (the Mayor). 1652[-7] token. 5.14 Oxford; C O|date|R. BW 111-12; Leeds 7. [?Baldwin]. Same rev. die as 3669-73
3668b	1.16	17.9	M	180°	Same dies. [?Baldwin]
3668c	1.15	17.7	M	180°	Same dies. [?Baldwin]
3668d	1.06	16.3	M	180°	Same dies. [?Baldwin]
3668e	1.05	16.1	M	180°	Same dies. Nott
3668f	1.00	15.5	M	180°	Same dies. [?Baldwin]
3668g	1.00	15.4	M	180°	Same dies. [?Baldwin]
3668h	0.85	13.1	M	180°	Same dies. [?Baldwin]
3668i	0.84	13.0	M	180°	Same dies. [?Baldwin]
3668j	0.78	12.1	M	180°	Same dies. [?Baldwin]
3669	0.81	12.4	M	180°	*Oxford,* City (the Mayor). 1652[-7] token. 5.14 Oxford; C O|date|R. BW 111-12; Leeds 8. [?Baldwin]. Same rev. die as 3668, 3670-3
3670a	1.12	17.3	M	180°	*Oxford,* City (the Mayor). 1652[-7] token. 5.14 Oxford; C O|date|R. BW 111-12; Leeds 3. [?Baldwin]. Same rev. die as 3668-9, 3671-3
3670b	0.97	15.0	M	180°	Same dies. [?Baldwin]
3671a	1.03	15.9	M	180°	*Oxford,* City (the Mayor). 1652[-7] token. 5.14 Oxford; C O|date|R. BW 111-12; Leeds 4. [?Baldwin]. Same rev. die as 3668-70, 3672-3
3671b	0.95	14.6	M	180°	Same dies. [?Baldwin]
3672a	1.37	21.1	M	0°	*Oxford,* City (the Mayor). 1652[-7] token. 5.14 Oxford; C O|date|R. BW 111-12; Leeds 5. [?Baldwin]. Same rev. die as 3668-71, 3673
3672b	1.26	19.4	M	180°	Same dies. [?Baldwin]. The axis here is an exception to the uniform die-position
	(chipped)				previously noted (Milne, p. xv)
3672c	1.19	18.3	M	0°	Same dies. Nott
3672d	1.10	16.9	M	0°	Same dies. [?Baldwin]
3673	1.17	18.1	M	180°	*Oxford,* City (the Mayor). 1652[-7] token. 5.14 Oxford; C O|date|R. BW 111-12; Leeds 6. [?Baldwin]. Same rev. die as 3668-72
3674a	1.32	20.4	M	180°	*Oxford,* City (the Mayor). 1652[-7] token. 5.14 Oxford; C O|date|R. BW 111-12; Leeds 10. [?Baldwin]. Same rev. die as 3675
3674b	1.29	19.9	M	180°	Same dies. [?Baldwin]
3674c	0.85	13.1	M	180°	Same dies. [?Baldwin]
3675a	1.09	16.9	M	180°	*Oxford,* City (the Mayor). 1652[-7] token. 5.14 Oxford; C O|date|R. BW 111-12; Leeds 12. [?Baldwin]. Same rev. die as 3674
3675b	1.04	16.1	M	180°	Same dies. [?Baldwin]
3675c	0.94	14.5	M	180°	Same dies. [?Baldwin]
3675d	0.89	13.7	M	180°	Same dies. [?Baldwin]

	Weight			Die
	g	*gr*		*axis*
3676a	1.07	16.4	Br	0°	*Applebee,* Edward, tallow-chandler. nd ¼d. A|EI; 5.77. BW 113; Leeds 13. [?Baldwin]
3676b	1.03	15.9	Br	0°	Same dies. [?Baldwin]
3676c	0.90	13.9	Br	0°	Same dies. Nott [?Baldwin]
3676d	0.49	7.5	Br	0°	Same dies. [?Baldwin]
3677	1.20	18.5	Br	0°	*Applebee,* Tho[mas]. nd. 'MALLIA CADREENE'. 5.14.94; A|TS. BW 114; Leeds —. Nott. Thomas Appleby apprenticed a chandler (Leeds, pp. 378-9). Rev. legend starts at 6 o'clock; explained as dog-latin *mali*, 'apple', *a*, 'by', and as obs. *quadrine*, 'farthing' (Fletcher 1901); cf. also the Italian quattrino, *Kateryns* 1547 (Frey 1947, p. 195). Same rev. die as 3678
3678a	0.95	14.6	Br	180°	*Applebee,* Tho[mas]. nd. 'MALLIA CADREENE'. 5.14.94; A|TS. BW 114; Leeds 15. [?Baldwin]. Same rev. die as 3677 (q.v.)
3678b	0.45	6.9	Br	180°	Same dies. [?Baldwin]
3679	1.14	17.6	Br	0°	*Applebee,* William. 1666. 3.3.13; A|WA. BW 115; Leeds 16. Nott. William Applebee, chandler, 1681 (Leeds, pp. 379-80)
3680	0.77	11.8	Cu	180°	*Barrett,* John. 1666. 2.3.8; B|IF. BW 117; Leeds 19. Nott. Ioh'es Barrett apprenticed a mercer 1649; John Barrett, milliner, licensed 1665 'to hange out and sett up at his house. . . the signe of the Halfe moone and seaven Starres' (Leeds, pp. 381-2)
3681a	2.12	32.7	Cu	0°	*Bird,* Michael, watchmaker. 1668 ½d. 3.101.1; M B|date. BW 119 but P^ENY; Leeds 21 but HALF ∙ P^ENY. Nott
3681b	2.10	32.4	Cu	0°	Same dies. [Baldwin]
3682a	1.21	18.7	Br	180°	*Bishop,* George, cutler. 1668. 5.42.31; B|GS. BW 120; Leeds 22. [Nott]. George Bishop licensed 1667 'to hang out & sett up at his house. . . the signe of the Cutlers Armes' (Leeds, p. 384)
3682b	1.03	15.9	Br	0°	Same dies. Nott
3682c	0.76	11.8	Br	90°	Same dies. [Baldwin]
3683a	1.10	16.9	M	180°	*Bodicott,* Humphry, vintner (VINTENER). nd. 5.3.90; 5.64.33. BW 124 but IN; Leeds 27. [Baldwin]. 'Five Taverns in Oxford in the Year 1636. They were kept by. . . [four others] and Humphry Budwit (or Bodicote); the signes were the Mermayd, the Swan, the other three were only Bushes', 1710 (Hearne 1889, p. 85). Bodicot (d. 1660) was lessee in 1639 of 'the tavern against All Souls', afterwards the Three Tuns (Leeds, pp. 385-9); see also 3712
3683b	0.88	13.6	M	180°	Same dies. [Baldwin]
	(pierced)				
3683c	0.88	13.5	M	180°	Same dies. Nott
3683d	0.88	13.5	M	180°	Same dies. [?Baldwin]
3683e	0.84	13.0	M	180°	Same dies. [?Baldwin]
3683f	0.62	9.6	M	180°	Same dies. [?Baldwin]
3684a	1.18	18.1	Br	0°	*Bodicott,* Humphry, vintner (VINTENER). nd. 5.3.90; 5.64.33. BW 124 but IN; Leeds 28. [?Baldwin]. See 3683
3684b	0.75	11.5	Br	0°	Same dies. [Baldwin]
3685a	1.42	21.9	Br	0°	*Carter,* Richard, brewer (BRVER). nd. 3.4.6; R C. BW 128; Leeds 34. Nott. Diameter 17.5 mm
3685b	0.90	13.9	M	0°	Same dies. [Baldwin]. Diameter 17.5-18.5 mm
3685c	0.87	13.4	Br	0°	Same dies. [?Baldwin]. Diameter 17-17.5 mm
3685d	0.51	7.8	Br	0°	Same dies. [?Baldwin]. Diameter 16.5 mm
	(chipped)				
3686a	1.63	25.1	Br	0°	*Cornish,* William, mercer. 1658. 5.14 Mercers; C|WE. BW 131 but A^T; Leeds 40. Nott. William Cornishe 'gent.' (Leeds, p. 398). Diameter 17 mm
3686b	1.25	19.2	Cu	0°	Same dies. [Baldwin]. Diameter 15.5 mm
3687	1.19	18.4	M	180°	*Daniell,* Nicholas, baker. 1657. 5.65.30; 5.76(N).1. BW 132; Leeds 41. Nott
3688a	0.87	13.4	Br	0°	*Goode,* Rich[ard], chandl[e]r. 1670. 3.3.13; R G. BW 136 but RICH:; Leeds 45. Nott
3688b	0.51	7.9	Br	0°	Same dies. [Baldwin]
3689a	1.08	16.7	Cu	180°	*Hall,* Anthony, vintner. nd. 3.10.19 (A H); H|AA. BW 137 but THE; Leeds 46. Nott. Anthony Hall was at the Mermaid from 1661 (Leeds, p. 405)
3689b	0.64	9.8	Cu	180°	Same dies. [Baldwin]
3690a	0.72	11.1	Br	0°	*Hanson,* Joseph, glover. 1670. 5.15 Leathersellers 2; 5.77. BW 138, Leeds 47, but obv. and rev. transposed. Nott
3690b	0.52	8.0	Br	0°	Same dies. [Baldwin]
	(chipped)				

[*continued overleaf*]

PLATE 29

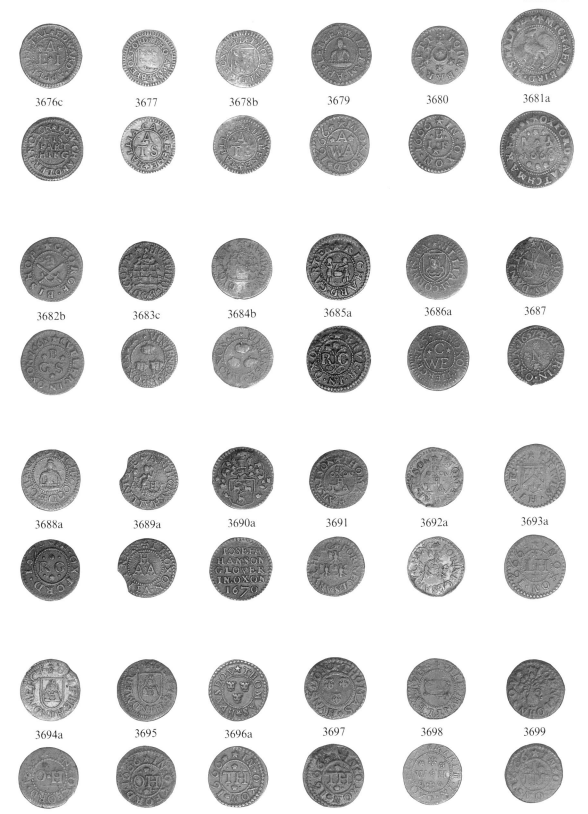

3676c 3677 3678b 3679 3680 3681a

3682b 3683c 3684b 3685a 3686a 3687

3688a 3689a 3690a 3691 3692a 3693a

3694a 3695 3696a 3697 3698 3699

Plate 29 (*cont.*)

	Weight			Die	
	g	gr		axis	
3691	1.07	16.5	M	270°	*Harrison,* Thomas. nd, 'for necessary change (NECESARY CHENG)'. 5.77 (H|TA); 3.88.3. BW 140; Leeds 49. Nott. Thomas Harrison apprenticed a mercer 1633; d. 1665 (Leeds, pp. 407-8). Same dies as 3692, the rev. in earlier state reading CHENG
3692a	1.15	17.8	Br	0°	*Harrison,* Thomas. nd, 'for necessary change (NECESARY CHANG)'. 5.77 (H|TA); 3.88.3. BW 139; Leeds 48. [Baldwin]. Same dies as 3691, with the rev. recut to show feathers in wings and tail more clearly, and E of CHENG altered to A
3692b	0.91	14.1	M	90°	Same dies. [?Baldwin]
3692c	0.91	14.0	Cu	90°	Same dies. Nott
3693a	1.03	15.8	Br	0°	*Hine,* Lewis. 1666. 5.14 Grocers; L H. BW 144; Leeds 54. Nott. Lewis Hine or Hind, chandler (Leeds, p. 410)
3693b	0.94	14.4	Br	0°	Same dies. [Baldwin]
3694a	1.36	20.9	Br	180°	*Hine* (HIND), Oliver (OLIFFE), mercer (MERC[R]). 1657. 5.14 Mercers; O H. BW 142; Leeds 52. [?Baldwin]. Oliffe, Olivar, Olive or Ollave Hind, Hine, or Hyne; brother of Lewis (Leeds, pp. 409-10), whence choice of surname form. Same obv. die as 3695
3694b	1.13	17.5	Br	0°	Same dies. Nott [?Baldwin]
3694c	0.95	14.7	Br	0°	Same dies. [?Baldwin]
3695	1.15	17.8	M	180°	*Hine* (HIND), Oliver (OLIFFE), mercer (MERC[R]). 1666. 5.14 Mercers; O H. BW 143; Leeds 53. Nott. Same obv. die as 3694
3696a	1.15	17.8	Cu	180°	*Hunsdon,* Thomas. 1666. 3.44.3; T H. BW 145; Leeds 55. Nott. Thomas Hunsdon, chandler, 1665 (Leeds, p. 411). Same rev. die as 3697
3696b	1.12	17.3	Cu	180°	Same dies. [Baldwin]
3697	1.20	18.5	M	90°	*Hunsdon,* Thomas. 1666. 3.44.3; T H. BW 145; Leeds 56. Nott. Same rev. die as 3696
3698	0.66	10.1	Br	90°	*Huntley,* Will[iam], rug-maker. 1670. 5.64.50; W H. BW 147 but WILL:; Leeds 59. Nott. William Huntley, rug-maker, Master of the City Workhouse 1660-87/8. . ., clothier 1693/4 (Leeds, pp. 412-15)
3699	1.31	20.2	Br	0°	*Johnson,* John. 1666. 4.11.24; I|IM. BW 149; Leeds 62. Nott [?Baldwin]. John Johnson, barber and confectioner (Leeds, p. 417)

	Weight			Die
	g	gr		axis
3700a	1.13	17.5	Br	0°	*King,* Lawrence (LAWRANCE), glover. nd. L K; 3.6.2. BW 150; Leeds 63. Nott [ex Seaby 1960]
3700b	0.45	7.0	Br	180°	Same dies. [?Baldwin]
	(chipped)				
3701	1.00	15.5	Br	90°	*King,* Lawrence (LAWRANCE), glover. nd. L K; 3.6.2. BW 150; Leeds 64. Nott
	(chipped)				
3702	0.98	15.1	Br	90°	*Knibb,* Joseph, clockmaker. nd. 5.50.19 (I K); 5.77.1. BW 151 but *Joseph|Knibb:*, clock dial = I[hands]K, obv. and rev. transposed; Leeds 65 but obv. and rev. transposed. Clark. Joseph Knibb fl. Oxford 1663-9, London 1670-97 (Leeds, pp. 418-21; Beeson 1962, pp. 122-4; Lee 1964)
3703	0.99	15.2	Br	0°	*Lambe,* Hugh, hosier. 1668. 3.7.1; H L|date. BW 152; Leeds 66. Nott
3704	1.02	15.7	Br	90°	*Lambe,* Hugh, hosier. 1668. 3.7.1; H L|date. BW 152; Leeds 67. Nott
3705	0.82	12.6	Cu	0°	*Lant,* Al[i]ce. 1667. 3.7.34; A L. BW 153; Leeds 68. Nott. James Launt, cordwayner, 1658; widow Alce, 1667 (Leeds, pp. 421-2)
3706	0.85	13.1	Br	0°	*Madle,* Arthur, chandler. 1666 ¼d. 5.77; M|AS. BW 154 but ARTHVR; Leeds —, cf. 69 (same obv. die). Nott. Arthur Madle, hempdresser, 1656-88/9 (Leeds, p. 422)
3707a	0.86	13.3	Br	0°	*Madle* (MADEL), Arthur (ARTHER). 1667 ¼d. M|AS; 5.77. BW 155 but FARTHINGE; Leeds 70. [Baldwin]. Form of surname as on 3706
	(pierced)				
3707b	0.63	9.7	Br	0°	Same dies. [?Baldwin]
3708	1.10	17.0	Br	180°	*Orum,* Nich[olas], fishmonger. 1659. 3.111.1; N O. BW 158 but NICH:; Leeds 73. Nott. Nicholas Oram, 1658/9 etc. (Leeds, p. 426). Same rev. die as 3709
3709a	1.05	16.2	Br	270°	*Orum,* Nich[olas], fishmonger. 1659. 3.111.1; N O. BW 158 but NICH:; Leeds 72. Nott. Same rev. die as 3708
3709b	0.91	14.0	Br	270°	Same dies. Nott
3709c	0.76	11.8	Br	270°	Same dies. [Baldwin]
3710a	0.74	11.4	Br	120°	*Orum,* Nich[olas], fishmonger. 1659. 3.111.1; N O. BW 158; Leeds 74. Nott. Same rev. die as 3711
3710b	0.72	11.2	Br	30°	Same dies. [Baldwin]
3711	0.71	10.9	Br	90°	*Orum,* Nicholas, fishmonger. 1659. 3.111.1 (· NICHOLAS · ORVM · IN.OXON around); N O (···|N ·O|···; · FISHMONGER · I659 around). BW —, cf. 158; Leeds 75. Nott. Same rev. die as 3710
3712a	1.08	16.7	M	90°	*Peirson,* Ann. 1669. 5.43.20; date. BW 159; Leeds 76. [Baldwin]. Ann, widow of William Pierson or Pearson, tailor, 1667 (Leeds, p. 427)
3712b	0.90	13.8	M	0°	Same dies. Nott
3713	1.22	18.8	Br	180°	*Pont,* Richard. 1668. 5.14 Vintners; P|RE. BW 160; Leeds 77. Nott. Richard Pont, vintner, at the Three Tuns tavern 1666-71 (Leeds, p. 428); see also 3683-4. Same rev. die as 3714
3714a	1.73	26.7	Br	240°	*Pont,* Richard. 1668. 5.14 Vintners; P|RE. BW 160; Leeds 78. Nott. Same rev. die as 3713
3714b	0.81	12.4	Br	240°	Same dies. [Baldwin]
3715a	0.97	15.0	Br	180°	*Potter,* William, apothecary. nd. 5.14 Apothecaries; P|WA. BW 161; Leeds 79. Nott
3715b	0.67	10.3	Br	180°	Same dies. [Baldwin]
3716	1.21	18.7	Br	180°	*Prince,* Daniel (DANIELL). 1667. 3.5.23; 5.35.27 (P|DK). BW 162; Leeds 80. Nott. Daniell Prince licensed 1661 to set up the sign of Prince James Duke of York, and to keep an inn (Leeds, p. 430)
3717a	1.02	15.7	Br	180°	*Prince,* Edward, chandler. nd. 3.3.13; P|EE. BW 163; Leeds 81. [Baldwin]. Edward Prince licensed 1650 to set up or hang out the sign of the Tallow-Chandler (Leeds, p. 432)
3717b	0.95	14.6	Br	180°	Same dies. Nott
3717c	0.86	13.3	Br	180°	Same dies. [Nott]
3718a	1.20	18.5	Br	270°	*Robinson,* Will, goldsmith (GOVLDSMITH). 1668. 5.14 Goldsmiths; R|WM. BW 165; Leeds 83. [Baldwin]
3718b	1.13	17.5	Br	270°	Same dies. Nott
3718c	0.97	15.0	Br	270°	Same dies. [Nott]
3719a	1.06	16.3	Br	0°	*Ryland,* John. 1659. 5.34.8; R|IA. BW 166; Leeds 84. Nott. John Ryland apprenticed a whitebaker 1620 (Leeds, p. 434). Obv. legend starts at 11 o'clock, rev. legend at 10 o'clock
3719b	0.93	14.4	Br	0°	Same dies. [Baldwin]
3720a	1.01	15.6	M	180°	*Souch* (SHOVCH), John, milliner (MILLENER). 1657. 5.35.15 (· IOHN · SHOVCH · MILLENER around); I S (I · S; · IN · OXFORD · I657 around). BW —, cf. 168; Leeds 89. Nott. John Souch licensed 1659 to hang out the sign of the Fan (Leeds, p. 437)
3720b	0.75	11.5	M	180°	Same dies. [Baldwin]

[*continued overleaf*]

PLATE 30

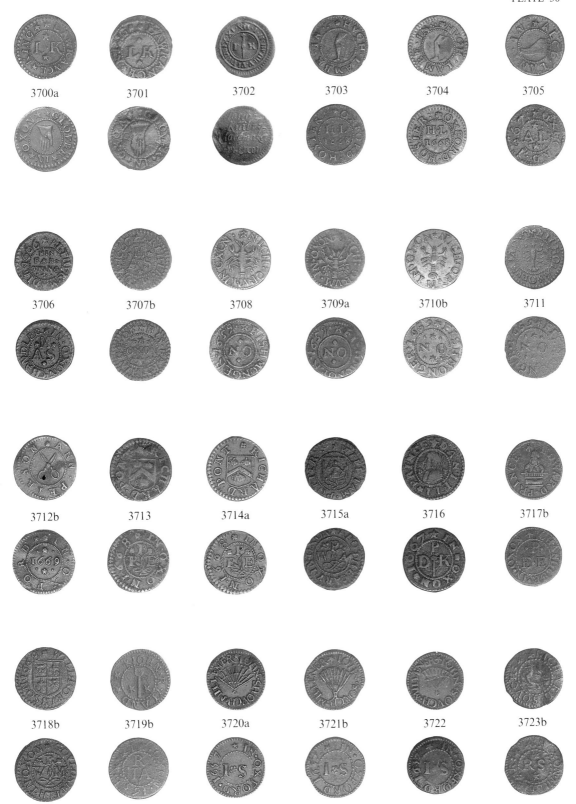

3700a 3701 3702 3703 3704 3705

3706 3707b 3708 3709a 3710b 3711

3712b 3713 3714a 3715a 3716 3717b

3718b 3719b 3720a 3721b 3722 3723b

Plate 30 (*cont.*)

	Weight			Die	
	g	gr		axis	
3721a	1.16	18.0	M	0°	*Souch,* John, milliner (MILLENER). 1657. 5.35.15; I S. BW 168 but MILLENER, OXFORD[no stop]I657; Leeds 88. Nott. See 3720. Same rev. die as 3722
3721b	1.06	16.4	M	0°	Same dies. [Baldwin]
3722	1.01	15.6	M	180°	*Souch,* John, milliner (MILLENER). 1657. 5.35.15; I S. BW 168 but MILLENER, OXFORD[no stop]I657; Leeds 87. Nott. See 3720. Same rev. die as 3721
3723a	1.45	22.3	Br	180°	*Souch,* Richard, milliner. nd. 3.101.21; R S. BW 169; Leeds 90 but MILLINER. [Baldwin]. Richard Souch licensed 1661 to set up the sign of the Hen and Chickens (Leeds, p. 438)
3723b	0.95	14.6	Br	180°	Same dies. Nott
3723c	0.88	13.6	Br	0°	Same dies. [?Baldwin]

	Weight			Die
	g	*gr*		*axis*
3724a	1.44	22.2	M	0°	*Spencer,* Edward, chandler. nd. 3.108.20; E S. BW 170; Leeds 91. [Baldwin]. 'The said Mr Spencer. . . tells me that this was one of his Farthings, and that he well remembers his Coyning them, but cannot tell the Year. . . he put upon them 3 Doves, with Olive Branches in their Mouths, those being his Arms', 1713 (Hearne 1898, p. 207)
3724b	1.30	20.0	M	0°	Same dies. Nott
3725	0.72	11.2	Cu	180°	*Stevenson,* Thomas. 1664. 5.14 'Upholsterers'; S|TA. BW 171; Leeds 92. Nott [?Baldwin]. Thomas Stevenson apprenticed an upholster, 1655 (Leeds, p. 439). Same rev. die as 3726
3726a	0.84	12.9	Cu	0°	*Stevenson,* Thomas. 1664. 5.14 'Upholsterers'; S|TA. BW 171; Leeds 93. [Baldwin]. Same rev. die as 3725
3726b	0.70	10.8	Cu	0°	Same dies. Nott
3727	0.98	15.1	Br	180°	*Toldervey,* John, milliner. 1660. 5.14.95; I T|date. BW 173; Leeds 97 but MILLINER. [Baldwin]. Same obv. die as 3728
3728	1.29	20.0	M	330°	*Toldervey,* John, milliner. 1660. 5.14.95; I T|date. BW 173; Leeds —. Nott. Same obv. die as 3727
3729a	0.99	15.2	Br	180°	*Tonge,* William, skinner (SKINER). 1657. T|WI; date. BW 174; Leeds 98. Nott. William Tonge, Chamberlain, 1653-61 (Leeds, p. 442)
3729b	0.97	15.0	Br	180°	Same dies. [Baldwin]
3730a	1.20	18.6	Br	0°	*Tonge* (TONGVE), William. 1661. 5.14 Cordwainers 2; T|WG. BW 175; Leeds 99. Nott. William Tongue, cordwainer, son of issuer of 3729 (Leeds, p. 443), whence form of surname
3730b	0.90	14.0	Br	0°	Same dies. [Baldwin]
3731a	0.87	13.4	Br	180°	*Turner,* Will[iam]. nd. 3.2.11; T|WE. BW 177 but WILL.; Leeds 100 but TVRNER. Nott. Issuer ?William Turner, mercer, Chamberlain 1654-67 (Leeds, pp. 443-4). Obv. legend starts at 10 o'clock, rev. at 7 o'clock
3731b	0.60	9.3	Br	180°	Same dies. [Baldwin]
3732a	0.90	14.0	Cu	180°	*Turton,* Ann. 1657. 5.14 Ironmongers; A T. BW 178; Leeds 101. [Nott or Baldwin]. Ann Turton, widow, ironmonger 1652-9, kept the Crown Tavern (Leeds, pp. 423, 445); afterwards Mrs William Morrell, see 3745; see also 3733. Diameter 16-16.5 mm
3732b	0.67	10.4	Cu	0°	Same dies. Nott. Diameter 16 mm
3732c	0.38	5.8	Cu	180°	Same dies. [?Baldwin]. Diameter 15 mm
	(pierced, worn)				
3733a	1.57	24.2	Br	60°	*Turton,* Rich[ard]. 1668. 5.14 Ironmongers; T|RM. BW 179; Leeds 102 but RICH. Nott. Richard, son of Ann Turton (Leeds, pp. 446-7), see 3732
3733b	1.10	17.0	Br	240°	Same dies. [Baldwin]
3734a	0.84	12.9	Br	90°	*Walker,* William. 1668. 3.53.1 (·WILLIAM·WALKER around); W|WM (·IN·OXON·I668 around). BW —; Leeds 105; Dickinson 181A. [?Baldwin]. Will. Walker at the Roebuck, 1667-70; innholder, 1667-8 (Leeds, p. 449)
3734b	0.62	9.5	Br	90°	Same dies. Baldwin
3735	0.83	12.9	Br	0°	*Wallis,* Samuel (SAMVELL). nd. 5.82.1; W|SA. BW 182; Leeds 106. Nott
3736a	0.58	9.0	Br	180°	*White,* Rob[ert], silk-weaver (SILK WEVE^R). 1657. 5.83.30; R W|date. BW 184 but ROB ·WHITE:SILK:WEVE^R; Leeds 108. Nott. Forename as on 3737
3736b	0.55	8.5	Br	180°	Same dies. Nott
3737a	1.11	17.1	Br	270°	*White,* Robert, silk-weaver (SILKE|WEAVER). 1657. 5.83.1; R W|date. BW 183; Leeds 107 but R·W 1657. Nott. Overstruck on a token with shield device on one side, initials E S on the other
3737b	1.06	16.3	Br	270°	Same dies. [Nott]. Overstruck on a token with shield device
3737c	0.82	12.7	Br	270°	Same dies. [?Baldwin]
3737d	0.78	12.1	Br	270°	Same dies. [?Baldwin]
3737e	0.41	6.3	Br	270°	Same dies. [?Baldwin]
	(chipped)				
3738a	1.17	18.1	Br	0°	*Wilson,* Robert, brewer. nd. 5.81.15; 5.14 Brewers. BW 186; Leeds 110. Baldwin. Same rev. die as 3739
3738b	0.69	10.7	Br	0°	Same dies. [?Baldwin]
3739a	0.62	9.6	Br	0°	*Wilson,* Robert, brewer. nd. 5.81.15; 5.14 Brewers. BW 186; Leeds 111. [?Baldwin]. Robert Wilson died 1663 (Leeds, p. 451). Same rev. die as 3738
	(chipped)				
3739b	0.56	8.7	Br	0°	Same dies. [Nott]
	(chipped)				

[*continued overleaf*]

PLATE 31

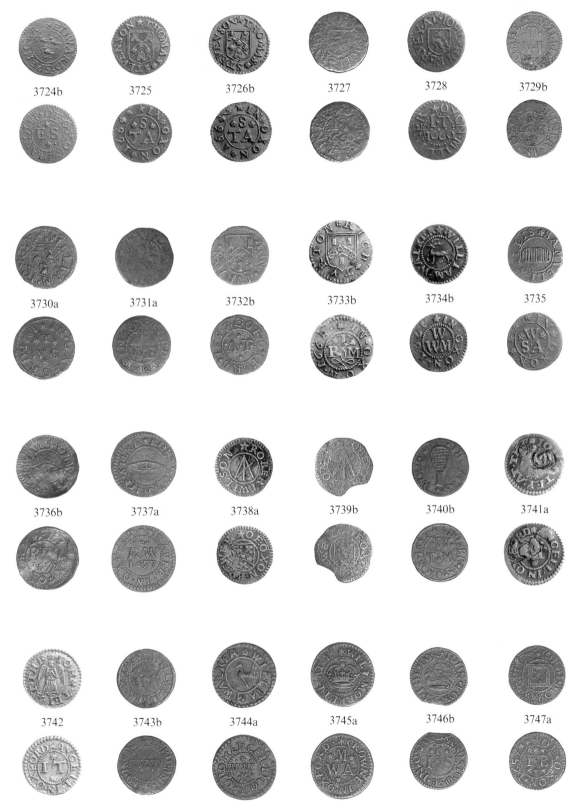

3724b   3725   3726b   3727   3728   3729b

3730a   3731a   3732b   3733b   3734b   3735

3736b   3737a   3738a   3739b   3740b   3741a

3742   3743b   3744a   3745a   3746b   3747a

Plate 31 (*cont.*)

	Weight			Die axis	
	g	gr			
3740a	1.04	16.0	M	180°	*Wood,* Thomas, vintner. 1652. 5.35.10; W|TM. BW 187; Leeds 112. Nott. Thomas Wood, occupier 1651-63 of two tenements in St Mary's parish, behind which stretched the (Oriel College) tennis or racket court (Leeds, pp. 452-3); see also 3777
3740b	0.80	12.3	M	180°	Same dies. [?Baldwin]

Named signs

3741a	1.06	16.3	Br	0°	*Angel* (AT THE ANGELL): Tey, John. nd. 3.10.1; I T. BW 172; Leeds 96 but rev. die different from 95. [Baldwin]. John Tey, innholder (Leeds, pp. 440-1). Countermarked on rev. with crown above ?rose
3741b	0.50	7.7	Br	0°	Same dies. [Baldwin]
	(chipped)				
3742	0.69	10.6	Br	0°	*Angel* (AT THE ANGELL): Tey, John. nd. 3.10.1; I T. BW 172; Leeds 95. Nott. See 3741
3743a	1.04	16.0	Br	180°	*Bird & Hand* (AT THE BVRD AND HAND): Walker, Will[iam] (Sir), [mercer]. nd. 3.6.22; WW. BW 180 but AT[no stop]THE; Leeds 103. Nott. Trade as on 3744 (q.v. for knighthood). William Walker, mercer, licensed 1648 to use the sign of the Bird in Hand (Leeds, p. 447)
3743b	0.77	11.9	Br	180°	Same dies. [Baldwin]
3744a	1.29	19.9	Br	180°	[*Bird & Hand*]: Walker, William (Sir), mercer. nd. 3.6.22; W W. BW 181; Leeds 104. [?Baldwin]. Sign name from 3743. Issuer mayor, and knighted Feb. 1685 as butler of the King's wine-cellar and beer seller at the Coronation (Shaw 1906, ii. 260; Leeds, pp. 447-8)
3744b	1.16	17.9	Br	180°	Same dies. Nott
3745a	1.74	26.9	Cu	270°	*Crown* (AT YᴱCROWNE): Morrell, Will[iam]. nd. 5.60.1; M|WA. BW 156 but WILL.; Leeds 71. [?Baldwin]. William Morrell, vintner 1659, and ironmonger 1661 (Leeds, pp. 423-4); see also 3732, and 3733
3745b	1.07	16.5	Br	90°	Same dies. Nott
3745c	0.85	13.2	Br	90°	Same dies. Nott [?Baldwin]
3746a	1.23	18.9	M	180°	*Fox & Goose* (AT THE): Fox, John. nd. 3.66.3; F|IS. BW 135; Leeds 44. Nott. John Fox, tailor and alehouse keeper (Leeds, p. 403)
3746b	0.94	14.5	M	180°	Same dies. [Baldwin]
3747a	1.38	21.3	Br	0°	*Gilt* [*Looking-glass*] (AT Yᴱ GVILT): Bishop, Joh[n]. 1657. 5.3.70; I B. BW 121 but IOH:, Aᵀ; Leeds 24. [Baldwin]. John Bishop, milliner, licensed 1667/8 to hang out the sign of the Looking Glass (Leeds, p. 385)
3747b	0.98	15.1	Br	0°	Same dies. [?Baldwin]

Names signs (*cont.*)

	Weight			Die	
	g	gr		axis	
3748a	1.70	26.2	Br	210°	*Gilt* [*Looking-glass*] (AT Y^E GVILT): Bishop, Joh[n]. 1657. 5.3.70; I B. BW 121 but IOH:, A^T; Leeds 23. [?Baldwin]. Sign and forename as for 3747
3748b	0.91	14.1	Br	210°	Same dies. Nott
3748c	0.90	13.9	Br	210°	Same dies. Baldwin
3749	0.97	14.9	Br	0°	*Gilt* [*Looking-glass*] (AT THE GILT): Bishop, John. 1663. 5.3.70; I B. BW 122 but IOHN, THE · GILT; Leeds 25. Nott. Sign-name as on 3747
3750a	0.87	13.4	Br	0°	[*Gilt*] *Looking-glass* (LOOKINGGLAS): Bishop, Joh[n], milliner (MILENER). 1669. 5.3.70; I B|date. BW 123 but IOH:, LOOKINGGLAS; Leeds 26 but LOOKINGGLAS. Brand [or Nott ex Seaby]. John Bishop, chamberlain, 1666-71 (Leeds, p. 385). Sign-name completed from 3747 (q.v.). Struck from clashed dies
3750b	0.74	11.5	Br	0°	Same dies. [Nott]
3750c	0.72	11.0	Br	0°	Same (clashed) dies. [?Baldwin]
3751a	0.99	15.3	Br	180°	*Golden Key* (AT THE GOVLDING KEY): Ireland, Seth. nd. 5.66.1; 3.9.11 (S I). BW 148; Leeds 60. Nott [ex Seaby 1960]. Seth Ireland, mercer, 1646; died 1660 (Leeds, p. 416)
3751b	0.84	12.9	Br	180°	Same dies. [Baldwin]
3752	0.81	12.5	Cu	270°	*Golden Key* (AT THE GOVLDING KEY): Ireland, Seth. nd. 5.66.1; 3.9.11 (S I). BW 148 but THE; Leeds 61. Nott. See 3751
					Looking-glass see *Gilt Looking-glass*
3753a	1.05	16.3	Br	180°	*Mortar & Pestle* (AT THE MORTER AND PEST): Baley, William. nd. 5.64.80; W B. BW 116; Leeds 17. [?Baldwin]. William Baylie, mercer, 1644; licensed 1650/1 to set up and hang out the sign of the Pestle & Mortar (Leeds, p. 380)
3753b	0.97	15.0	Br	180°	Same dies. Nott
3754	0.97	14.9	Br	180°	*Mortar & Pestle* (AT THE MORTER AND PEST): Baley, William. nd. 5.64.80; W B. BW 116; Leeds 18. [?Nott]. See 3753
3755	0.94	14.5	Br	180°	*Racket & Ball* (AT Y^E RACKIT & BALL): Butler, Thomas. nd. 5.35.11; B|TM. BW 127 but BVTLER; Leeds 33. Nott. Thomas Butler, apprenticed 1659/60 to Thomas Burnham, see 3777; licensed for alehouse, 1670-5; occupied the (City) racket court near Smith Gate, 1671-80 (Leeds, pp. 394-5)
3756a	1.06	16.4	Br	180°	*Salmon* (AT THE): Raulins, Samson. nd. 3.109.10; R|SM. BW 164 but RAVLINS; Leeds 82. Nott. Sampson Rawlins apprenticed a chandler 1639; licensed 1650/1 to hang out or set up the sign of the Salmon (Leeds, p. 433)
3756b	0.95	14.7	Br	180°	Same dies. Nott [?Baldwin]
3757	1.22	18.8	Br	90°	*Spectacles* (AT Y^E): Williams, Tho[mas]. nd. 5.86.1; T W. BW 185 but THO:; Leeds —. [Baldwin]. Issuer ?Thomas Williams, milliner, fl. 1637-72 (Leeds, p. 451); Whittet 1986a, p. 112, prefers Thomas Williams, apothecary (d. 1668), but Robert Liford, milliner (see 57) also displayed spectacles. Same rev. die as 3758
3758a	1.18	18.2	Br	90°	*Spectacles* (AT Y^E): Williams, Tho[mas]. nd. 5.86.1; T W. BW 185 but THO:; Leeds 109. [?Baldwin]. Same rev. die as 3757, q.v.
3758b	1.11	17.1	Br	270°	Same dies. [?Baldwin]
3758c	0.96	14.8	Br	180°	Same dies. Nott
3759a	1.20	18.5	M	0°	*Sugar-loaf* (LOFE): Bowell, John, mercer. 1657. I B|date; 5.64.1. BW 125; Leeds 31. [Baldwin]
3759b	1.10	16.9	M	0°	Same dies. Brand [or Nott]
3759c	1.09	16.8	M	0°	Same dies. [?Baldwin]
3759d	0.76	11.7	M	0°	Same dies. [Baldwin]
3760a	1.19	18.4	M	180°	*Sugar-loaf* (LOFE): Bowell, John, mercer. 1657. I B|date; 5.64.1. BW 125; Leeds 29. [?Baldwin]. Same rev. die as 3761-2
3760b	1.06	16.3	M	180°	Same dies. [?Baldwin]
3760c	1.06	16.3	M	180°	Same dies. [?Baldwin]
3760d	1.03	15.9	M	180°	Same dies. [?Baldwin]
3760e	0.89	13.8	M	180°	Same dies. [?Baldwin]
3760f	0.75	11.5	M	180°	Same dies. [?Baldwin]
3761	1.05	16.2	M	180°	*Sugar-loaf* (LOFE): Bowell (BOWEL), John, mercer. 1657. I B|date (I · B|I657; · IOHN · BOWEL · MERCER around); 5.64.1 (· SVGAR · LOFE · IN · OXON around). BW —; Leeds —. [?Baldwin]. Same rev. die as 3760, 3762, whence form of surname

[*continued overleaf*]

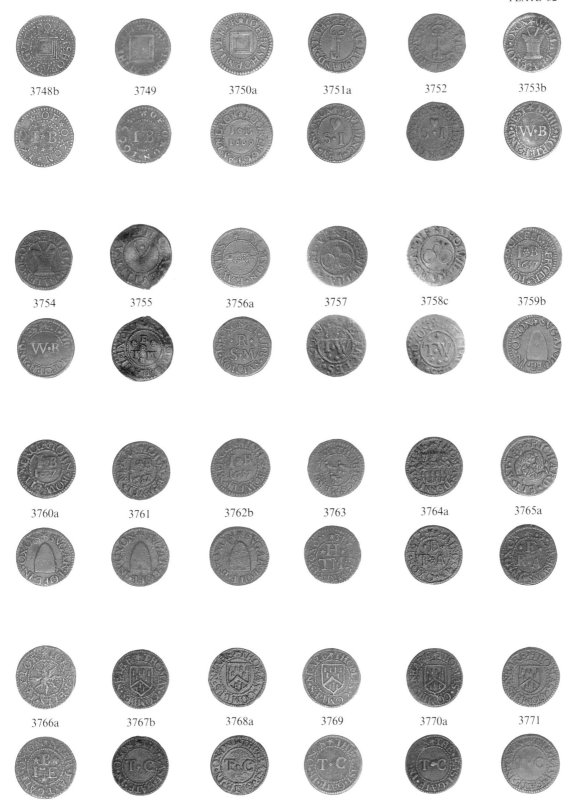

PLATE 32

3748b	3749	3750a	3751a	3752	3753b

3754	3755	3756a	3757	3758c	3759b

3760a	3761	3762b	3763	3764a	3765a

3766a	3767b	3768a	3769	3770a	3771

Plate 32 (*cont.*)

	Weight			Die	
	g	gr		axis	
3762a	1.20	18.5	M	180°	*Sugar-loaf* (LOFE): Bowell, John, mercer. 1657. I B|date; 5.64.1. BW 125; Leeds 30. [Baldwin]. Same rev. die as 3760-1
3762b	1.19	18.4	M	180°	Same dies. [?Baldwin]
3762c	1.16	17.8	M	180°	Same dies. [?Baldwin]
3762d	1.09	16.8	M	180°	Same dies. [Baldwin]
3762e	0.88	13.5	M	180°	Same dies. [?Baldwin]
	(chipped)				
3763	0.71	10.9	Br	0°	*Three Blackbirds* (AT 3 BLACKBIRDS): Higgs, Tho[mas], mercer. nd. 3.108.16; H|TM. BW 141 but THO:, BLACKBIRDS; Leeds 50. Nott. Thomas Higgs apprenticed to Thomas Combes (see 3767-72) 1648-56 (Leeds, p. 408)
3764a	1.13	17.4	M	180°	*Three Kings* (AT THE 3 KINGS): Dennis, Thomas. 1652. 3.4.21; D|TA. BW 133; Leeds 42. Nott. Thomas Dennis, mercer (Leeds, p. 401)
3764b	1.06	16.4	M	180°	Same dies. [Baldwin]
3764c	0.73	11.3	M	180°	Same dies. [Nott]
3765a	1.28	19.7	M	180°	*Three Salmons* (AT THE 3 SAMMONS): Ely, Richard. nd. 3.109.16; E|RA. BW 134; Leeds 43. Nott. Richard Ely, chandler, 1653; d. 1661 (Leeds, pp. 402-3)
3765b	1.16	17.9	M	180°	Same dies. [Baldwin]

OXFORD. East Gate neighbourhood

The reading is NEER EAST GATE OXON on 3766; NEARE THE EAST GATE IN OXON on the remainder

3766a	0.76	11.8	Br	90°	*Betts,* John, tailor (TAYLOR). nd. 2.4.3; B|IE. BW 118; Leeds 20. Nott. John Bett(s) also held an alehouse licence 1659-69 (Leeds, pp. 382-3)
3766b	0.69	10.7	Br	90°	Same dies. [?Baldwin]
	(chipped)				
3767a	0.79	12.1	M	180°	*Combes,* Thomas. nd. 5.14 Grocers; T C. BW 129; Leeds 35. [Baldwin]. Mr Thomas Combes, mercer; d. 1661 (Leeds, p. 396). Same rev. die as 3768
3767b	0.75	11.5	M	180°	Same dies. [?Baldwin]
3768a	1.14	17.6	M	180°	*Combes,* Thomas. nd. 5.14 Grocers; T C. BW 129; Leeds 36. Brand [or Nott]. Same obv. die as 3769; same rev. die as 3767
3768b	1.10	17.0	M	180°	Same dies. [?Baldwin]
3768c	0.77	11.9	M	180°	Same dies. [?Baldwin]
3768d	0.76	11.7	M	180°	Same dies. [?Baldwin]
3769	1.08	16.6	M	180°	*Combes,* Thomas. nd. 5.14 Grocers; T C. BW 129; Leeds —. [?Baldwin]. Same obv. die as 3768
3770a	1.03	15.9	M	180°	*Combes,* Thomas. nd. 5.14 Grocers; T C. BW 129; Leeds 38. [?Baldwin]. See 3767. Same obv. die as 3771-2
3770b	1.01	15.6	M	180°	Same dies. [?Baldwin]
3771	1.16	17.9	M	180°	*Combes,* Thomas. nd. 5.14 Grocers; T C. BW 129; Leeds 37. [?Baldwin]. Same obv. die as 3770, 3772

OXFORD. East Gate neighbourhood (*cont.*)

	Weight			Die	
	g	gr		axis	
3772a	1.00	15.4	M	180°	*Combes,* Thomas. nd. 5.14 Grocers; T C. BW 129; Leeds —. [Nott]. Same obv. die as 3770-1
3772b	0.81	12.5	M	180°	Same dies. [?Baldwin]

OXFORD. New College neighbourhood

The reading is NE(A)R(E) NEW COLLEDG IN OXON

3773	1.15	17.7	Cu	90°	*Short,* Lawrence. nd. 3.6.51 (·LAWRENCE·SHORT·NER around); S|LE (·S·|L·E; ·NEW·COLLEDG·IN·OXON around). BW —, cf. 167; Leeds 86. Nott. Lawrence Short, coffee man, 1670-3 (Leeds, pp. 435-6). Same rev. die as 3774
3774a	1.54	23.8	Br	270°	*Short,* Lawrence. nd. 3.6.51; S|LE. BW 167; Leeds 85. [Baldwin]. Same rev. die as 3773
3774b	1.46	22.6	Br	270°	Same dies. Nott [ex Daniels]

OXFORD. North Gate neighbourhood

The reading is AT NORTH GATE IN OXON

3775a	1.10	17.0	Br	180°	*Wrigglysworth,* Edmund. 1652. Date; E W. BW 188; Leeds 113. [Baldwin]. Edmund Wrigglysworth apprenticed a white baker 1640; 'mercer' 1654 (Leeds, p. 453)
3775b	1.04	16.1	Br	180°	Same dies. Nott
3775c	0.98	15.2	Br	180°	Same dies. [?Baldwin]
3775d	0.96	14.8	Br	180°	Same dies. [?Baldwin]
	(chipped)				

OXFORD. St Mary the Virgin neighbourhood

The reading is AT S^{T}MARY IN OXON, which Leeds takes to mean 'in St Mary's parish' (p. 397); but the meaning 'near St Mary's church' finds support in Richard Cony's proximity 1667 to the West end of St Mary's Church (Salter 1923, p. 242)

3776	2.04	31.5	Br	0°	*Cony,* Richard. 1666 ½d. 5.77; C|RM. BW 130 but S^{T}MARYS, OXON·I666; Leeds 39 but S^T. Nott

OXFORD. 'The Tennis Court'

The reading is AT Y^{E}TENIS COVRT IN OXON, i.e. the Merton College tennis court in St John's parish? the Oriel College tennis court in St Mary's parish? or the Christ Church College tennis court in St Aldate's parish?

3777a	0.72	11.1	Br	90°	*Burnham,* Thomas. nd. 5.35.10; B|TI. BW 126; Leeds 32. Nott. Thomas Burnham, licensed alehouse-keeper; kept the tennis court in St John's parish 1647-63; held the racket court in St Mary's parish 1664-70, cf. 3740; kept the tennis court in St Aldate's parish 1670-76 (Leeds, pp. 391-4); see also 3755
3777b	0.70	10.8	Br	90°	Same dies. [?Baldwin]
	(chipped)				
3777c	0.69	10.6	Br	90°	Same dies. No provenance

OXFORD. The Turl Gate neighbourhood

The reading is IN OXON AT THE TVRLE GATE on both, cf. *Turl Gate Street* 1661-6, subsequently *Turl Street.* The first element is the word *tirl,* a turnstile; the gate was in the City Wall, leading out into what is now Broad Street (EPNS 1954, p. 44)

3778a	1.23	19.0	Br	0°	*Hunt,* Edward. nd. 5.77; E H. BW 146; Leeds 57. Nott. Edward Hunt apprenticed to Edmund Wrigglesworth, mercer (see 3773), 1654-61 (Leeds, p. 412). Same rev. die as 3779
3778b	0.78	12.0	Br	180°	Same dies. [Nott]
3779a	1.11	17.1	Br	180°	*Hunt,* Edward. nd. 5.77; E H. BW 146; Leeds 58. [Baldwin]. Same rev. die as 3778
3779b	0.77	11.8	Br	90°	Same dies. Nott
3779c	0.40	6.2	Br	90°	Same dies. Nott
	(chipped)				

SHIPTON UNDER WYCHWOOD

The reading is SHIPTON VNDER WHITCHWOOD

3780	0.53	8.2	Br	0°	*Wells,* Joh[n]. nd. 5.14 Grocers; W|ID. BW 190 but IOH:, WHITCHWOOD; Milne 117. Nott.
	(pierced)				Forename completed from Milne, p. 41

SONNING *see* Berkshire

[*continued overleaf*]

PLATE 33

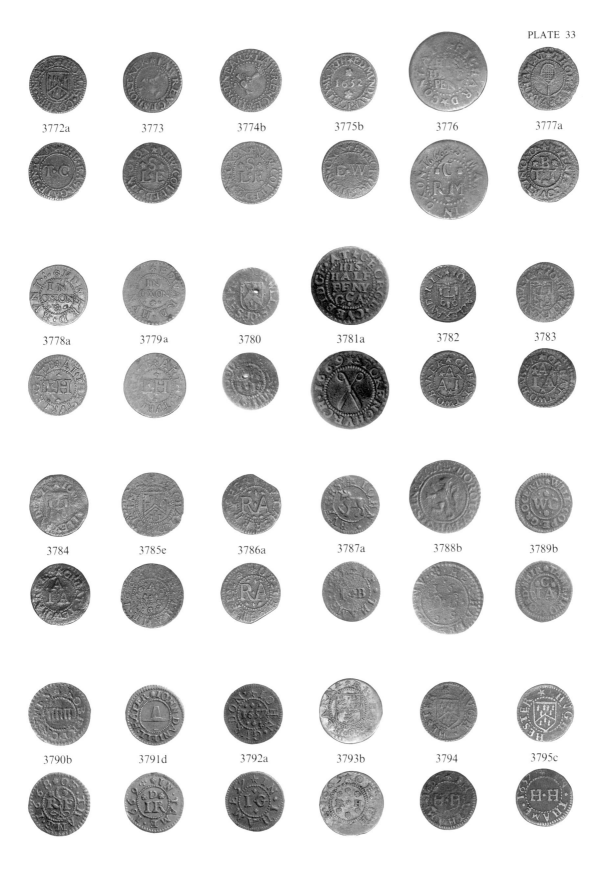

3772a   3773   3774b   3775b   3776   3777a

3778a   3779a   3780   3781a   3782   3783

3784   3785e   3786a   3787a   3788b   3789b

3790b   3791d   3792a   3793b   3794   3795c

Plate 33 (*cont.*)

STOKENCHURCH (Oxon., Aston Rowant parish *subsequently* Buckinghamshire)

The reading is STOKENCHVRCH

	Weight			Die	
	g	gr		axis	
3781a	1.51	23.2	Br	0°	*Cubbidge,* George. 1669 ½d. 5.77 (C|GA); 5.43.24. BW 189; Milne 118. Nott [?Baldwin]. George Cubbidge trained as a tailor; kept a mercery and chandler's shop (Delafield *c.*1750, see Milne, pp. xx, 41)
3781b	0.90	13.8	Br	0°	Same dies. [?Baldwin]
	(chipped)				

TEW, Great

The reading is GREAT TWO on 3782-3; GREAT TEW on 3784

3782	1.35	20.9	Cu	0°	*Allexander,*John,baker.nd.5.14Bakers(·IOHN·ALLEXANDER·INaround);A|AI(·A·|A·I|·; ·GREAT·TWO·BAKER around). BW —, cf. 89; Milne —. Nott. Same dies as 3783, in earlier state with forename initials A·I [*sic*]; same obv. die as 3784
3783	0.89	13.8	Cu	180°	*Allexander,* John, baker. nd. 5.14 Bakers; A|IA. BW 89; Milne 93. Nott. Same dies as 3782, with I·A cancelling A·I; same obv. die as 3784
3784	0.94	14.5	M	180°	*Allexander,* John, baker. nd. 5.14 Bakers; A|IA. BW 90 but TEW; Milne —, cf. p. 27. Nott. Same obv. die as 3782-3

THAME

The reading is TAME on 3791; TAME IN OXFORD SHIR on 3789; THAME on the remainder

3785a	1.52	23.5	Br	0°	*Adkins,* Richard. 1669. 5.14 Grocers; A|RS. BW 191 but ADKINS; Milne 119. Brand [or Baldwin]
3785b	1.29	19.8	Br	0°	Same dies. [?Baldwin]
3785c	0.97	15.0	Br	0°	Same dies. [?Baldwin]
3785d	0.77	11.9	Br	0°	Same dies. [?Baldwin]
3785e	0.75	11.5	Br	0°	Same dies. [?Baldwin]
3785f	0.72	11.2	Br	0°	Same dies. [Nott]
3786a	0.79	12.2	M	180°	*Aeris,* Ruth. nd. R A; R A. BW 193 but AERIS; Milne 121. [Nott]. Ruth Ayres married Edward Bowry 1665/6. Overstruck on Moulton (Northants.): Peryn, John, nd (dies and axis as 3398). Diameter 16 mm
3786b	0.78	12.0	Br	90°	Same dies. [Baldwin]. Diameter 17 mm
3786c	0.69	10.6	Br	180°	Same dies. Nott. Diameter 16 mm
3786d	0.61	9.4	Br	0°	Same dies. [?Baldwin]. Diameter 16 mm
	(chipped)				
3786e	0.59	9.1	Br	180°	Same dies. Nott. Diameter 15.5 mm
3787a	1.21	18.7	M	180°	*Burges,* John. 1653. 3.61.1; I B. BW 195; Milne 123. Nott
3787b	0.86	13.2	M	180°	Same dies. [?Baldwin]
	(worn)				
3787c	0.85	13.1	M	180°	Same dies. [Baldwin]
3788a	1.17	18.0	Br	0°	*Burgis,* Dorothy. 1669 ½d. 3.11; 5.77 (*D B*). BW 194; Milne 122. [Baldwin]
	(chipped)				
3788b	1.01	15.5	Br	0°	Same dies. Nott
3789a	1.24	19.1	Cu	180°	*Cope,* Will—, grocer. nd. W C; C|IA. BW 196 but WILL:, OXFORD·SHIR; Milne 124. [Baldwin]
3789b	0.70	10.7	Cu	180°	Same dies. Nott
3789c	0.30	4.6	Cu	180°	Same dies. [?Baldwin]
	(chipped)				
3790a	0.79	12.1	Br	60°	*Crewes,* Robert. 1668. 5.32.9; C|RF. BW 197; Milne 125. [?Baldwin]. 'Robert Crues' d. 1688/9 (Milne, p. 42)
3790b	0.68	10.5	Br	240°	Same dies. Nott [?Baldwin]
3790c	0.67	10.3	Br	240°	Same dies. [?Baldwin]
3790d	0.66	10.1	Br	60°	Same dies. [?Baldwin]
3790e	0.63	9.7	Br	240°	Same dies. [Nott]
3791a	0.98	15.2	Cu	270°	*Daniell,* John, hatter (HATER). 1669. 5.61.1; D|IR. BW 198 but DANIELL; Milne 126. [?Baldwin]
3791b	0.98	15.1	Cu	0°	Same dies. Nott [?Baldwin]
3791c	0.90	13.9	Cu	0°	Same dies. [?Baldwin]
3791d	0.89	13.8	Cu	0°	Same dies. Nott
3791e	0.84	13.0	Cu	0°	Same dies. [?Baldwin]

| | Weight | | Die | | |
	g	gr		axis	
3792a	1.82	28.1	Br	180°	*Gurdon,* John. 1657. Date; I G. BW 199 but THAME[no stop]57; Milne 127. Nott. John Gurdon, draper, 1681 (Milne, p. 42)
3792b	1.08	16.6	Cu	90°	Same dies. [?Baldwin]
3793a	1.61	24.9	Br	90°	*Hearne,* Richard. 1669. 5.14 Drapers; R H. BW 201; Milne 130. [?Baldwin]. Diameter 17.5 mm
3793b	1.56	24.1	Br	90°	Same dies. [Nott]. Diameter 17.5 mm
3793c	1.54	23.8	Br	90°	Same dies. Nott [?Baldwin]. Diameter 17.5 mm
3793d	0.65	10.0	Br	90°	Same dies. [?Baldwin]. Diameter 16 mm
3794	1.15	17.8	Br	180°	*Hester,* Hugh. 1657. 5.14 Grocers; H H. BW 202; Milne 132. [?Baldwin]. Same obv. die as 3795
3795a	1.13	17.5	Br	180°	*Hester,* Hugh. 1657. 5.14 Grocers; H H. BW 202; Milne 131. [Nott]. Same obv. die as 3794
3795b	1.08	16.7	Br	180°	Same dies. [Baldwin]
3795c	1.06	16.3	Br	180°	Same dies. Nott
3795d	1.02	15.8	Br	180°	Same dies. [Nott]
3795e	0.90	13.9	Br	0°	Same dies. [?Baldwin]
3795f	0.59	9.0	Br	0°	Same dies. [?Baldwin]
	(chipped)				

THAME (*cont.*)

	Weight			Die	
	g	gr		axis	
3796	0.87	13.4	Br	0°	*Jemet,* William. 1669. 5.61.26; I|WI. BW 203 but WILLIAM · IEMET; Milne 133. Nott
	(chipped)				
3797a	1.34	20.7	Cu	210°	*Leaver,* Edward. nd. 5.14 Merchant Taylors; L|EI. BW 204; Milne —. [?Baldwin]. Same obv. die as 3798
3797b	1.08	16.7	Cu	210°	Same dies. Nott
3797c	0.71	11.0	Cu	210°	Same dies. [?Baldwin]
	(chipped)				
3798a	1.01	15.6	Cu	30°	*Leaver,* Edward. nd. 5.14 Merchant Taylors; L|EI. BW 204; Milne 134. [?Baldwin]. Same obv. die as 3797
	(pierced)				
3798b	0.80	12.4	Cu	30°	Same dies. [Baldwin]
3799	0.66	10.2	Br	90°	*Rastell,* Rich[ard]. nd. 5.14 Mercers (· RICH: · RASTELL around); R R̨ (· ̨|R R̨|: ; · IN · THAME ····· around). BW —, cf. 205; Milne —, cf. 136 (same obv. die). [?Baldwin]. Forename completed from 3800-2. Same obv. die as 3800, in earlier state reading RICH:
3800a	1.16	17.9	Br	180°	*Rastell,* Richard. nd. 5.14 Mercers (· RICH^ARD^RASTELLaround);RR(· |RR| · ;IN:THAME · · · around). BW —; Milne 137. [?Baldwin]. Same obv. die as 3799, altered to read RICH^ARD^; same rev. die as 3801
3800b	1.15	17.8	Br	0°	Same dies. Nott [?Baldwin]
	(chipped)				
3800c	1.08	16.6	Br	90°	Same dies. [Nott]
3800d	1.04	16.0	Br	90°	Same dies. [?Baldwin]
3800e	1.01	15.6	Br	0°	Same dies. [?Baldwin]
	(chipped)				
3801	1.37	21.1	Br	0°	*Rastell,* Richard. nd. 5.14 Mercers; R R. BW 205; Milne 135. [?Baldwin]. Same rev. die as 3800
3802a	1.11	17.1	Br	270°	*Rastell,* Richard. nd. 5.14 Mercers; R R. BW 205; Milne 138. Nott [?Baldwin]
3802b	0.97	14.9	Br	270°	Same dies. [?Baldwin]
3802c	0.85	13.1	Br	270°	Same dies. [?Baldwin]
	(chipped)				
3802d	0.70	10.9	Br	270°	Same dies. [?Baldwin]
3803a	0.57	8.8	Br	0°	*Tripp,* William, chandler. nd. 5.32.9; T|WE. BW 206 but CHANDLER · IN · THAME; Milne 140. Nott. Legends both sides start at 10 o'clock. Same obv. die as 3804-5
3803b	0.55	8.5	Br	0°	Same dies. [?Baldwin]
3804a	0.71	10.9	Br	120°	*Tripp,* William, chandler. nd. 5.32.9; T|WE. BW 206 but CHANDLER · IN · THAME; Milne —, cf. p. 28. [?Baldwin]. Rev. legend starts at 5 o'clock. Same obv. die as 3803, 3805
3804b	0.71	10.9	Br	120°	Same dies. [?Baldwin]
3805a	0.87	13.4	Br	90°	*Tripp,* William, chandler. nd. 5.32.9; T|WE. BW 206 but CHANDLER · IN · THAME; Milne 139. [?Baldwin]. Rev. legend starts at 6 o'clock. Same obv. die as 3803-4. Diameter 16.5 mm
	(worn)				
3805b	0.72	11.0	Br	0°	Same dies. Nott [?Baldwin]. Diameter 16-16.5 mm
3805c	0.69	10.7	Br	0°	Same dies. [Baldwin]. Diameter 17-17.5 mm
3805d	0.61	9.4	Br	270°	Same dies. [?Baldwin]. Diameter 16.5 mm
3806a	1.21	18.6	Br	0°	*Watters,* Matthew (MATHEW), mercer. nd. 5.14 Mercers; M W. BW 207 but WATTERS; Milne 141. [?Baldwin]. Mathew Warters d. c.1658 (Milne, p. 43)
3806b	1.09	16.8	Br	0°	Same dies. Nott
3806c	1.06	16.4	Br	180°	Same dies. [?Baldwin]
3806d	0.99	15.2	Br	0°	Same dies. Nott [?Baldwin]
	(chipped)				
3806e	0.84	12.9	Br	0°	Same dies. [?Baldwin]
3807a	2.21	34.1	Br	180°	*Weekes,* Isaac, gardener. 1667 ½d. 4.1.1; 5.77. BW 208; Milne 142 but GARDENER · IN. [?Baldwin]. 'Isaac Wicks' 1684 (Milne, p. 43)
3807b	1.93	29.7	Br	180°	Same dies. Nott
3807c	1.87	28.8	Br	180°	Same dies. [?Baldwin]
3807d	1.59	24.5	Br	180°	Same dies. [?Baldwin]

Named signs

3808	1.92	29.6	Br	0°	*Black Lion* (THE BLACKE LION): Adkens, William. 1669 ½d. 5.77; 3.39.20. BW 192; Milne 120. Nott. William Adkins 'yeoman' (Milne, p. 42)
3809a	1.17	18.1	Br	90°	*Red Lion* (AT THE READ LYON): Harris, John. nd. 3.11; I H. BW 200; Milne 129. [?Baldwin]. Obv. legend starts at 3 o'clock. Same obv. die as 3810
3809b	1.08	16.7	Br	90°	Same dies. [Baldwin]
3809c	0.87	13.4	Br	90°	Same dies. [?Baldwin]

[*continued overleaf*]

PLATE 34

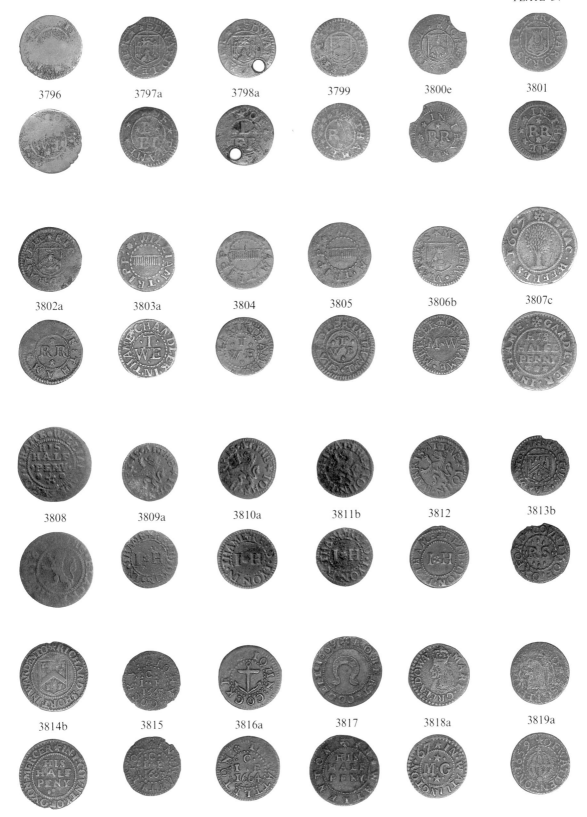

3796   3797a   3798a   3799   3800e   3801

3802a   3803a   3804   3805   3806b   3807c

3808   3809a   3810a   3811b   3812   3813b

3814b   3815   3816a   3817   3818a   3819a

Plate 34 (*cont.*)

	Weight			Die	
	g	gr		axis	
3810a	1.24	19.2	Br	90°	*Red Lion* (AT THE READ LYON): Harris, John. nd. 3.11; I H. BW 200; Milne —. [?Baldwin]. Same obv. die as 3809; same rev. die as 3811
3810b	1.04	16.1	Br	90°	Same dies. [Baldwin]
3810c	1.03	16.0	Br	90°	Same dies. [?Baldwin]
3811a	1.13	17.4	Br	90°	*Red Lion* (AT THE READ LYON): Harris, John. nd. 3.11; I H. BW 200; Milne 128. [?Baldwin]. Obv. legend starts at 3 o'clock. Same obv. die as 3812; same rev. die as 3810
3811b	0.77	11.8	Br	90°	Same dies. [?Baldwin]
3812	1.36	21.0	Br	0°	*Red Lion* (AT THE READ LYON): Harris, John. nd. 3.11; I H. BW 200; Milne —. Nott. Same obv. die as 3811

WARDINGTON (Cropredy parish)

The reading is WARDENTON COVNTY OF OXFORD on 3813; WARDENTO^{N}IN Y^{E}COVNTY OF OXON on 3814

3813a	0.77	11.8	Br	0°	*Short*, R[ichard]. nd. 5.14 Grocers; R S. BW 210 but R:SHORT; Milne 143 but R:SHORT·IN etc., cf. Milne 1945, p. 105. [?Baldwin]. Forename completed from 3814
3813b	0.74	11.4	Br	0°	Same dies. Nott
	(chipped)				
3814a	2.37	36.6	Br	180°	*Short*, Richard, mercer. nd ½d. 5.14 Grocers; 5.77. BW 209 but WARDENTO^N; Milne 144. [Nott]
3814b	1.21	18.7	Br	180°	Same dies. Nott [?Baldwin]
	(chipped)				

WATLINGTON

The reading is WATLENTON on 3817, 3819-20; WATTLETON on 3815-16; WATLINGTON on the remainder

3815	0.69	10.7	M	180°	*Cocky*, John. 1663. C|IE|date; C|IE|date. BW 213; Milne —, cf. p. 28. Nott. John Cockey, brazier, 1693/4 (Milne, p. 43)
	(chipped)				
3816a	1.36	21.0	Cu	330°	*Cocky* (COCKEE), John. 1664. 5.38.1; C|IE|date. BW 211; Milne 145. Nott. Form of surname from 3815
3816b	0.92	14.2	Cu	150°	Same dies. [Baldwin]
3816c	0.77	11.9	Br	150°	Same dies. [?Baldwin]
3817	1.84	28.4	Br	0°	*Cogell*, Robert. 1669 ½d. 5.68.10; 5.77. BW 212; Milne 146. Nott
3818a	1.44	22.2	Br	270°	*Greendown*, Mary. [16]67. 3.5.105; M G. BW 214; Milne 147. Nott. Mary Greendown kept the King's Head tavern (Delafield *c*.1750, see Milne, p. 43); see also 3819-20
3818b	1.40	21.6	Br	270°	Same dies. [?Baldwin]
3818c	0.39	6.0	Br	180°	Same dies. [Baldwin]
	(chipped)				
3818d	0.36	5.5	Br	90°	Same dies. [?Baldwin]
	(chipped)				
3819a	1.32	20.4	Br	0°	*Greendown* (GREENDOVNE), Thomas. 1659. 5.64.1; 5.3.96. BW 216 but GREENDOVNE, WATLENTON, rev. a vintner's bush; Milne 148 but THOMAS:GREENDOVNE. Nott. Form of surname as on 3820
3819b	0.50	7.7	Br	180°	Same dies. [?Baldwin]

WATLINGTON (*cont.*)

	Weight			Die	
	g	gr		axis	
3820	1.20	18.5	Br	0°	*Greendown,* Tho[mas]. 1664 ½d. 5.3.96; 5.64.1. BW 215 but THO:; Milne 149. Nott. Forename completed from 3819. Thomas Greendowne, innkeeper, 1665, widow Mary (Milne, p. 43); see also 3818
3821	0.52	7.9	Br	180°	*Haines,* Richard. nd. 5.14 Grocers; H|RM. BW 217; Milne 150. Nott
3822a	0.75	11.6	Br	0°	*Harris,* Richard. nd. 5.82.1; H|RE. BW 218; Milne 151. Nott
3822b	0.67 (chipped)	10.3	Br	0°	Same dies. [?Baldwin]
3822c	0.64	9.9	Br	0°	Same dies. [Baldwin]
3822d	0.42	6.5	Br	0°	Same dies. [?Baldwin]
3823a	0.73	11.3	Br	270°	*Haynes,* Robert. 1664. 5.14 Mercers; H|RD. BW 219; Milne 152. [?Baldwin]. Robert Haynes, mercer, 1662 (Milne, p. 44)
3823b	0.71	11.0	Br	270°	Same dies. Nott
3824	1.72	26.6	Br	0°	*Langford* (LANKFORD), Nicholas. nd. 5.45.6; L|NG. BW 220; Milne 153. Nott. Nicholas Langford junior, 1662; wife Grace, 1695; 'butcher' 1703/4 (Milne, p. 44). Rev. legend starts at 6 o'clock
3825	1.05 (chipped)	16.2	Br	180°	*Langford,* Nicholas. 1670 ½d. 3.1.50 (· NICHOLAS · LANGFORD ❧ around); 5.77 (L|NG) (HIS|HALF|PENY|L|N.G; · IN · WATLINGTON · I670 ❧ around). BW —, cf. 220; Milne 154; Dickinson 220A. Nott. See also 3824
3826a	1.99	30.7	Br	90°	*Nash,* Mary. 1669 ½d. 5.77 (M N); 5.14 Mercers. BW 221; Milne 155. [?Baldwin]. Widow Nash, mercer, 1662 (Milne, p. 44). Diameter 21-21.5 mm
3826b	1.47	22.7	Br	90°	Same dies. Nott. Diameter 21-21.5 mm
3826c	1.31	20.3	Br	90°	Same dies. [?Baldwin]. Diameter 21-21.5 mm
3826d	1.00	15.4	Br	90°	Same dies. [Baldwin]. Diameter 20-20.5 mm
3827a	0.72 (chipped)	11.1	Br	180°	*Seeley,* Richard. nd. 4.12.2; S|RA. BW 222; Milne 156. [Baldwin]
3827b	0.58	8.9	Br	180°	Same dies. Nott
3828a	0.87	13.4	Br	0°	*Seeley,* Richard. nd. 4.12.2; S|RA. BW 222; Milne 157. [?Baldwin]. Rev. legend starts at 3 o'clock
3828b	0.72 (chipped)	11.1	Br	0°	Same dies. Nott [?Baldwin]

WHEATLEY (Cuddesdon parish)

The reading is WHVTELY [*sic*]

3829	0.72 (chipped)	11.1	Br	180°	*Temple,* Thomas. nd. 5.64.81; T|TE. BW 223 but WHVTELY; Milne 158. Nott. Thomas Temple 'chapman' 1669, 'grocer' 1691 (Milne, p. 45)

WITNEY

The reading is WITTNEY on 3832, 3836, 3847, 3849-50; WITTNY on 3834-5, 3839, 3842-3; WITNY on 3848; WITNEY on the remainder, with IN THE COVNTY OXON on 3844

3830a	1.17	18.0	M	180°	*Ashfield,* Richard, clothier. nd. 3.58.1; A|RM. BW 224 but · OF · WITNEY · CLOTHIER; Milne 160. [Baldwin]. Same obv. die as 3831
3830b	1.03	15.8	M	180°	Same dies. Nott
3831	0.86	13.2	M	180°	*Ashfield,* Richard, clothier. nd. 3.58.1; A|RM. BW 224 but · OF · WITNEY · CLOTHIER; Milne 159. [Baldwin]. Same obv. die as 3830
3832a	1.88	29.0	Br	0°	*Brice,* Thomas. nd ½d. 5.83.50; B|TI. BW 225; Milne 161. [?Baldwin]. Issuer ?Thomas Brice, clothier, 1663 (Milne, p. 45)
3832b	1.87	28.8	Br	0°	Same dies (clashed). Nott [ex Daniels]
3833a	2.50	38.5	Cu	0°	*Chamberlin,* William. 1666 ½d. 5.77. C|WI. BW 226; Milne 162. [?Baldwin]
3833b	1.84	28.4	Cu	0°	Same dies. Nott
3834	0.85	13.2	Br	90°	*Collier,* Tho[mas], clothier. nd. 3.58.1; 5.76.84 (T C). BW 227; Milne 163. Nott. Thomas Collier senior, 1662-5 (Milne, p. 45). Obv. legend starts at 1 o'clock
3835	1.09	16.8	Br	0°	*Dutton,* Richard, clothier (CLOTHER). [16]68 ½d. 5.77 (R D); 5.14 Clothworkers. BW 228 but CLOTHER; Milne 164. Nott. Richard Dutton the elder, blanketmaker, 1682 (Milne, p. 45)
3836	0.92	14.2	Br	0°	*Dutton,* Thomas. nd. 5.81.16; 5.64.50. BW 229; Milne —, cf. 165 (same rev. die), but merchant's mark pierces a heart. Nott. Issuer ?Thomas Dutton, blanketer, 1694 (Milne, pp. 45-6)

[*continued overleaf*]

PLATE 35

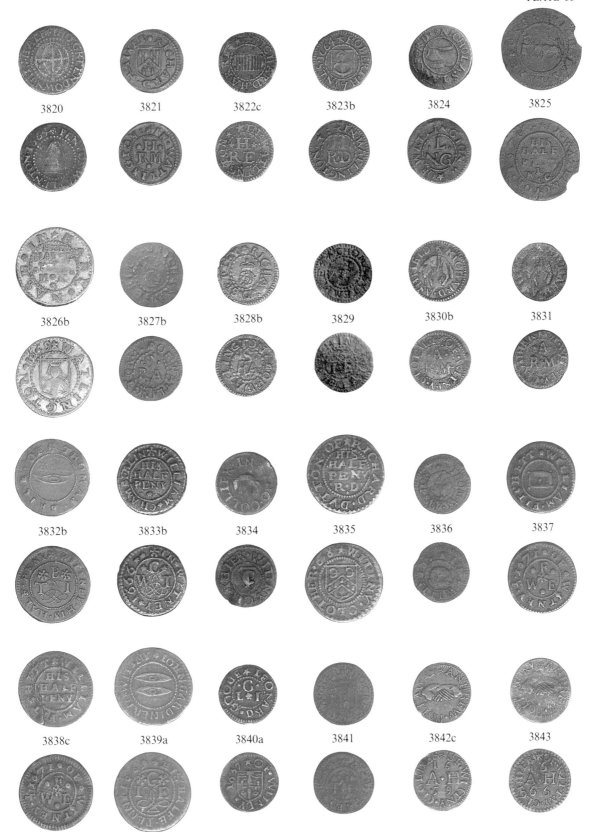

3820   3821   3822c   3823b   3824   3825

3826b   3827b   3828b   3829   3830b   3831

3832b   3833b   3834   3835   3836   3837

3838c   3839a   3840a   3841   3842c   3843

Plate 35 (*cont.*)

	Weight			Die	
	g	gr		axis	
3837	1.71	26.5	Cu	0°	*Fitchett,* William. 1671 ½d. 5.64.50 (·WILLIAM ·FITCHETT around); F|WE (·F·|·|W E|·; ·OF· WITNEY · ½ ·I67I around). BW —, cf. 230; Milne —; Dickinson 230A. Nott. William Fitchett, supervisor of highways, 1671 (Milne, p. 46). Same rev. die as 3838; this obv. published in Milne 1945, p. 104, but with suggestion that 'the centre of the original die. . . was repunched'
3838a	1.95	30.1	Br	90°	*Fitchett,* William. 1671 ½d. 5.77; F|WE. BW 230; Milne 166. [Nott]. Obv. die larger than that on 3837, q.v.; same rev. die as 3837
3838b	1.71	26.4	Br	90°	Same dies. [?Baldwin]
3838c	1.65	25.4	Br	90°	Same dies. Baldwin
3839a	1.53	23.6	Br	270°	*Gardiner,* John. 1669 ½d. 5.83.4; G|IE. BW 231; Milne 167. Nott
3839b	1.33	20.5	Br	270°	Same dies. [?Baldwin]
3839c	0.98	15.2	Br	270°	Same dies. [?Baldwin]
3839d	0.96	14.8	Br	270°	Same dies. [Baldwin]
3840a	1.29	20.0	M	180°	*Goode,* Leonard. 1657. G|LI; 5.14 Bakers. BW 232 but D in LEONARD (as well as GOODE) inverted; Milne 168. [?Baldwin]. Leonard Goode, baker, 1668 (Milne, p. 46)
3840b	1.24	19.1	M	0°	Same dies. [?Baldwin]
3840c	1.06	16.3	M	180°	Same dies. [Nott ex Daniels]
3840d	0.93	14.4	Br	180°	Same dies. Seaby 1961
3841	1.36	20.9	M	270°	*Gregory,* Tho—, chandler. 1664. 5.14 Tallow Chandlers; G|TI. BW 233 but THO:; Milne 169. Nott
3842a	1.98	30.5	Br	180°	*Hollaway,* Andrew, clothier (CLOTHYER). 1659. 3.6.60; 5.77 (A H). BW 236; Milne 172. Nott. Same obv. die as 3843
3842b	1.13	17.4	Br	90°	Same dies. [?Baldwin]
3842c	0.70	10.8	Br	180°	Same dies. [?Baldwin]
3842d	0.65	10.0 (chipped)	Br	180°	Same dies. [Baldwin]
3843	0.56	8.6	Br	270°	*Hollaway,* Andrew, clothier (CLOTHYER). 1666. 3.6.60; 5.77 (A H). BW 237; Milne 173. Nott. Same obv. die as 3842

WITNEY (*cont.*)

	Weight			Die	
	g	gr		axis	
3844a	1.34	20.7	Br	180°	*Jorden,* Jo[hn]. nd. 5.76.85 (IGI?); I|IG. BW 238; Milne 174. [Baldwin]. John Jordan or Jordaine 'gentleman' 1691/2 (Milne, p. 46)
3844b	1.11	17.1	Br	180°	Same dies. Nott
3844c	1.08	16.7	M	180°	Same dies. [?Baldwin]
3845a	1.36	21.0	Br	180°	*Palmer,* John. 1656. 5.64.50; P|IA. BW 240; Milne 176. [Baldwin]. John Palmer 'gentleman' 1711 (Milne, p. 47)
3845b	1.02	15.7	Br	180°	Same dies. Nott
3846a	1.67	25.7	Cu	0°	*Sanders,* William and *Sanders,* Mary. nd ½d. S|WM; 5.77. BW 241; Milne 177. Brand [or Nott]
3846b	1.55	23.8	Cu	0°	Same dies. [Baldwin]
3846c	1.17	18.0	Cu	0°	Same dies. [?Baldwin]
3846d	1.15	17.7	Cu	0°	Same dies. [?Baldwin]
3847a	1.27	19.5	Br	180°	*Smith,* Paul, draper. 1656. 5.59.7; S|PS. BW 242; Milne 178. Nott
3847b	1.16	17.8	Br	180°	Same dies. [?Baldwin]
3847c	0.94	14.5	Br	180°	Same dies. [Baldwin]
3848a	1.97	30.3	Br	270°	*Ward,* Thomas. 1668 ½d. 5.14 Tallow Chandlers; 5.77. BW 243; Milne 179. Nott
3848b	1.60	24.8	Br	270°	Same dies. [Baldwin]
3848c	1.19	18.3	Br	270°	Same dies. [?Baldwin]
	(chipped)				
3849a	1.11	17.2	Br	180°	*Werge,* Ralph. 1653. 5.14 Mercers; W|RM. BW 244; Milne 180 but same rev. die as 181 (cf. p. 29). [Nott]. Ralph Wyrg(e) or Werge 1642-61, Werdg 1662, Wirge 1665 (Milne, p. 47). Same rev. die as 3850
3849b	0.74	11.4	Br	180°	Same dies. [?Baldwin]
3850a	1.16	17.8	Br	180°	*Werge,* Ralph. 1653. 5.14 Mercers; W|RM. BW 244; Milne 181 but same rev. die as 180 (cf. p. 29). Baldwin. Same rev. die as 3849
3850b	1.03	16.0	Br	180°	Same dies. [?Baldwin]
	(chipped)				
3851a	3.02	46.6	Br	0°	*White,* Andrew senior. 1667 ½d. W|AM; 5.77. BW 245; Milne 182. [Baldwin]. Andrew White, clothier, 1678 (Milne, p. 47). Diameter 21 mm
3851b	2.30	35.5	Br	270°	Same dies. [?Baldwin]. Diameter 20 mm
	(chipped)				
3851c	1.54	23.8	Br	0°	Same dies. [Nott]. Diameter 20.5 mm
3851d	1.35	20.8	Br	270°	Same dies. [?Baldwin]. Diameter 19 mm
	(chipped)				
3851e	1.26	19.5	Br	0°	Same dies. Nott. Diameter 20.5 mm
	(pierced)				
3852a	2.27	35.1	Br	270°	*Willy,* Robert senior. nd ½d. 5.77; 5.47.1 (W|RP). BW 246 but W|RP on a signboard; Milne 183. Nott. Issuer ?Robert Wyly, tailor, 1632 (Milne, p. 47). Diameter 21 mm
3852b	0.97	14.9	Br	270°	Same dies. [Baldwin]. Diameter 19.5 mm
	(corroded)				
3853a	1.52	23.5	Br	0°	*Young,* John. 1655. 3.3.13; Y|IA. BW 247; Milne 184. [Baldwin]. John Young 'innkeeper' 1700, but also followed the trade of chandler (Milne, p. 48)
3853b	1.46	22.5	Br	0°	Same dies. [?Baldwin]
3853c	1.32	20.3	Br	0°	Same dies. [?Baldwin]
3853d	1.25	19.3	Br	0°	Same dies. Nott
3853e	0.86	13.2	Br	0°	Same dies. [?Baldwin]
	(pierced)				
3853f	0.45	6.9	Br	0°	Same dies. [?Baldwin]

Named signs

3854a	2.09	32.2	Br	0°	*Three Leopards' Heads* (AT THE 3 LIBBETS HEADS): Katte, Peter. 1670 ½d. 3.44.5 (K|PA); 5.77. BW 239; Milne 175. Nott. Issuer ?Peter Keat(e) senior, 'blanketer' 1684 (Milne, pp. 46-7)
3854b	1.67	25.7	Br	0°	Same dies. [?Baldwin]
3854c	1.05	16.3	Br	0°	Same dies. [?Baldwin]
	(chipped)				
3855a	1.34	20.6	Br	0°	*White Swan* (AT THE): Hearn, William. nd. 3.102.1; H|WI. BW 234 but THE; Milne 170. [?Baldwin]. Diameter 17.5 mm
3855b	1.17	18.0	Br	270°	Same dies. [?Baldwin]. Diameter 16.5 mm
3855c	0.94	14.4	Br	270°	Same dies. Nott. Diameter 16.5 mm
3855d	0.91	14.0	Br	180°	Same dies. [?Baldwin]. Diameter 16.5 mm

[*continued overleaf*]

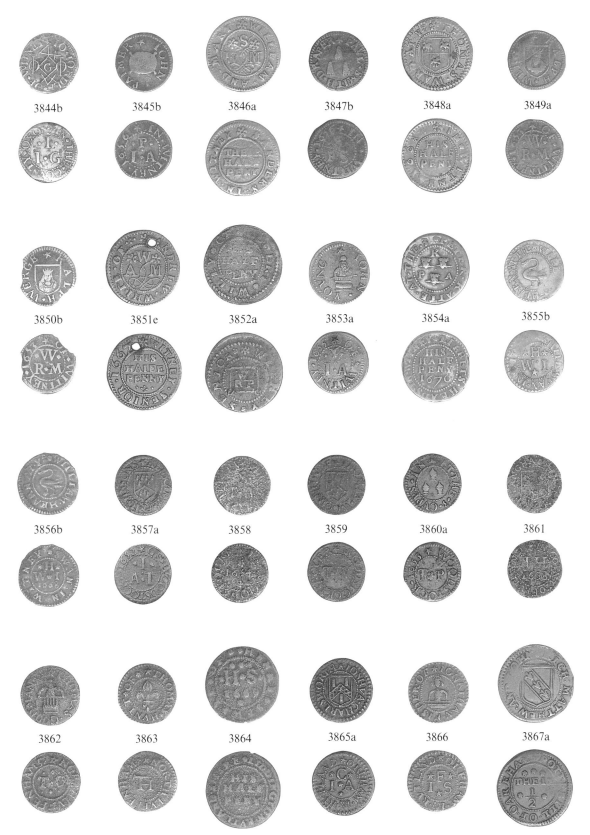

PLATE 36

3844b 3845b 3846a 3847b 3848a 3849a

3850b 3851e 3852a 3853a 3854a 3855b

3856b 3857a 3858 3859 3860a 3861

3862 3863 3864 3865a 3866 3867a

Plate 36 (*cont.*)

	Weight			Die	
	g	gr		axis	
3855e	0.90	13.8	Br	270°	Same dies. [Baldwin]. Diameter 16.5 mm
3855f	0.83	12.8	Br	180°	Same dies. [?Baldwin]. Diameter 16 mm
3856a	1.03	15.9	Cu	0°	[*White*] *Swan* (AT Y^E): Hearn, William. 1668. 3.102.1; H|WI|date. BW 235; Milne 171. Nott. Sign name completed from 3855
3856b	0.91	14.1	Cu	0°	Same dies. [?Baldwin]

WOODSTOCK (Wootton parish)

The reading is WOODSTOCK on 3859-60; WOODSTOCKE on 3857-8

3857a	1.15	17.7	M	180°	*Johnsons,* Alexander. 1652. 5.14 Grocers; I|AI. BW 248; Milne 185. Nott. Alexander Johnson, mercer; Chamberlain. . . 1651/2 (Milne, p. 48). IOHNSONS not necessarily for 'Johnson's', but perhaps from the continuing process of surnames acquiring an -s suffix (McKinley 1977, pp. 220-32); see also 1601, Edward IOHNSONS of Cheltenham
3857b	0.77	11.8	M	180°	Same dies. [Baldwin]
3858	0.87	13.5	Br	180°	*Sparrow,* Thomas. 1654. S|TA; date. BW 250; Milne 187. Nott. Thomas Sparrow, mercer, 1678 (Milne, p. 48)
3859	1.13	17.4	Br	180°	*Woodard,* Thomas, grocer. nd. 5.14 Grocers; T W. BW 251; Milne 188. Nott. Thomas Woodward 'gentleman' 1665 (Milne, p. 48)

Named signs

3860a	1.23	19.0	M	180°	*Three Cups* (AT THE 3 CVPPS): P[aynter], T[homas]. 1653. 5.64.107; T P. BW 249; Milne 186. Baldwin. 'T.P. (i.e. Tho. Paynter). . .' (Willis *c*.1740, see Milne, pp. 30, 48)
3860b	0.97	14.9	Br	180°	Same dies. [Nott]
3860c	0.85	13.1	Br	180°	Same dies. [?Baldwin]

WOOTTON

See also WOODSTOCK

Wallington, Edward *see* 1775 (Glos.: Wotton under Edge)

RUTLAND

The county occurs as RVTLAND on 3865-6, 3870; COVNTY OF RVTLAND on 3861; RVTLAND SHIRE on 3864

LANGHAM (Oakham parish)

The reading is LANGHA^M IN Ƴ COVNTY OF RVTLAND

3861	0.56 (corroded)	8.6	Br	0°	*Homes,* John. 1658. 5.14 Tallow Chandlers; I H|date. BW 1 but LANGHA^M. Nott. Between IN and COVNTY a stop and possibly the Y of Y^E

LIDDINGTON *see* LYDDINGTON

LUFFENHAM, North

The reading is NORTH LVFFENHAM on both

3862	1.02	15.7	Br	270°	*Goodman,* Thomas. [16]57. 3.3.13; T G. BW 3. Nott [ex Carthew]
3863	0.63	9.7	Br	270°	*Huntt,* Thomas. nd. 4.13.1; 5.76.86 (T H). BW 4. Nott. The arms *Azure a fleur de lis argent* were borne by Digby, North Luffenham etc. (Papworth 1874, p. 846)

LYDDINGTON

The reading is LIDDINGTON RVTLAND SHIRE

3864	1.90	29.3	Br	180°	*Sewell,* Henry. 1669 ½d. H S|date; 5.77. BW 2 but RVTLAND · SHIRE. Nott [ex Carthew]. Small cut in edge, perhaps an identification mark

NORTH LUFFENHAM *see* LUFFENHAM, North

OAKHAM

See also LANGHAM. The reading is OKEHAM on 3865-6, 3869, with IN RVTLAND on 3865-6; OAKEHAM on 3867-8

	Weight			Die	
	g	gr		axis	
3865a	1.71	26.3	Cu	180°	*Charlsworth,* Joshua. nd. 5.14 Ironmongers; C|IA. BW 6. Baldwin [or Nott]
3865b	0.56	8.7	Cu	0°	Same dies. [?Baldwin]
	(corroded)				
3866	0.90	13.9	Br	180°	*Fisher,* Jonathan. nd. 3.3.13; F|IS. BW 7. Nott
3867a	3.47	53.4	Cu	0°	*Matthew,* Rich[ard] and *Potterill*, John. nd ½d. 5.14.96; 5.77. BW 8 but RICH:MATTHEW. [?Baldwin]. Richard Matthewes, barber-surgeon, and John Potterill, apothecary (Whittet 1987b, pp. 249-50); nothing to be found for justification of arms on seal left by Richard Matthew's father, of King Street, Westminster (Vis. Rutland 1681-2, p. 20); mother Catherine, see BW London 1614. Same rev. die as 3868
3867b	2.74	42.3	Cu	0°	Same dies. [?Baldwin]

OAKHAM (*cont.*)

	Weight			Die	
	g	gr		axis	
3868a	4.35	67.1	Cu	180°	*Matthew,* Rich[ard] and *Potterill,* John. nd ½d. 5.14.96; 5.77. BW 8 but RICH:MATTHEW. Nott. Same rev. die as 3867
3868b	3.32	51.3	Cu	180°	Same dies. [?Baldwin]
3868c	1.62	24.9	Cu	180°	Same dies. [?Baldwin]
3868d	1.26	19.4	Cu	180°	Same dies. [Baldwin]

Named signs

3869a	0.96	14.8	Br	180°	*Bell* (AT THE): Reeve, Samuel (SAMVELL). 1655. 5.70.1; 5.32.11. BW 9 but I655|candles. Nott
3869b	0.85	13.1	Br	180°	Same dies. Nott

UPPINGHAM

The reading is VPPINGHAM on 3870-6, with IN RVTLAND on 3870; VPINGHAM on 3877-8

3870a	1.78	27.5	Br	0°	*Barriffe,* Peter. 1668 ½d. 5.59.3; 5.77. BW 10. Nott
3870b	1.43 (pierced)	22.1	Br	0°	Same dies. [?Baldwin]
3871	0.77	11.9	Cu	90°	*Butler,* Thomas. nd. 5.14.97; T B. BW 11. Nott
3872	0.55 (chipped)	8.5	Br	180°	*Clipsam,* Henry. 1657. 5.14 Grocers; M|HC [*sic*]. BW 12 but H.C.M. [?Baldwin]. Same obv. die as 3873. Cf. 'Widdow Clipsham' 1665 (Bourne 1991, p. 40)
3873a	0.98	15.2	Cu	0°	*Clipsam,* Henry. 1657. 5.14 Grocers; M|HC [*sic*]. BW 12 but H.C.M. [?Baldwin]. Same obv. die as 3872
3873b	0.80	12.3	Cu	0°	Same dies. [Baldwin]
3873c	0.61	9.4	Cu	0°	Same dies. Nott
3874	1.00	15.5	Br	180°	*Farbecke,* Edmond. nd. 5.82.1; E F. BW 13. [?Baldwin]. Cf. 'Mr Ferbecke' 1665 (Bourne 1991, p. 40)
3875	1.31	20.2	M	180°	*Farbecke,* Edmond. nd. 5.82.1; E F. BW 13. Nott. Same rev. die as 3876
3876	1.24	19.2	Br	270°	*Farbecke* (FARBECK), Edmond. nd. 5.82.1 (·EDMOND:FARBECK around); E F (E·F; ·OF·VPPINGHAM around). BW —; Young 1913/14, 13½. Nott. Form of surname from 3874-5. Same rev. die as 3875
3877	0.86	13.3	Cu	0°	*Goodwin,* Elizabeth. 1666. 5.51.10; E G. BW 14. Nott. 'Widdow Goodwyn' 1665 (Bourne 1991, p. 39)
3878	1.10	17.0	Br	180°	*Hull,* John, chandler. 1666. 5.14 Tallow Chandlers 2; H|IM. BW 16. Nott. John Hull 'grocer' 1691; bequeathed a shop (BW 16 n.)

SHROPSHIRE

The county occurs as SHROPSHIRE on 3882, 3884-5; SHROPSHEIRE on 3909; SHROPSHE[R] on 3903; Y[E]COVNTY OF SALOP on 3902, cf. *Salopescira* 1094-8, 1156 (Ekwall 1960, p. 421), 'Salop' having been long in unofficial use, and the official name of the county 1974-80 (Room 1983, p.108).

BISHOP'S CASTLE

The reading is BISHOPS CASLLE

3879	1.38	21.3	Br	0°	*Wollaston,* Edward junior. 1670 ½d. 5.14.98; 5.77. BW 5. Nott. First S in BISHOPS cancels C

BRIDGNORTH

The reading is BRIDG\|NORTH on 3881; BRIDGNORTH on 3880

3880	0.77	11.9	M	0°	*Bridgnorth,* Borough (The Chamberlains (CHAMBERLAYNES)). nd. 5.5.12; 5.17.1. BW 8-9. Baldwin
3881	2.09	32.2	Br	60°	*Bridgnorth,* Borough (The Chamberlains (CHAMBERLINS)). 1665 ½d. 5.5.4; date. BW 7. Baldwin

BROSELEY

The reading is BROSLEY IN SHROPSHIRE

3882	1.20 (pierced)	18.5	Br	180°	*Okes,* William. 1669 ½d. 4.1.4; 5.77. *BW 14 (PENNY). Nott

[*continued overleaf*]

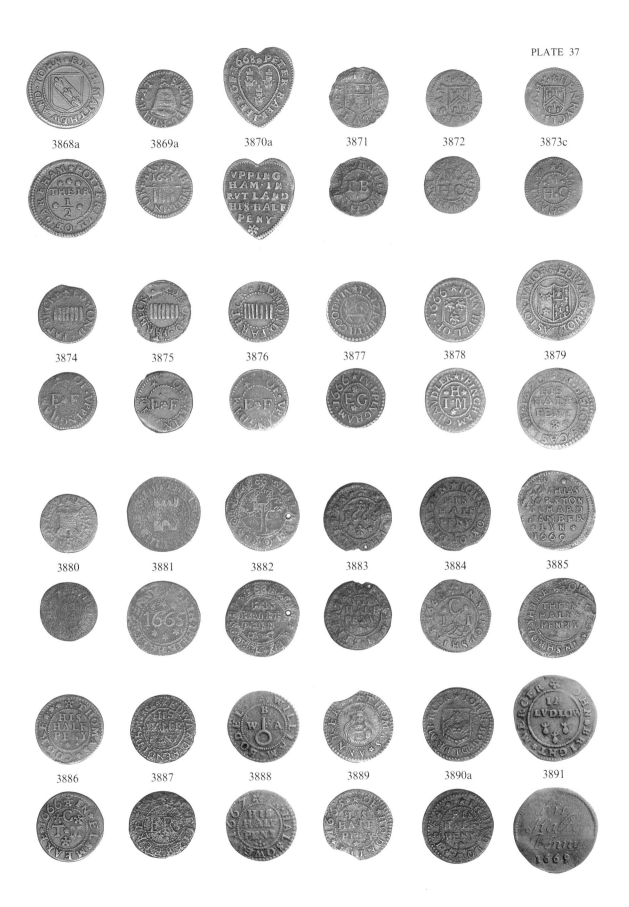

PLATE 37

3868a 3869a 3870a 3871 3872 3873c

3874 3875 3876 3877 3878 3879

3880 3881 3882 3883 3884 3885

3886 3887 3888 3889 3890a 3891

Plate 37 (*cont.*)

CHURCH STRETTON

The reading is CHVRCH STREATEN

	Weight		Die		
	g	*gr*	*axis*		
3883	2.02	31.1	Br	180°	*Phillipps,* Ann. 1666 ½d. Date (· · · |I666| · · · ; · ANN · PHILLIPPS · around); 5.77
	(pierced, chipped)				(HIR|HALF|PENY| · · · ; · IN · CHVRCH · STREATEN around). BW —; Dickinson 14A.
					Baldwin. Reading completed from specimen in Spink Sale 7, lot 106; the R of HIR may cancel
					S. Issuer probably the widow of John Phillip(p)s, see BW 15

COLMAN HILL (Halesowen parish) *see* Worcestershire

DRAYTON IN HALES [*subsequently* MARKET DRAYTON] (Shropshire *and* Staffordshire)

The reading is DRAYTON IN SHROPSHIRE on both

3884	1.97	30.3	Cu	180°	*Cox,* John. 1668 ½d. 5.77; C|II. BW 18. Nott
3885	2.71	41.8	Cu	0°	*Thurston,* Matthias [and] *Chamberlyn,* Richard. 1669 ½d. 5.77; 5.77. BW 20 but
					CHAMBER:|LYN. Nott. Reading confirmed from specimen in Spink Sale 7, lot 108.
					Double-struck

ELLESMERE (Shropshire *and* Wales, Flintshire)

The reading is ELIZMEERE on 3887; ELSMEARE on 3886

3886	1.56	24.1	Cu	90°	*Cooke,* Thomas. 1666 ½d. 5.77; C|TM. BW 21. Nott
3887	1.66	25.6	Cu	90°	*Renolds,* Edward, mercer. nd ½d. 5.77; E R. BW 22 but M^ERCER. Nott
	(chipped)				

HALESOWEN (Shropshire *and* Worcs., *subsequently* entirely Worcestershire)

The reading is HALSOWEN. See also COLMAN HILL (Worcs.)

3888	2.38	36.8	Cu	0°	*Bodely,* William. 1667 ½d. 5.50.41 (B|WA); 5.77. BW Worcs. 62. Baldwin. E of HALSOWEN
					double-struck or over L

HODNET

The reading is HODNITT

3889	1.36	20.9	Cu	180°	*Annker,* Thomas. 1665 ½d. 3.5.96; 5.77. BW 23. Seaby [1972+]

LUDLOW

The reading is LVDLOE on 3897; LVDLOV on 3896; LVDLOWE on 3900-1; LVDLOW on the remainder

3890a	1.43	22.1	Cu	0°	*Bowdler,* John, mercer. 1664 ½d. 5.14 Mercers; 5.77. BW 25. Nott [ex Daniels]
3890b	1.35	20.9	Cu	180°	Same dies. [?Baldwin]
3891	2.39	36.9	Cu	0°	*Bright,* John, mercer. 1669 ½d. 4.15.5; 5.77.1. BW 26 but *Halfe|Penny.* Nott

LUDLOW (*cont.*)

	Weight			Die	
	g	*gr*		*axis*	
3892	2.47	38.0	Br	0°	*Davies,* Edward, apothecary. 1669 ½d. 5.14 Apothecaries; 5.77 (D|E—). BW 27 but D|E.— [letter missing]. Nott
3893	0.90	13.9	Br	0°	*Davies,* Tamerlane (TAMBERLAYN). nd. 5.14 Mercers; D|TM. BW 29. Spink
3894	1.61	24.8	Br	270°	*Davies,* Tamerlane (TAMBERLAINE), mercer. 1669 ½d. 3.5.98 (T D); 5.77. BW 28. [Spink]
3895	1.73	26.7	Cu	0°	*Haughton,* George. 1666 ½d. 5.5.15; 5.77. BW 31 but obv. the Royal Exchange (?); Thompson 1993, p. 78. Nott
3896	2.27	35.0	Cu	180°	*Haughton,* George, mercer. 1669 ½d. 5.77; 5.8.3. BW 32 but rev. the Royal Exchange; Thompson 1993, p. 78. Spink 1975
3897	0.71	10.9	Br	180°	*Jones,* Walter. nd. 3.5.96; I|WM. BW 33. Baldwin. Obv. legend starts at 10 o'clock, rev. legend at 11 o'clock
3898	1.97	30.4	Br	90°	*Miels,* Edward. 1665 ½d. 5.77; M|EM. BW 35. Spink 1975 [ex ? ex Baldwin]. Reading confirmed from specimen in Spink Sale 7, lot 111
3899	1.53	23.6	Br	30°	*Miels,* Edward. 1665 (I665) ½d. 5.77; M|EM. *BW 34 (HALFE|PENY) but I665; *Boyne 1858, Shropshire 25 (I665). Spink 1975 [ex ? ex Baldwin]
3900	0.88	13.6	Br	180°	*Pearce,* John. 1656 [or later]. 5.14 Ironmongers; date. BW 36. Baldwin. John Pearce, ironmonger, leaseholder of 18-19 Broad Street 1669 (Lloyd 1979, p. 41). Mullet i.m. and stops on obv.; rev. previously paired with Will. Richards, see 3901
3901	0.74	11.4	Br	180°	*Richards,* Will—. 1656. 5.14 Haberdashers; date. BW 37 but WILL:. Spink 1975. Cinquefoil i.m. and pellet stops both sides; rev. subsequently paired with John Pearce, see 3900

MADELEY

The reading is MADELY IN SHROPSHE^R on 3903; MADLY IN Y^{E}COVNTY OF SALOP on 3902

3902	1.76	27.1	Br	180°	*Holland,* John. 1667 ½d. 5.33.1; 5.77. BW 40. Nott
3903	1.40 (chipped)	21.6	Br	270°	*Lewis,* Edward. 1669 ½d., 'Madeley (MADELY) Wood yields coal (YEILDS COLE) that's good'. 5.77; 5.33.4. BW 42 but SHROPSHE^R. [Clark]

NEWPORT

Clarke, Samuel *see* 'NEWPORT' (Uncertain I)
Legg, Arthur *see* 1909 (Isle of Wight)
Rowe, Arthur *see* 'NEWPORT' (Uncertain I)
Rowe, William *see* Uncertain II
Thornton, John *see* 325 (Bucks.: Newport Pagnell)
Younge, Thomas junior *see* 'NEWPORTE' (Uncertain I)

OSWESTRY

The reading is OSWALSTREY on 3904-5; OSWESTRE on 3906-7; OSWESTRIE IN SHROPSHEIRE on 3909; OS-ALDSTREE on 3908

3904a	2.71	41.8	Br	0°	*Edwards,* Hugh. 1669 1d. 3.7.33; 5.77. BW 56 but I^D. [Baldwin]
3904b	2.40	37.0	Br	180°	Same dies. [?Baldwin]
3904c	2.05	31.6	Br	180°	Same dies. Nott
3904d	1.88	29.0	Br	180°	Same dies. [?Baldwin]
3905	2.39	36.9	Br	270°	*Edwards,* Richard. 1668 1d. 5.64.50; 5.77. BW 57. Nott
3906	2.81	43.3	Cu	270°	*Jones,* John. 1666 1d. 5.55.13; 5.77. BW 59 but I^D. Nott. Reading confirmed from *NCirc* 1976, 7651
3907	2.44 (chipped)	37.6	Cu	180°	*Jones,* John. 1666 1d. 5.55.13; 5.77. BW 59 but I^D. [Baldwin]. Reading confirmed from specimen in Spink Sale 7, lot 115
3908	1.57 (corroded)	24.2	Br	270°	*Payne,* Richard. 1667 1d. 5.64.81; 5.77. BW 61 but OS-ALDSTREE, I^D. No provenance
3909	2.52	38.9	Cu	90°	*Ward,* Arthur (ARTHE^R). 1668 1d. 5.77; 5.40.12. BW 62 but I^D. Nott

SHIFNAL

The reading is SHIFNALL

3910a	1.92	29.6	Br	90°	*Manwaring,* Arthur. 1664 ½d. 3.5.96; 5.77. BW 65. Nott. Diameter 20.5-21 mm
3910b	1.70	26.2	Cu	180°	Same dies. [Baldwin]. Diameter 19.5 mm

[continued overleaf]

PLATE 38

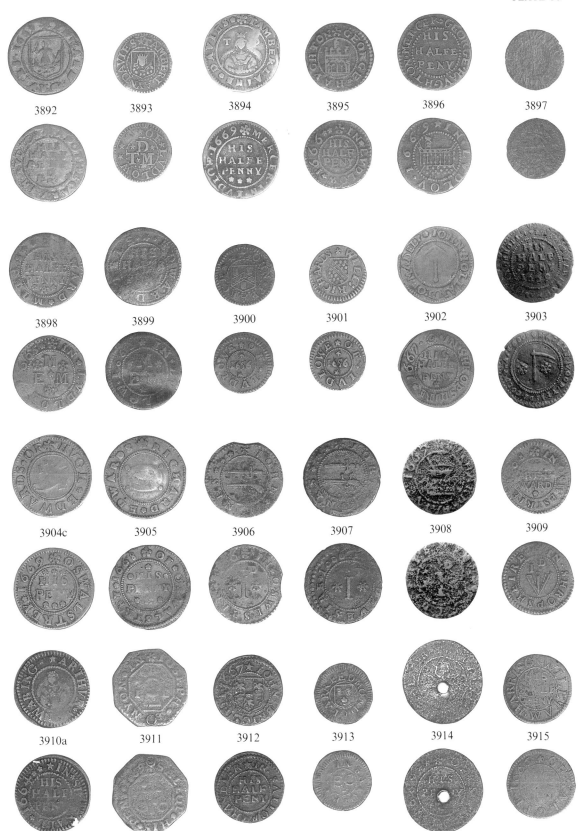

3892 3893 3894 3895 3896 3897

3898 3899 3900 3901 3902 3903

3904c 3905 3906 3907 3908 3909

3910a 3911 3912 3913 3914 3915

Plate 38 (*cont.*)

SHREWSBURY

The reading is SALLOP on 3911-12, 3917, 3926, 3931, SALOP on 3914, 3916, 3921, 3928-30, SALOPE on 3915, SALOPP on 3913, 3918-20, 3924-5, cf. *Salopesberia* 1094-8 (Ekwall 1960, p. 420); SHREWSBVRY on 3922-3, 3927

	Weight			Die	
	g	*gr*		*axis*	
3911	2.61	40.3	Cu	180°	*Benyon,* Joseph. 1669 1d. 4.10.7 (B|IE); 5.65.3. BW 69 but PENY · I669, I[D]. Spink 1971
	(pierced and plugged)				
3912	1.93	29.8	Cu	0°	*Brigdell,* John, chandler. 1667 ½d. 5.14 Tallow Chandlers; 5.77. BW 71. Baldwin
3913	1.46	22.5	Br	90°	*Clarke,* Edmond. nd. 5.14.99; E C. BW 72. Spink [1975 ex ? ex Baldwin]
3914	1.78	27.5	Br	0°	*Coney,* Samuel, innkeeper (INKEEPER). 1669 1d. 2.4.3; 5.77. *BW 73 (SAMVELL). Nott.
	(pierced)				Reading largely completed from specimen in Spink Sale 7, lot 118
3915	1.70	26.2	Br	180°	*Harrison,* William. 1666 ½d. 5.77; 5.14 Stationers 2. BW 75; Spink Sale 7, lot 118 (pl. 6).
					Baldwin. Harrison, William, bookseller, 1655 (Forrest 1924, p. 134)

SHREWSBURY (*cont.*)

	Weight			Die	
	g	*gr*		*axis*	
3916a	1.08	16.7	Br	90°	*Hinde,* Benjamin. nd. 5.14.99; B H. BW 76 but HINDᴱ. [Nott]. Obv. legend starts at 1 o'clock, rev. legend at 6 o'clock
3916b	0.67 (chipped)	10.3	Br	180°	Same dies. Clark [1977]
3917	2.00	30.9	Cu	0°	*Hollier,* John, mercer. 1668 ½d. 5.14 Mercers; 5.77. BW 77. Spink 1971
3918	1.42	21.9	Br	90°	*Machen* (MACHEN), Samuel (SAMVELL), baker. nd ½d. 4.10.6 (-|SH); 5.77. *BW 78 (M|SH). Nott
3919	1.47	22.7	Br	90°	*Meyricke* (MEYRICHE), Thomas. 1663. 5.14 Vintners; 5.76.87 (T M). BW 80. Spink 1975. Form of surname from 3920. Meyrick, Thomas, vintner, 1634 (Forrest 1924, p. 204)
3920	1.74	26.9	Cu	180°	*Meyricke,* Tho[mas]. 1663 ½d. 5.14 Vintners; 5.77. BW 81. Seaby [1972+]. Forename completed from 3919. Thomas Meyrick 'gent' 1667 (BW 81 n.)
3921a	2.81	43.4	Cu	180°	*Millard,* John, distiller (A·DISTILLER). 1667 ½d. 5.64.68; 5.77. BW 83 but MILLARD, A·DISTILLER. Nott. 'John Milward Distiller for encroaching. . .at his Shopp. . .' 1667 (BW 83 n.)
3921b	1.61 (chipped)	24.9	Cu	180°	Same dies. Nott
3922	1.81	27.9	Cu	180°	*Millington,* John. 1664 ½d. 5.65.7 (M|IM); 5.77. BW 82. [?Baldwin]. Same rev. die as 3923. Millington, John, baker, 1638; John junior, baker, 1662 (Forrest 1924, p. 205)
3923a	1.86	28.6	Cu	0°	*Millington,* John. 1664 ½d. 5.65.7 (M|IM); 5.77. BW 82. [Baldwin]. Same rev. die as 3922. 'John Mellington, sen[ior], baker, for encroaching. . .[at] his Shop' (BW 82 n.)
3923b	1.34	20.7	Cu	0°	Same dies. Nott
3924	1.54	23.8	Cu	90°	*Overton,* Constantine. 1663 ½d. 5.14 Cordwainers; 5.77. BW 84. Nott. 'Constantine Overton corvisor [*i.e.* cordwainer]' (BW 84 n.)
3925	1.35	20.8	Cu	0°	*Roberts,* Owen. 1666 ½d. 4.10.6 (O R); 5.77. BW 86. Nott
3926	1.64	25.3	Cu	0°	*Selby,* Job, distiller. 1667 ½d. 5.77; I S. BW 87. Nott. Reading confirmed from specimen in Spink Sale 7, lot 118
3927	3.88	59.9	Cu	0°	*Studley,* Thomas. nd 1d. 5.77; S|TE. BW 88. Spink 1975 [ex ? ex Baldwin]. Studley, Richard & Edward, butchers, sons of Thomas, butcher, deceased, 1721 (Forrest 1924, p. 276)
3928	1.84	28.5	Cu	270°	*Thomas,* William, mercer. 1666 ½d. 5.14 Mercers; 5.77. BW 90. Spink 1975 [ex ? ex Baldwin]. Overstruck
3929	0.75	11.5	Cu	0°	*Wilding* (WILDINGE), Michael (MICHAELL), mercer. nd. 5.14 Mercers; W|MI. BW 92 but IN·SALOP. Nott. Form of surname from 3930
3930	1.98	30.6	Cu	90°	*Wilding,* Michael (MICHAELL). 1664 ½d. 5.14 Mercers; 5.77. BW 91. Spink 1975 [ex ? ex Baldwin]
3931	2.09	32.3	Br	180°	*Willis,* Joshua, mercer. nd ½d. 5.14.99; 5.77. BW 93. Nott. Punctuation formed by cloves

WELLINGTON

The reading is WELLINGTON on both

3932	2.11	32.6	Cu	0°	*Sockett,* Andrew, mercer. 1666 ½d. 3.5.96; 5.77. BW 95. Baldwin. Andrew Sockett, c.1648-1721, father of Andrew Sockett (d. 1725), mercer (Trinder 1980, pp. 25-26, 362-63)
3933a	1.86	28.7	Cu	0°	*Wright,* Stephen, mercer. 1668 ½d. 3.67.20; 5.77. BW 96; BW Somerset 299; Spink Sale 7, lot 119 (pl. 6). Baldwin [or Nott]. Attribution from the occurrence of Mr Stephen Wright, 1660 (BW 96 n.)
3933b	1.58	24.4	Cu	0°	Same dies. [?Baldwin]. Partly obscured on obv. by flattening, on rev. by (negative) impression from token reading. . .NGECHI -H. . . around HIS|HA. . .|PENY|I668

WEM

The reading is WEM on 3934, 3936-8; WE- on 3935

3934	2.21	34.2	Cu	180°	*Alanson,* William. 1666 ½d. 5.14.100; 5.77. BW 97. [Clark ex Spink Sale 7 lot 120 ex Tatton ex Daniels 1911]
3935	1.60	24.7	Br	0°	*Chettwood,* John, mercer. nd ½d. 5.14.101; I C. *BW 98 (WEM) but Arms three single crowns. Nott
3936	2.28	35.2	Cu	0°	*Roycroft,* Samuel (SAMVELL). 1665 ½d. 5.14 Ironmongers; 5.77. BW 100. [Clark ex Spink Sale 7 lot 120 ex H. Lowe ex Sare 1933]
3937	2.11	32.6	Cu	0°	*Shenton,* John, mercer. 1666 ½d. 5.14.102; 5.77. BW 101. [Baldwin]. Same rev. die as 3938
3938	1.14	17.6	Cu	180°	*Shenton,* John, mercer. 1666 ½d. 5.14.102; 5.77. BW 101. Seaby 1969. Same rev. die as 3937

[continued overleaf]

PLATE 39

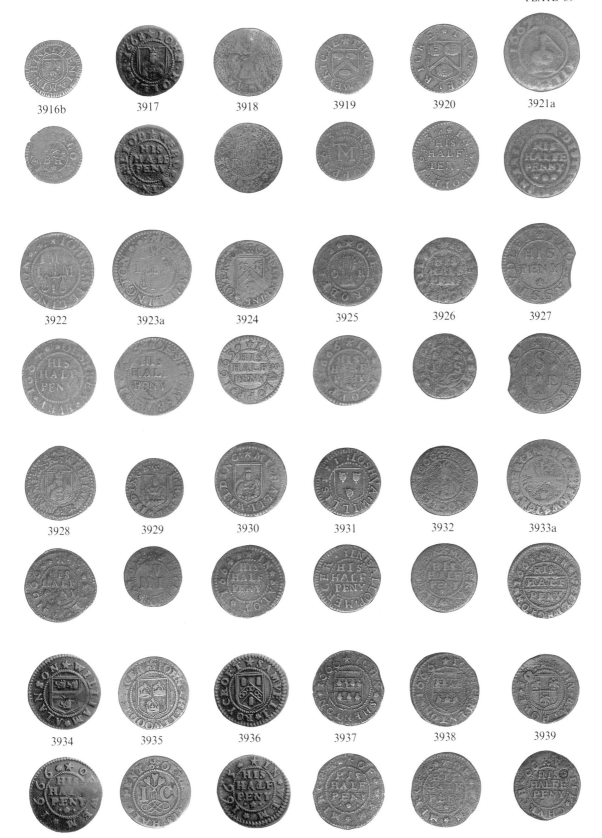

3916b   3917   3918   3919   3920   3921a

3922   3923a   3924   3925   3926   3927

3928   3929   3930   3931   3932   3933a

3934   3935   3936   3937   3938   3939

Plate 39 (*cont.*)

WHITCHURCH (Shropshire *and* Cheshire)

The reading is WHIT CHVRCH on 3940; WHITE CHVRCH on 3939

	Weight		*Die*		
	g	*gr*	*axis*		
3939	1.94	29.9	Cu	0°	*Bathowe,* John. [16]66 ½d. 5.14 Tallow Chandlers (· IOHN · BATHOWE · IN: around); 5.77
	(pierced, chipped)				(HIS|HALFE|PENY; · WHITE · CHVRCH · 66 around). BW —, cf. 104. Nott. Attributed to
					John Bathoe, Whitchurch, 1672 (Watkins-Pitchford 1949, p. 71)

	Weight			Die	
	g	*gr*		*axis*	
3940	1.58	24.3	Cu	60°	*Newton,* Edw— [and] *Rowly* , Humphry. nd. 5.77; 5.14 Mercers. BW 106. Nott. Attribution not
	(chipped)				assured

SOMERSET

The county occurs as SOMERSET on 4007, 4071 (SHIRE), 4076 (C SOMERSET), 4143 (SHIER), 4181, 4188-90; SVMMERSET on 3987 (SHEIRE), 4029 (-SHIR), 4157-61 (THE COVNTY OF); SVMERSET on 4004 (SHEIR), 4038 (SHEIRE), 4079; SOMMERSET on 4146; SVMERSETT on 4010

ASHCOTT (Shapwick parish)

The reading is ASHCOTE on both

3941	0.79	12.2	Br	90°	*Milles,* Richard. 1666. 3.95.1; R M. BW 1. Nott. Reading confirmed from Taunton specimen.
	(chipped)				Same rev. die as 3942
3942	0.59	9.1	Br	180°	*Milles,* Richard. 1666. 3.95.1; R M. BW 1. [Baldwin]. Same rev. die as 3941

AXBRIDGE

The reading is AXBRIDGE on 3943, 3945; ARBEIDGE [*sic*] on 3944

3943a	0.87	13.5	M	180°	*Hopkins,* William. 1656. 4.13.1; W H. BW 2. Nott
3943b	0.72	11.0	M	180°	Same dies. [Baldwin]
3944	0.95	14.7	M	180°	*Tuthill* (TVTHILE), John. 1652. I T (I·T; ·IOHN·TVTHILE around); I T (I·T;
					·IN·ARBEIDGE·I652 around). BW —; Dickinson 3A. Nott. Convincingly associated with
					3945, whence form of surname
3945	1.03	15.9	Cu	0°	*Tuthill,* John. 1669. T|ID; 3.10.1. BW 3. Baldwin

BATH

The reading is BATHE on 3946-54, 3960-1, 3963-5, 3967, 3970, and *Bathe* on 3962; BATH on 3955-7, 3966, 3968-9; THE CITTY OF BATH on 3971. The place is unnamed on 3958-9. Note on 3946-54: The arms of the City of Bath as usually blazoned are *Party per fess embattled azure and argent the base masoned in chief two bars wavy of the second over all a sword in pale gules hilt and pommel or* (Fox-Davies 1915, p. 66; 1985, p. 70)

3946a	2.02	31.2	Cu	0°	*Bath,* City. 1659 Bath (BATHE) ¼d. 5.42.8 (THE ARMES OF BATHE around); C B|date. BW
	(chipped)				5 but obv. and rev. transposed. [?Nott]. Same rev. die as 3947. Issue authorised 26 March
					(Sydenham 1905, pp. 12-13)
3946b	1.70	26.2	Cu	0°	Same dies. [?Baldwin]
3946c	1.46	22.5	Cu	0°	Same dies. [?Baldwin]
	(chipped)				
3947a	2.11	32.5	Cu	90°	*Bath,* City. 1659 Bath (BATHE) ¼d. 5.42.8 (THE ARMES OF BATHE around); C B|date. BW
					5 but obv. and rev. transposed. Nott [?Baldwin]. Same rev. die as 3946
3947b	1.40	21.6	Cu	90°	Same dies. [Nott]
3948a	2.49	38.4	Br	180°	*Bath,* City. 1670 Bath ¼d. (BATHE FARTHINGE). 5.14 Bath (THE ARMES OF BATHE
					around); C B|date. BW 6 but obv. and rev. transposed. Nott. Issue authorised 7 March 1669/70
					(Sydenham 1905, p. 15)
3948b	2.32	35.8	Cu	180°	Same dies. [?Baldwin]
3948c	2.01	31.0	Cu	90°	Same dies. [Baldwin]
3948d	1.70	26.3	Cu	90°	Same dies. [?Baldwin]
3948e	1.49	23.0	Cu	90°	Same dies. [?Baldwin]
3949	2.55	39.4	Cu	0°	*Bath,* City. 1670 Bath ¼d. (BATHE FARTHINGE). 5.14 Bath (THE ARMES OF BATHE
					around); C B|date. BW 6 but obv. and rev. transposed. [?Baldwin]. Same rev. die as 3950-1
3950a	3.05	47.0	Cu	0°	*Bath,* City. 1670 Bath ¼d. (BATHE FARTHINGE). 5.14 Bath (THE ARMES OF BATHE
					around); C B|date. BW 6 but obv. and rev. transposed. [?Baldwin]. Same rev. die as 3949, 3951.
					Diameter 20-20.5 mm
3950b	2.61	40.2	Cu	0°	Same dies. [Baldwin]. Diameter 20.5-21 mm
3950c	1.98	30.6	Cu	0°	Same dies. [?Baldwin]. Diameter 20-21.5 mm. Collector's number 1470 inked below date
3950d	1.65	25.4	Cu	0°	Same dies. [?Baldwin]. Diameter 20.5-21 mm

[*continued overleaf*]

PLATE 40

3940   3941   3942   3943a   3944   3945

3946a   3947b   3948a   3949   3950b   3951a

3952b   3953   3954   3955b   3956   3957b

3958a   3959a   3960   3961   3962   3963

Plate 40 (*cont.*)

	Weight			Die	
	g	gr		axis	
3951a	3.27	50.5	Cu	0°	*Bath,* City. 1670 Bath ¼d. (BATHE FARTHINGE). 5.14 Bath (THE ARMES OF BATHE around); C B|date. BW 6 but obv. and rev. transposed. [?Baldwin]. Same obv. die as 3952; same rev. die as 3949-50
3951b	2.34	36.2	Cu	0°	Same dies. [?Baldwin]
3952a	3.27	50.4	Cu	180°	*Bath,* City. 1670 Bath ¼d. (BATHE FARTHINGE). 5.14 Bath (THE ARMES OF BATHE around); C B|date. BW 6 but obv. and rev. transposed. [?Baldwin]. Same obv. die as 3951
3952b	2.46	37.9	Cu	180°	Same dies. Nott
3952c	1.63	25.1	Cu	180°	Same dies. [?Baldwin]
3952d	1.53	23.6	Cu	180°	Same dies. [?Baldwin]
		(chipped)			
3952e	1.45	22.4	Cu	180°	Same dies. [?Baldwin]
		(corroded)			
3953	2.16	33.4	Cu	0°	*Bath,* City. 1670 Bath ¼d. (BATHE FARTHINGE). 5.14 Bath (THE ARMES OF BATHE around); C B|date. BW 6 but obv. and rev. transposed. [?Baldwin]. Same obv. die as 3954. Struck off-centre
3954	3.00	46.3	Cu	0°	*Bath,* City. 1670 Bath ¼d. (BATHE FARTHINGE). 5.14 Bath (THE ARMES OF BATHE around); C B|date. BW 6 but obv. and rev. transposed. [?Baldwin]. Same obv. die as 3953. Struck off-centre
3955a	1.35	20.9	Cu	330°	*Bigges,* Richard, mercer. nd. 5.14 Mercers; B|RH. BW 10. [Baldwin]
		(chipped)			
3955b	1.00	15.4	Cu	330°	Same dies. Nott
3956	0.94	14.5	Br	0°	*Burton,* James. nd. 5.14 Mercers; I B. BW 11 but N of BVRTON retrograde. Nott
3957a	0.98	15.1	M	180°	*Bush,* John, mercer. 1656. 5.14 Mercers; B|IA. BW 12. Nott
3957b	0.84	13.0	M	180°	Same dies. [?Baldwin]
3957c	0.75	11.6	M	180°	Same dies. [Baldwin]
3958a	1.95	30.0	Br	0°	*Chapman,* Henry (HENERY), 'quondam esquire'. nd. 2.1; H C. BW 13; BW Uncertain 32. Nott [ex Seaby]. Attributed to Henry Chapman, captain of the Bath trained bands 1644/5. . . 1661, his house called the Sunne 1653, 1670; one of his tokens the undertype to John Bush 1656; 'gent.' 1670, 1672 (Sydenham 1905, pp. 43-60; Vis. Som. 1672, p. 19). Legends start at 10 o'clock both sides
3958b	1.27	19.6	Br	0°	Same dies. Deane 1976
3959a	0.98	15.2	M	30°	*Chapman,* Henry, 'quondam esquire (ESQ^R)'. nd. 2.1; H C. BW 14; BW Uncertain 33. Nott [ex Carthew]. See 3958. Overstruck
3959b	0.67	10.3	Br	30°	Same dies. [Baldwin]. Double-struck
3960	0.83	12.9	M	180°	*Chapman,* mercer. nd. 5.14 Mercers; C|WA. BW 15. [Baldwin]. Walter Chapman 'gent.', died 1655 (Vis. Som. 1672, p. 19; Sydenham 1905, pp. 60-3). Same rev. die as 3961
3961	1.28	19.7	M	180°	*Chapman,* Walter, mercer. nd. 5.14 Mercers; C|WA. BW 15. Nott. Same rev. die as 3960
3962	0.73	11.3	Br	0°	*Collins,* Richard, 'a clothier'. 1669. 5.77.1 (C|RE); 5.77.1. *BW 17. Nott
		(chipped)			
3963	0.59	9.1	Cu	0°	*Horler,* Richard. 1664. 5.14 Tallow Chandlers; H|RS. BW 22 but BATHE. Baldwin. Richard Horler, chandler (Sydenham 1905, p. 73)

BATH (*cont.*)

	Weight			Die	
	g	gr		axis	
3964a	1.04	16.1	M	180°	*Pearce,* John, mercer. 1652. 5.14 Mercers; P|II. BW 26. Nott. Same rev. die as 3965
3964b	1.02	15.7	M	180°	Same dies. [Baldwin]
3964c	1.00	15.4	M	180°	Same dies. [?Baldwin]
3964d	0.83	12.8	M	180°	Same dies. [?Nott]
3964e	0.78	12.0	M	180°	Same dies. [?Baldwin]
	(chipped)				
3964f	0.69	10.7	M	180°	Same dies. [?Baldwin]
	(chipped)				
3964g	0.61	9.4	M	180°	Same dies. [Baldwin]
	(pierced, chipped)				
3965a	1.15	17.7	Br	180°	*Pearce,* John, mercer. 1652. 5.14 Mercers; P|II. BW 27 but MERCE^R. [Nott]. Same rev. die as 3964. Diameter 16.5-17.5 mm
3965b	1.01	15.6	Br	0°	Same dies. [Baldwin]. Diameter 15 mm
	(chipped)				
3965c	0.99	15.3	Br	0°	Same dies. Baldwin. Diameter 16 mm. Struck off-centre
3966a	1.10	16.9	M	180°	*Penny,* Robert, mercer. nd. 5.14 Mercers; P|RI. BW 28. Nott. Mr Robert Penny buried 1663 (Sydenham 1905, p. 88)
3966b	0.98	15.1	M	180°	Same dies. [Baldwin]
3967	0.56	8.7	Br	330°	*Rance,* Francis. 1659. 3.10.17; R|FE. BW 30. Nott. Reading confirmed from Taunton specimen
	(chipped)				
3968	0.69	10.7	Br	0°	*Reve,* Geo[rge], goldsmith. 1658. 5.14 Goldsmiths; R|GM. BW 32 but GEO:. Nott. Reading completed from Taunton specimen; legends start at 10 o'clock both sides
3969	1.50	23.1	Br	0°	*Salmon,* Thomas. 1667. 5.85.1; 5.85.2 (T S). BW 33. [Longman] 1958, lot 452. Mr Thomas Salmon, bookseller etc. (Sydenham 1905, pp. 98-9)
3970a	1.07	16.6	M	270°	*Smith,* William. 1666. 5.43.30; S|WI. BW 34. Nott. William Smith, clothier (Sydenham 1905, p. 100)
3970b	0.77	11.9	M	270°	Same dies. [Baldwin]

Named signs

| 3971 | 0.45 | 6.9 | Cu | 180° | *White [Hart]* (AT WHIT): Masters, John. nd. 3.53.1; M|IE. BW 25 but A^T. Nott. Reading completed from Taunton specimen. 'Mr John Masters for ye White Hart' 1668 (Sydenham 1905, p. 80) |
| | (chipped) | | | | |

BECKINGTON

The reading is BECKINGTON

| 3972 | 0.80 | 12.3 | M | 180° | *Horler,* John. nd. 5.14 Haberdashers; I H. BW 42. Spink 1975 |

BRIDGWATER

The reading is BRIDGWATER on 3975-80, 3982-3, 3986, 3988-90, 3994; BRIDG|WATER on 3974; BRIDG WATER on 3984-5, 3987, 3991-2, with SVMMERSET SHEIRE on 3987; BRIDGEWATER on 3993; BRIDGE|WATER on 3973; BRIDGEWATE^R on 3981. Note on 3973-80: The ancient seal of Bridgwater incorporates a castle standing on a bridge with water underneath (Fox-Davies 1915, p. 110)

3973	1.62	25.0	Br	0°	*Bridgwater,* Borough. nd. 5.7.23; 5.77 (· · ·	BRIDGE	WATER	· · ·). BW —, cf. 50; Gray 1915, 50a. [Baldwin]. Punches similar to those on 3976
3974a	1.34	20.7	Br	0°	*Bridgwater,* Borough. nd. 5.7.23; 5.77. BW 50 but obv. and rev. transposed. [?Baldwin]. Punches similar to those on 3978
3974b	1.27	19.6	Br	0°	Same dies. [?Baldwin]
3974c	1.24	19.1	Br	0°	Same dies. Nott [?Baldwin]
3974d	1.04	16.0	Br	0°	Same dies. [Nott]
3974e	0.88	13.5	Br	0°	Same dies. [?Baldwin]
3975a	3.47	53.5	Cu	270°	*Bridgwater,* Borough. 1666 Bridgwater ¼d. 5.7.22 (THE ARMES OF BRIDGWATER around); date. BW 49 but obv. and rev. transposed. [?Baldwin]
3975b	2.44	37.6	Cu	270°	Same dies. [?Baldwin]
3976a	3.37	51.9	Cu	0°	*Bridgwater,* Borough. 1666 Bridgwater ¼d. 5.7.22 (THE ARMES OF BRIDGWATER around); date. BW 49 but obv. and rev. transposed. [?Baldwin]. Same obv. die as 3977
3976b	3.29	50.8	Cu	0°	Same dies. [Baldwin]
3976c	3.26	50.3	Cu	0°	Same dies. Brand [or Nott]
3976d	3.00	46.3	Cu	0°	Same dies. [Baldwin]
3976e	2.32	35.8	Cu	0°	Same dies. [?Baldwin]

[*continued overleaf*]

PLATE 41

3964b   3965c   3966a   3967   3968   3969

3970a   3971   3972   3973   3974c   3975a

3976c   3977d   3978a   3979   3980a   3981

3982a   3983a   3984a   3985   3986   3987

Plate 41 (*cont.*)

	Weight			Die	
	g	gr		axis	
3977a	3.03	46.7	Cu	270°	*Bridgwater,* Borough. 1666 Bridgwater ¼d. 5.7.22 (THE ARMES OF BRIDGWATER around); date. BW 49 but obv. and rev. transposed. [?Baldwin]. Same obv. die as 3976
3977b	2.77	42.7	Cu	270°	Same dies. [?Baldwin]
3977c	2.64	40.7	Cu	270°	Same dies. [?Baldwin]
3977d	1.97	30.4	Cu	270°	Same dies. Brand [or Nott]
3978a	1.99	30.7	Cu	0°	*Bridgwater,* Borough. 1666 Bridgwater ¼d. 5.7.22 (THE ARMES OF BRIDGWATER around); date. BW 48 but obv. and rev. transposed. Brand [or Baldwin ex Gilbert]. Same rev. die as 3979-80
3978b	1.47	22.6	Cu	0°	Same dies. [Baldwin]
3979	1.73	26.8	Cu	180°	*Bridgwater,* Borough. 1666 Bridgwater ¼d. 5.7.22 (THE ARMES OF BRIDGWATER around); date. BW 48 but obv. and rev. transposed. [?Baldwin]. Same rev. die as 3978, 3980
3980a	1.86	28.7	Cu	180°	*Bridgwater,* Borough. 1666 Bridgwater ¼d. 5.7.22 (THE ARMES OF BRIDGWATER around); date. BW 48 but obv. and rev. transposed. [?Baldwin]. Same rev. die as 3978-9
3980b	1.82	28.0	Cu	180°	Same dies. [?Baldwin]
3981	0.45	6.9	Br	0°	*Atkins,* Alexand[e]r. 1656. A|AA; date. BW 52 but ALEXAND^R. Spink 1975
3982a	2.08	32.0	M	270°	*Crapp,* William. 1670. Date; C|WM. BW 55. Nott
3982b	1.18 (chipped)	18.2	M	270°	Same dies. [Baldwin]
3983a	2.20	34.0	Cu	90°	*Goodridge,* William. 1669. G|WI; 5.13.18. BW 58. [Baldwin]. Diameter 21-21.5 mm
3983b	2.01 (chipped)	30.9	Cu	90°	Same dies. Nott. Diameter 21 mm
3983c	1.78	27.5	Cu	270°	Same dies. [?Baldwin]. Diameter 20-20.5 mm
3984a	1.32	20.4	M	180°	*Haviland,* Robert. nd. 5.76.88 (h); H|RL. BW 59. Nott
3984b	1.15	17.8	Cu	180°	Same dies. [?Baldwin]
3985	0.96	14.8	Br	180°	*Hunt,* John. 1651. H|IS; date. BW 61. [?Baldwin]
3986	0.65	10.0	M	90°	*Linton,* John. 1656. 5.14 Salters; IL|E. BW 63 but I · L| · E · [*sic*]. Nott. Reading confirmed from Taunton specimen
3987	0.99	15.3	Br	270°	*Page,* Will—. 1669. Date; P|WE. BW 66 but WILL:, IN · SVMMERSET. Baldwin. Reading completed from Taunton specimen. Rev. struck off-centre from clashed dies

BRIDGWATER (*cont.*)

	Weight			Die	
	g	*gr*		*axis*	
3988	1.08	16.6	Cu	0°	*Palmer,* John. 1664. 5.14 Drapers; P|IA. BW 67. Nott. Reading completed from Taunton specimen
3989	1.23	19.0	Br	0°	*Pettitt,* Edmond. 1654. P|EI; date. BW 68 but BRIDGWATER. Nott
3990	0.60	9.2	Br	180°	*Roberts,* Christopher. 1664. 5.64.100; R|CF. BW 69. Nott. Issuer might be the goldsmith C R (Bird 1992, p. 192)
3991	0.82	12.7	Br	180°	*Safforde,* James. 1652. S|IE; S|IE. BW 71. Baldwin
3992a	1.21	18.7	M	180°	*Sealy,* William. 1652. W S; date. BW 72. [Baldwin]. Same obv. die as 3993
3992b	1.14	17.6	M	180°	Same dies. Nott
3993a	1.34	20.7	Br	90°	*Sealy,* William. 1654. W S; date. BW 73. Baldwin. Same obv. die as 3992. Overstruck on Blandford Forum: Stayner, as Norweb 862, die axis 225°; cf. Gray 1915, p. 119; referenced as BW 74, WILLIAM SERLLAND, which goes back to J. S. Smallfield (Gill 1879, pp. 100-1), but must derive from such an overstrike, obv. on rev. Diameter 17.5-18 mm
3993b	1.09	16.8	Br	90°	Same dies. Nott. Diameter 17-17.5 mm
3993c	0.51	7.9	Br	90°	Same dies. [Baldwin]. Diameter 16.5 mm

BRIDGWATER. High Cross neighbourhood

The High Cross was a 15th-century hexagonal market cross (butter cross) in the market place, subseqently Cornhill (Bridgwater 1973, pp. 48-9, 53: reproduction of John Chubb watercolour, 63, 65). The reading is AGAINST THE HIGH CROSS IN BRIDGWATER

3994a	2.73	42.2	Cu	0°	*Rogers,* John. 1669. 5.14.103; R|IT|date. BW 70. [?Baldwin]
3994b	1.41	21.8	Cu	0°	Same dies. [Nott]
3994c	1.12	17.2	Cu	0°	Same dies. Baldwin

BRISTOL *see* Gloucestershire

BRUTON

The reading is BREWTON on 3995 (THE TOWNE OF), 3997; BRVTON on 3996

3995a	2.56	39.4	Cu	0°	*Bruton,* Borough (THE TOWNE). 1669 'necessary change (CHAINGE) for [Bruton]'. 5.3.5; 5.76(B).1. BW 75 but FOR:, obv. and rev. transposed. [?Baldwin]. Obv. legend taken as identifying the issuer, rev. as continuing into the field: 'B'tun'. Diameter 20 mm
3995b	2.04	31.5	Cu	0°	Same dies. [?Nott]. Diameter 21.5 mm
3995c	1.97	30.4	Cu	0°	Same dies. Baldwin. Diameter 20.5-21 mm
3995d	1.70	26.2	Cu	0°	Same dies. [Baldwin]. Diameter 20.5 mm
3995e	1.56	24.1	Cu	0°	Same dies. [Nott]. Diameter 20.5 mm
3995f	1.52	23.4	Cu	0°	Same dies. [?Nott]. Diameter 20.5 mm
3995g	1.46	22.5	Cu	0°	Same dies. [?Baldwin]. Diameter 20.5-21 mm
3996	1.01	15.6	Br	0°	*Brayne,* James. 1659. Date; B|IE. BW 76. Nott
3997	1.32	20.4	Br	180°	*Ludwell,* Robert, mercer. nd. 5.14 Grocers; 5.76.89 (L R). BW 77 but ROBERT · LVDWELL. Baldwin. Legends start at 10 o'clock on both sides

CASTLE CARY

The reading is CASTELL CARY

3998	1.06	16.4	Br	0°	*Russe,* Edward. 1666. Date; R|EM. BW 81. Baldwin

CHARD

Unnamed on 4003. The reading is CHARDE on 4005, 4010, with SVMERSETT on 4010; CHARD on the remainder, with IN SVMERSET SHEIR on 4004, SOMERSET on 4007. Note on 3999: The 1570 seal of Chard represents two peacocks (?), one on either side of a central floriated ornament adorned with two acorns (Fox-Davies 1915, p. 164)

3999a	2.26	34.8	Br	90°	*Chard,* Borough (BVRROVGH) (made by the portreeve (Y[E]PORTRIFF) for the poor (Y[E]POORE)). 1669. 4.4.7; C B|date. BW 82 but THE · BVRROVGH, Y[E]PORTRIFF. Baldwin
3999b	1.79	27.6	Br	90°	Same dies. [Nott]
3999c	1.72	26.6	Br	90°	Same dies. [?Baldwin]
3999d	1.57 (chipped)	24.3	Br	90°	Same dies. [?Baldwin]. For the 1671 Chard ¼d. see 4004

[*continued overleaf*]

PLATE 42

3988 3989 3990 3991 3992b 3993c

3994c 3995c 3996 3997 3998 3999d

4000 4001 4002 4003b 4004c 4005

4006 4007 4008 4009 4010a 4011

Plate 42 (*cont.*)

	Weight			Die	
	g	gr		axis	
4000	2.77	42.7	Br	270°	*Able,* Humphry. nd ½d. (A · BRASSE · HALFE:PENNY). 5.14 Innholders 2; A|HM. BW 84 but HALFE:, obv. and rev. transposed. Baldwin. Double-struck; flan deformed by a third impression. Reading confirmed from Young specimen
4001	0.85 (chipped)	13.1	Br	0°	*Bartly,* George. nd. 3.8.1; B|GA. BW 85. Nott
4002	0.63 (chipped)	9.7	Cu	90°	*Buridg,* William. 1665. 5.43.20; B|WA. BW 86 but BVRIDG. Baldwin
4003a	1.52	23.5	Br	180°	*Chapman,* John. nd, 'for necessary change (CHANG)'. 4.15.4; 4.15.4. BW 87, BW Uncertain 61, but IOHN[no stop]CHAPMAN:FO^R. [Baldwin]. Attributed, from finds in Chard, to John Chapman, mayor 1657 (Gill 1879, p. 102). Issuer 'merchant' 1652/3, 'mercer' 1679-80 (Whittet 1986b, p. 129)
4003b	1.10 (chipped)	17.0	Br	180°	Same dies. Spink 1975
4003c	1.08	16.6	Br	270°	Same dies. [Nott]
4004a	3.19	49.2	Br	0°	*?H—,* I/J—. 1671 Chard ¼d. (A CHARD FARTHINGE). Date; I H. BW 83. Baldwin. Previously considered a corporation token, but nothing more than a private issuer is indicated
4004b	1.80	27.8	Br	0°	Same dies. [Nott]
4004c	1.79	27.7	Br	180°	Same dies. [Nott]
4004d	1.57	24.2	Br	0°	Same dies. [?Baldwin]
4004e	1.49	23.0	Br	180°	Same dies. [?Nott]
4004f	1.49	23.0	Br	0°	Same dies. [Baldwin]
4005	0.43 (chipped)	6.6	Br	300°	*J[ohnson],* P[eter]. nd, 'receive the crown in every town'. 4.12.2; 5.77. BW 89 but P · I:, CHARDE. Baldwin. Issuer identified by Gray 1915, p. 125
4006	1.36	20.9	Br	0°	*Legg,* John. 1660. 5.43.30; L|IA. BW 90. Baldwin [or Spink]. Obv. legend starts at 11 o'clock, rev. legend at 10 o'clock
4007	1.03	15.9	M	90°	*Lock,* Roger. nd. 4.15.4; L|RA. BW 91. Baldwin
4008	0.75	11.6	Br	0°	*Mason,* Abraham, bookseller. nd. 5.85.10; M|AE. BW 92 but BOOKSELLE^R. [Longman] 1958, lot 452
4009	1.18	18.2	M	0°	*Sayer,* William. 1660. 5.64.50; S|WS. BW 95. Spink 1971
4010a	0.70	10.7	Br	0°	*Seldred,* Henry. nd. 5.57.40; S|HI. BW 96 but a wool card; Boyne 1858, pl. 27.4. Nott
4010b	0.64 (chipped)	9.8	Br	0°	Same dies. [Baldwin]
4011	0.93	14.3	Cu	90°	*Way,* John. nd. 5.61.10; I W. BW 98. Baldwin. Reading completed from Taunton specimen

SOMERSET (cont.)

CHARD (cont.)

	Weight			Die	
	g	gr		axis	
4012	0.88	13.6	Br	180°	*Way,* Peter. nd. 4.11.1; W|PS. BW 99. Baldwin
4013	1.34	20.6	M	180°	*Williams,* Thomas. 1656. 3.2.8; W|TM. BW 100. Nott

CHEDDAR

The reading is CHEDDER

4014	1.15	17.8	Br	180°	*Gardner,* John. 1652. 3.3.13; G|II. BW 101. Nott

COKER, East

The reading is EAST COKER

4015a	1.08	16.6	Br	0°	*Gyles,* John. nd. 3.67.25; I G. BW 122. [Baldwin]
4015b	0.93	14.4	Br	0°	Same dies. Nott

CREECH ST MICHAEL

The reading is CREECH

4016	0.68	10.5	Br	270°	*Bobbett,* Robert. [16]60. 5.34.1; R B. BW 103. Nott

CREWKERNE

The reading is CREWKERNE on 4020-3; CREWCOVRNE on 4019; CROOKEHORNE on 4018; CROOKHORNE on 4017, 4024

4017	0.96	14.9	Br	180°	*Bennet,* William. 1666. 3.11; W B. BW 105. Nott
4018	0.54	8.3	Br	0°	*Brewer,* Roger. 1668. 3.11; B|RR. BW 106. Nott
	(chipped)				
4019a	1.28	19.8	Br	90°	*Cossenes,* Edward. 1670. 5.14 Haberdashers; E C. BW 107. [Baldwin]
4019b	1.20	18.5	Br	90°	Same dies. Nott
4020a	1.00	15.4	M	180°	*Grenway,* John. nd. 5.14.104; G|II. BW 109. [Baldwin]
4020b	0.96	14.9	M	180°	Same dies. Nott
4021a	1.30	20.1	M	180°	*Grenway,* John. nd. 5.14.104; G|II. BW 109. [?Baldwin]. Same rev. die as 4022
4021b	0.58	9.0	M	180°	Same dies. [?Baldwin]
	(chipped)				
4022	1.18	18.2	Cu	90°	*Grenway,* John. nd. 5.14.104; G|II. BW 109. [Baldwin]. Same rev. die as 4021
4023	0.96	14.9	Cu	90°	*Grenway,* John. nd. 5.14.104; G|II. BW 109. [?Baldwin]
4024	1.42	21.9	Br	270°	*Shire,* John. 1666. 5.64.81; S|IA. BW 111. Baldwin. Issuer an apothecary (Whittet 1986b, p. 128)

CROSCOMBE

The reading is CRASCOMBE on 4026-7; CROSCOMB on 4025, 4028

4025a	1.21	18.7	M	0°	*Blinman,* George. 1656. G B; G B. BW 113. Baldwin
4025b	0.96	14.8	M	180°	Same dies. [Nott]
4026	0.96	14.8	Cu	180°	*George,* James. 1666. 3.2.9; G|II. BW 115. Baldwin
4027a	1.09	16.8	Cu	90°	*Luffe,* Onesiphorus. 1666. 4.12.2; O L. BW 116 but IN·CRASCOMBE. Nott. The name Onesiphorus occurs in 2 Timothy 1:16 and 4:19
4027b	0.71	10.9	Cu	270°	Same dies. [Baldwin]
4028a	1.21	18.6	Br	0°	*Plimton,* Anthony. 1656. 3.67.4; A P. BW 117. Nott. Struck from flawed dies. Diameter 17.5 mm
4028b	0.85	13.1	Br	180°	Same dies. Baldwin. Diameter 15.5 mm

DULVERTON

The reading is DELVERTON. . . IN SVMMERSETSHIR

4029	1.50	23.2	Br	0°	*Crase,* Nich—, mercer. 1669 ½d. 5.77; N C|date. BW 120 but NICH:. Baldwin

EAST COKER *see* COKER, East

[*continued overleaf*]

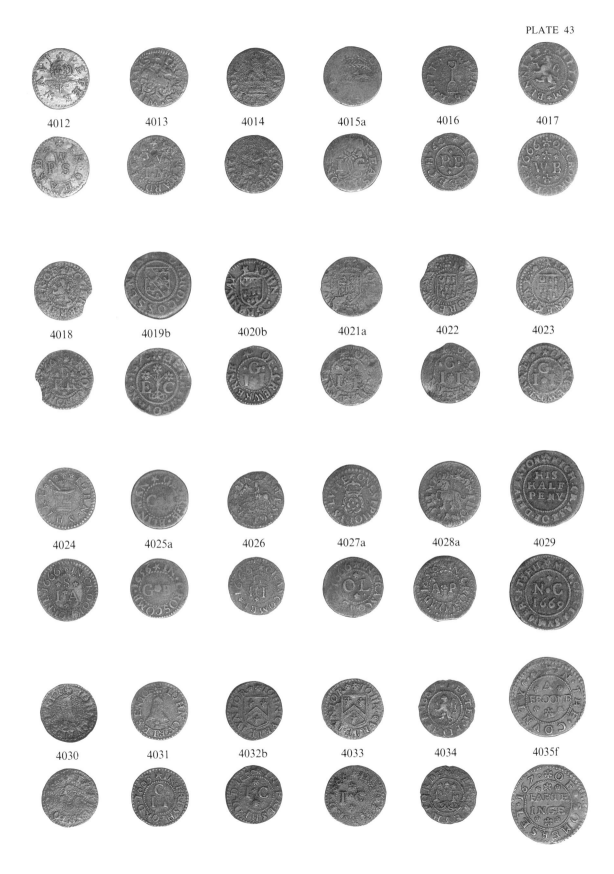

PLATE 43

4012 4013 4014 4015a 4016 4017

4018 4019b 4020b 4021a 4022 4023

4024 4025a 4026 4027a 4028a 4029

4030 4031 4032b 4033 4034 4035f

Plate 43 (*cont.*)

FRESHFORD

The reading is FRESHFORD throughout

	Weight			Die	
	g	gr		axis	
4030	0.64	9.9	Cu	0°	*Curle,* John senior. 1663. 5.70.1; C|II. BW 124. Nott. Same obv. die as 4031
4031	0.84	13.0	Cu	90°	*Curle,* John senior. 1663. 5.70.1; C|II. BW 124. Baldwin. Same obv. die as 4030
4032a	1.19	18.4	Cu	180°	*Curle,* John junior. 1666. 5.14.105; I C. BW 125. Nott. Same obv. die as 4033
4032b	0.93	14.4	Cu	180°	Same dies. [?Baldwin]
4033	0.81	12.4	Cu	0°	*Curle,* John junior. 1666. 5.14.105; I C. BW 125. [?Baldwin]. Same obv. die as 4032
4034	0.65	10.1	M	0°	*Fisher,* Peter (PEETER). 1669. 3.11; P F. BW 126; BW Ireland 451. Spink 1975. Attributed to
	(chipped)				Peter Fisher, fl. Freshford, Som., 1688 (Gray 1915, p. 125)

FROME

The reading is FROOMB on 4035; FROVME IN SVMERSET SHEIRE on 4038; FROOME on the remainder

4035a	2.34	36.0	Cu	270°	*Frome,* [Parish]. 1670 Frome ¼d. (FROOMB FARTHINGE). 5.77; 5.77. BW 127 but
					OF · SOMERSET.[?Baldwin]
4035b	2.27	35.0	Cu	270°	Same dies. [Baldwin]
4035c	2.23	34.4	Cu	270°	Same dies. [?Baldwin]
4035d	1.94	29.9	Cu	270°	Same dies. [Baldwin]
4035e	1.84	28.4	Cu	270°	Same dies. [?Baldwin]
4035f	1.52	23.5	Cu	270°	Same dies. Nott [ex Daniels]

FROME (*cont.*)

	Weight			Die	
	g	gr		axis	
4036	1.05	16.2	M	180°	*Marchant,* Henry. 1654. H M; date. BW 129. Baldwin. Subsequently gilt. Same obv. die as 4037
4037	1.40	21.5	Cu	0°	*Marchant,* Henry. 1664. H M; date. BW 131. Baldwin [or Spink]. Same obv. die as 4036
4038	1.37	21.2	Br	270°	*Sanders,* John. 1671 ¼d. 3.7.1; 5.77. BW 133. Nott
4039	0.99	15.3	M	180°	*Whitchurch,* Robert (ROBART). 1651. 3.5.96; R W. BW 135. Baldwin [or Spink]
4040a	1.20	18.5	M	180°	*Whitchurch,* Samuel. nd. 5.14 Mercers; S W. BW 137. Nott
4040b	0.93	14.4	M	270°	Same dies. [?Baldwin]
4041	0.93	14.3	M	180°	*Whitchurch,* William. 1651. 5.14 Grocers; 5.76.90 (W W). BW 138. Nott

GLASTONBURY

The reading is GLASTONBVRY on 4048, 4051-2, 4054-6; GLASTON on 4042, 4045-7, 4053; GLASSENBVRY on 4049-50; GLOSTONBVRY on 4043-4

					Bishop, William Tricky *see* 4056
4042	1.22	18.8	Br	0°	*Cary,* George, hosier. [16]68. 3.7.1; C|GA. BW 141. Seaby 1973
4043	2.22	34.3	Cu	0°	*Cooper,* William. 1666 ½d. 5.77; 5.8.10. BW 142. Nott
4044a	2.02	31.1	Cu	0°	*Cooper,* William. 1668. C; 5.8.10. BW 143 but C within flowerknot. [?Baldwin]
4044b	1.43	22.0	Cu	90°	Same dies. Brand [or Nott]
4044c	1.21	18.6	Cu	0°	Same dies. [?Baldwin]
4044d	1.09	16.8	Cu	270°	Same dies. [?Nott]
4044e	0.80	12.3	Cu	270°	Same dies. [?Baldwin]
4045	0.54 (chipped)	8.4	Cu	0°	*Day,* Mary. 1668. 5.14.5; M D. BW 144. Nott. Same obv. die as 4046
4046a	1.12	17.3	Br	0°	*Day,* Mary. 1668. 5.14.5; M D. BW 144. [Baldwin]. Same obv. die as 4045
4046b	0.77 (chipped)	11.9	Br	0°	Same dies. [?Baldwin]
4047	0.86 (chipped)	13.3	Cu	0°	*Denham,* Thomas. 1666. 5.60.1; T D. BW 145. Nott. Reading completed from Taunton specimen
4048a	1.12	17.2	M	180°	*Gutch,* Henry, mercer. 1653. 2.5.1; G|HA. BW 148 but obv. device Glastonbury Tor (see Introduction). [?Baldwin]
4048b	0.98	15.1	M	180°	Same dies. Nott
4049	0.86 (chipped)	13.2	Br	180°	*Hancocke,* Sidricke. nd. 1.40.20; H|SM. BW 149 but IN · GLASSENBVRY. Nott. Reading completed from Young specimen. Same rev. die as 4050. The forename was perhaps Shadrach (Daniel 1-3); 'Cedric' seems to have been invented 1819 by Scott (Withycombe 1977, p. 61)
4050	1.07	16.5	M	180°	*Hancocke,* Sidricke. nd. 1.40.12 (· SIDRICKE· HANCOCKE around); H|SM (· H ·|S · M; · IN · GLASSENBVRY around). BW —, cf. 149; Gray 1915, p. 123. Baldwin. Same rev. die as 4049
4051	0.65	10.0	Cu	270°	*Hopkins,* James. 1656. 5.14 Mercers; I H. BW 150. [?Baldwin]. Same obv. die as 4052. Rev. legend starts at 6 o'clock
4052a	1.19	18.3	Cu	180°	*Hopkins,* James. 1656. 5.14 Mercers; I H. BW 150. Nott. Same obv. die as 4051. Rev. legend starts at 6 o'clock
4052b	0.91	14.1	Cu	180°	Same dies. [?Baldwin]
4053a	1.49	23.0	Br	180°	*Mabson,* Henry, hosier. nd ½d. 3.7.2 (· HENRY · MABSON · HOSIER · OF around); M|HM (· M ·|H · M| · · ·; · GLASTON · HIS · HALF · PENY · around).BW—,cf.153;Dickinson153A. [Baldwin]
4053b	1.32	20.4	Br	180°	Same dies. Nott [?Baldwin]
4054	0.90	14.0	Br	270°	*Roode,* Thomas. 1668. 3.53.20; R|TI. BW 154 but T I R. Nott
4055a	1.19	18.4	M	180°	*West,* Peter, draper. nd. 3.6.1; W|PM. BW 156. [Baldwin]. Diameter 15.5-16 mm
4055b	0.98 (chipped)	15.1	M	180°	Same dies. No provenance. Diameter 15.5 mm
4055c	0.85 (chipped)	13.1	Br	180°	Same dies. Nott. Diameter 17 mm

Named signs

4056	1.20	18.4	M	0°	*Bishop:* Tricky, William. 1656. 3.5.52; date|W T. BW 140. Baldwin. The surname Tricky still common in Somerset [ex inf. P.J. Seaby]

[*continued overleaf*]

PLATE 44

| 4036 | 4037 | 4038 | 4039 | 4040b | 4041 |

| 4042 | 4043 | 4044b | 4045 | 4046b | 4047 |

| 4048b | 4049 | 4050 | 4051 | 4052b | 4053a |

| 4054 | 4055c | 4056 | 4057a | 4058 | 4059b |

Plate 44 (*cont.*)

GODNEY (Meare parish)

The reading is GODNYE

	Weight			Die	
	g	gr		axis	
4057a	2.57	40.0	Br	0°	*Orgainer* (ORGAINER), Anne. 1665 ½d5.77(HER|HALF|PENY|···;·ANNE·ORGAINER· around); date (···|I665|···; ·OF·GODNYE··· around). BW —; Dickinson 156B. [Nott]. Diameter 20.5-21 mm
4057b	1.14	17.6	Br	180°	Same dies. Nott. Obv. struck off-centre. Diameter 19-19.5 mm

HENSTRIDGE

The reading is HENSTRIDG

4058	0.84	12.9	Br	0°	*Huson,* Rich—. mercer. nd. 5.14 Grocers; H|RM. BW 157. Baldwin. Reading confirmed from Taunton specimen. The S of HVSON double-entered in die, the earlier S faint

ILCHESTER

The reading is IVELCHESTE(?) on 4059-60; IVELCHESTER on 4061-2; cf. *Iuelcestr'* 1157 (Ekwall 1960, p. 262). Note on 4059-60: The seal of Ilchester bears within a crescent an estoile of sixteen points (Lewis 1845, ii. 594)

4059a	1.75	26.9	Br	180°	*Ilchester,* Borough (Y^EBVRROV) (By the Bailiff (Y^EBAYLIFF) ?G— B—). nd. 2.3.4 (THE ARMES OF IVELCHESTE(?) around); G B. BW 159 but IVELCHESTE(?), Y^EBVRROV. [?Baldwin]. Same obv. die as 4060, q.v.
4059b	1.62	25.0	Br	180°	Same dies. Nott

ILCHESTER (*cont.*)

	Weight			Die	
	g	*gr*		*axis*	
4060a	1.51	23.2	Br	150°	*Ilchester,* Borough (Y^EBVRROV) (By the Bailiff (Y^EBAYLIFF) ?G— B—). nd. 2.3.4 (THE ARMES OF IVELCHESTE(?) around); G B. BW 159 but IVELCHESTE(?), Y^EBVRROV. [Baldwin]. Same obv. die as 4059. This specimen possibly exhibits a minute R almost horizontal above the last E of IVELCHESTE
4060b	1.07	16.5	Br	150°	Same dies. [?Baldwin]
	(pierced)				
4060c	0.86	13.3	Br	150°	Same dies. [?Baldwin]
4061	1.44	22.3	Br	180°	*Lockier,* John, mercer. 1657. Date; I L. BW 160. Baldwin
4062a	0.87	13.4	Br	180°	*Lockyer,* John. nd. 2.3.4 (· IOHN:LOCKYER:OF around); L|IM (· L · |IM; · IVELCHESTER · around). BW —, cf. 161 (I658). Nott. Tinned. Obv. legend starts at 3 o'clock
4062b	0.68	10.5	Br	180°	Same dies. Nott [?Baldwin]. Perhaps originally tinned
	(chipped)				

ILMINSTER

The reading is ILMISTER on 4063, 4065, 4067; ILEMESTER on 4069-70; ILLMISTER on 4068; ILMNSTER on 4064; ITMISTER [*sic*] on 4066

					Ilminster, Corporation *see* 4068
4063	0.47	7.3	Br	0°	*Carter,* Thomas. nd. 5.43.27; C|TM. BW 165. Nott
	(chipped)				
4064	1.50	23.2	Br	180°	*Crosse,* William (C|WI). 1658. C|WI; date. BW 167 but better I658, the 'stop' in the middle of the date being a compass mark on the die. Baldwin
4065	0.73	11.2	Cu	0°	*Crosse,* William (W C). nd. 3.53.1; W C. BW 166. Spink 1972. Reading confirmed from Taunton specimen
4066	0.91	14.0	M	180°	*Horwood,* Robert, chandler. nd. 5.65.1; H|RM. BW 169 but CHANDLER. Spink [*NCirc* July-Aug. 1971, 7833]. Same dies as 4067, before alteration of rev.
4067	1.21	18.6	Cu	180°	*Horwood,* Robert, chandler. nd. 5.65.1; H|RM. BW 168. Spink [*NCirc* July-Aug. 1971, 7832]. Same dies as 4066 with L cancelling first T of ITMISTER
4068a	1.99	30.7	Br	180°	?P—, T— [and] S—, T—. nd Ilminster ¼d. (ILLMISTER FARDING). 5.42.34 (T P); 3.7.6 (T S). BW 164. Nott. Previously considered a corporate issue, but nothing more than a partnership is indicated
4068b	1.41	21.8	Br	180°	Same dies. [?Baldwin]
	(chipped)				
4069	0.56	8.6	Br	180°	*Raw* (ROW), Alice. 1664. A R; 3.2.9. BW 170. Nott. Same dies as 4070, before O of ROW cancelled
4070	1.21	18.7	Br	0°	*Raw,* Alice. 1664. A R (· · · |A°R| · · · ; · ALICE:°:RAW · OFaround); 3.2.9(· ILEMESTER · I664 around). BW —, cf. 170; Gray 1915, 170a but ILEMESTER. [Baldwin]. Same dies as 4069, with A in RAW cancelling O

KILMERSDON

The reading is KILMERSDON IN SOMER\|SET\|SHIRE

					?F—, T— *see* Uncertain III
4071	1.40	21.7	Br	270°	*Foster,* William. 1669. 5.14.106; 5.77. BW 173. Baldwin. Reading completed from Taunton specimen
	(chipped)				

KILVE

The reading is KILVE

4072	1.18	18.2	Br	180°	*Michell,* Charles (CHARLLS). 1670. C M; M E. BW 174. Nott. Reading confirmed from Taunton specimen

[*continued overleaf*]

PLATE 45

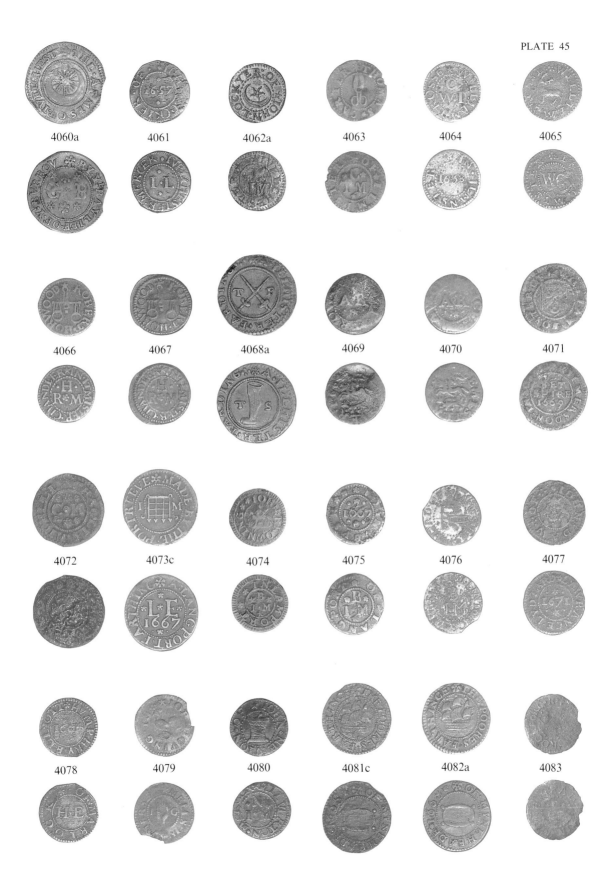

4060a   4061   4062a   4063   4064   4065

4066   4067   4068a   4069   4070   4071

4072   4073c   4074   4075   4076   4077

4078   4079   4080   4081c   4082a   4083

Plate 45 (*cont.*)

LANGPORT (Huish Episcopi parish)

The reading is LANGPORT on 4073, 4075; LAMPORT on 4074, as often (Ekwall 1960, p. 285)

	Weight			Die	
	g	gr		axis	
4073a	3.17	48.9	Br	30°	*Langport Eastover,* Borough. 1667 Langport ¼d., 'made by the portreeve' I M [*i.e.*John Michell]. 5.17.2 (I M); L E|date. BW 175 but obv. and rev. transposed. [?Baldwin]. Identification of portreeve from Bidgood 1886, 180 n.

4073b	2.54	39.2	Br	30°	Same dies. [?Baldwin]. Countermarked on reverse. See illustration above
4073c	2.12	32.7	Br	270°	Same dies. Nott
4073d	2.08	32.0	Br	90°	Same dies. [?Baldwin]
4073e	1.77	27.3	Br	0°	Same dies. [Baldwin]
4073f	1.40	21.6	Br	90°	Same dies. [?Baldwin]
4074	0.62	9.5	Br	0°	*Browning,* John. nd. 3.2.11; B|IM. BW Northants. 57; Dickinson 175A. Nott. Attribution from Gray 1915, p. 126
4075	1.30	20.1	M	180°	*Bush,* John. 1667. Date; B|IM. BW 176. Baldwin

LULLINGTON

The reading is LVLLINTON C SOMERSET

4076	1.31	20.2	Br	270°	*Bradford,* James. nd. 5.76.91 (I B); B|IM. BW 178 but [?no stop]C:SOMERSET. Baldwin. Tinned

LYDEARD ST LAWRENCE

The reading is LAWRANCE LYDIARD

4077	1.48	22.8	Br	270°	*Daw,* John. 1671. 3.5.96; date. BW 179. Baldwin

MARTOCK

The reading is MARTOCK

4078	1.08	16.6	Br	180°	*Elliott,* Humphry. 1664. Date; H E. BW 180. Baldwin

MELLS

The reading is MELLS IN SVMERSET

4079	0.71	11.0	Br	90°	*Guing,* John. nd. 3.101.4; 3.6.11 (I G). BW 182. Baldwin
	(chipped)				

MILVERTON

The reading is MILVERTON

4080	1.05	16.2	Br	180°	*Newton,* John, mercer. nd. 5.64.81; N|IM. BW 186. Nott

MINEHEAD

The reading is MINEHEAD on 4084-7; MYNEHEADE on 4081-2; MYNEHEAD on 4083

4081a	3.00	46.3	Cu	0°	*Minehead,* Borough. 1668 poor's ¼d. (THE POORES FARTHINGE). 5.13.18; 5.64.50. BW 187. [?Baldwin]. Same rev. die as 4082. Diameter 19 mm
4081b	2.90	44.7	Cu	270°	Same dies. [?Baldwin]. Diameter 20.5-21 mm
4081c	2.89	44.6	Cu	0°	Same dies. [Nott]. Diameter 19 mm
4081d	1.16	18.0	Cu	0°	Same dies. [Baldwin]. Diameter 19-19.5 mm
4082a	2.44	37.6	Cu	0°	*Minehead,* Borough. 1668 poor's ¼d. (THE POORES FARTHINGE). 5.13.18; 5.64.50. BW 187. Baldwin. Same rev. die as 4081
4082b	1.92	29.7	Cu	0°	Same dies. [?Baldwin]
4082c	0.88	13.6	Cu	0°	Same dies. [?Baldwin]
					Berry, John *see* TINHEAD (Wilts.)
4083	0.78	12.1	Br	180°	*Crockford,* Richard. nd. 5.13.18; C|RE. BW 189. Baldwin. Obv. field confirmed from Taunton specimen. Rev. legend starts at 4 o'clock
	(chipped)				

MINEHEAD (*cont.*)

	Weight			Die					
	g	gr		axis	
4084a	1.81	28.0	Br	0°	*Crockford,* Samuel. 1654. 5.65.1; 5.65.1. BW 190. Baldwin
4084b	0.95	14.7	Br	180°	Same dies. [Nott]
4085	1.09	16.8	Br	270°	*Streete,* John. 1666. 5.45.11; S|IM. BW 191. Baldwin. Reading completed from Taunton specimen. Reverse double-struck
4086	1.12	17.3	Br	180°	*Ugden,* Robert. nd. 5.37.5; V|RM. BW 193. Spink 1972
4087	1.27	19.6	Br	90°	*Ugden,* Robert. 1666. 5.37.5; M|RV. BW 192 but · M · |R · V| · · [*sic*]. Baldwin

MONTACUTE

The reading is MOVNTAGEW on 4089-90, MOVNTOGEW on 4088, cf. French *Montaigu*

4088	1.52	23.4	Cu	0°	*Blatchford,* Jane. nd. 5.64.80; 5.76.92 (?IHB). BW 194 but BLATCHFOR^D. Nott. Central bar of monogram cancels a mullet
4089a	0.83	12.7	Br	90°	*Clother,* John. 1655. 3.61.1; C|IM. BW 195 but a unicorn (no question). [Nott]. Diameter 14.5 mm
4089b	0.51	7.9	Br	0°	Same dies. Baldwin. Diameter 15-16 mm
4090	0.77	11.8	Br	180°	*Clothier,* John. nd. 5.71.1; C|ID. BW 196. Baldwin

NETHER STOWEY *see* STOWEY, Nether

NUNNEY

The reading is NUNNEY

4091	0.69	10.6	M	180°	*Ashe,* George. 1652. 5.14 Mercers; G A. BW 202. Clark 1977

PETHERTON, North

The reading is NORTH PETHERTON on 4092; NORTH PETHER-ON on 4093; NORTH PETHERTO^N on 4094

4092	0.88	13.6	Br	270°	*Hooper,* Tho—. 1668. H|TM; 5.14 Tallow Chandlers. BW 199 but THO:. Baldwin
4093	0.61	9.4	Br	0°	*Loueder,* Tho— (IHO:). 1657. L|TA|date; L|TA. *BW 201 (PETHERTON) but IHO: [*sic*]. Baldwin
4094	0.64	9.9	Br	0°	*Loueder,* Tho— (THO:). 1657. L|TA|date (· L · |T · A|I657; · THO: · LOVEDER · OF around); L|TA (· L · |T · A| ·; NORTH:PETHERTO^N around). BW —, cf. 201 (OF:); cf. Gray 1915, 201a (PETHERTO). Nott. Reading completed from Taunton specimen

PETHERTON, South

The reading is SOVTH PETHARTON on 4097; SOVTH PETHERTON on 4096; SOVTH PETHERTO^N on 4095

4095	0.47	7.3	Br	0°	*Anstie,* Edmond. 1668. 2.2; A|EA. BW 217 but PETHERTO^N; Gray 1915, 217a. Baldwin
4096a	0.88	13.6	Br	180°	*Willy,* John. nd. 5.64.15; W|ID. BW 218. Nott
4096b	0.84	13.0	Br	180°	Same dies. [?Baldwin]
4097	1.34 (chipped)	20.6	Br	270°	*Wintar,* William. 1669. 5.14.107; W|WE|date. BW 219 but three pellets one and two, W|WE|I669. Baldwin. Reading confirmed from Taunton specimen

SHEPTON MALLET

The reading is SHIPTON MALLETT on 4099-4101, MALLET on 4102-3; SHEPTON MALLETT on 4098

4098	0.73	11.3	M	180°	*Barnard,* Richard. nd. B|RM; B|RM. BW 207. Baldwin [or Nott]. Reading completed from Young specimen
4099a	1.37	21.2	Cu	0°	*Browne,* Will—, hosier. nd. 5.76.93 (B); W B. BW 208 but WILL:. Nott
4099b	0.61 (chipped)	9.4	Cu	180°	Same dies. [?Baldwin]
4100	0.78	12.0	Cu	90°	*Byrtt,* John. 1665. 5.76.94 (B); I6B65|IM. BW 209 but I6B65| · I · M ·	· . Baldwin. Obv. legend starts at 2 o'clock
4101	1.22	18.8	Br	270°	*Byrtt,* John. 1665. 5.76.94 (B); I6B65|IM. BW 209 but I6B65| · I · M ·	· . [Nott]. Obv. legend starts at 3 o'clock
4102	0.42	6.5	Br	0°	*James,* William. 1667. I|WI; I|WI|date. BW 210. [?Baldwin]
4103a	1.02	15.7	Br	180°	*Parfit,* Tho—, chandler. 1652. 3.3.13; date. BW 211. Nott
4103b	0.85	13.0	Br	180°	Same dies. [?Baldwin]

[*continued overleaf*]

PLATE 46

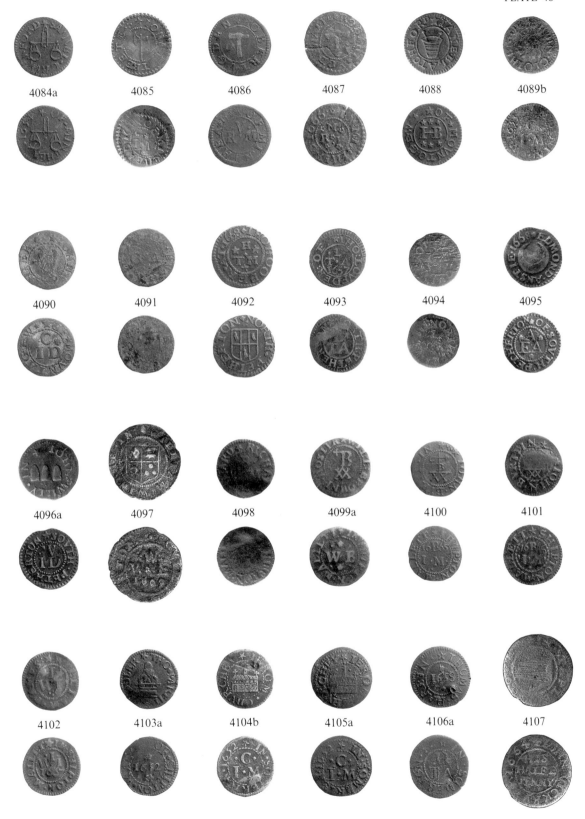

4084a 4085 4086 4087 4088 4089b

4090 4091 4092 4093 4094 4095

4096a 4097 4098 4099a 4100 4101

4102 4103a 4104b 4105a 4106a 4107

Plate 46 (*cont.*)

SOMERTON

The reading is SOMERTON throughout

	Weight			Die	
	g	*gr*		*axis*	
4104a	1.07	16.5	Br	180°	*Churchey,* Jerome (IEROM). 1652. 5.7.6; C|IM. BW 213. [?Nott]. Same rev. die as 4105
4104b	1.03	15.8	Br	180°	Same dies. Nott
4105a	1.24	19.2	Br	0°	*Churchey,* Jerome (IEROM). 1652. 5.7.6; C|IM. BW 213. Nott. Same rev. die as 4104, with all the letters and some of the outer circle recut; the obv. could be that of 4104 completely recut
4105b	0.89	13.7	Br	0°	Same dies. [Baldwin]
4106a	0.96	14.7	Br	90°	*Harbin,* Thomas. 1658. Date; H|TA. BW 214. Baldwin. Attached to the T in the rev. field, and parallel to its lower half, is a vertical stroke
	(pierced)				
4106b	0.93	14.3	Cu	–	Same dies. [?Baldwin]. Rev. brockage
4106c	0.77	11.9	Cu	270°	Same dies. [Nott]
4106d	0.77	11.9	Br	90°	Same dies. [?Baldwin]
	(chipped)				

STAPLEGROVE

The reading is STAPLE GROVE

4107	2.04	31.4	Cu	270°	*Vickry,* John. 1664 ½d. 5.77; 5.57.13. BW 221-2. Clark [1977]
	(chipped)				

STOGUMBER

The reading is STOGOMBER

Named signs

	Weight			Die	
	g	gr		axis	
4108	1.01	15.6	Br	150°	*Red Lion* (RE- LION): Phillips, John. nd. 3.11 (· IOHN · PHILLIPS · OF around); P‖IC (· P · ‖ I · C · STOGOMBER · RE - ·LION). BW —; *Dickinson 222A, *Gray 1915, p. 118 (both RED LION). Baldwin. Obv. legend starts at 1 o'clock

STOWEY, Nether

The reading is NETHERSTOY on both

4109	1.03	15.8	Cu	0°	*Hoopper,* John. nd. 5.64.80; H‖IG. BW 197. Nott
4110	0.89	13.7	Br	0°	*Patey,* William. nd. 4.13.1; P‖WA. BW 198. [?Baldwin]

TAUNTON

The reading is TANTON on 4124-5, 4130, 4138, 4142-3, 4146, 4149-52, with IN SOMERSET SHIER on 4143; TAVNTVN on 4136; TAWNTON on 4118; TAVNTON on the remainder, with IN SOMMERSET on 4146. Note on 4112-16: the Constables in 1667 were Stephen Savage and Henry Crosse (Symonds 1911, p. 56). He presumes (p. 55) that the farthings were issued by the Constables on behalf of the manor court; but the officers of the Borough Courts included two Constables, who supervised the alms-houses, the work-house, and the distribution of the borough charities (Whitty 1934, pp. 75-6)

4111a	2.65	40.9	Cu	0°	*Taunton,* Borough. nd. 5.5.10; 5.64.30. BW 226. [?Baldwin]
4111b	2.56	39.5	Cu	0°	Same dies. Brand [or Nott]
4112a	4.00	61.7	Br	270°	*Taunton,* Borough. 1667 Taunton ¼d., 'by the constables'. 5.5.12; 5.64.47. BW 227 but I667, obv. and rev. transposed. [?Baldwin]. Same rev. die as 4113. Diameter 21.5-22 mm (edges hammered up)
4112b	3.24	50.0	Br	270°	Same dies. [Baldwin]. Diameter 22 mm
4112c	3.18	49.1	Br	90°	Same dies. Nott. Diameter 22-22.5 mm
4112d	2.87	44.3	Br	270°	Same dies. [Nott]. Diameter 23 mm
4112e	2.58	39.8	Br	270°	Same dies. [?Baldwin]. Diameter 22-22.5 mm
4112f	2.51	38.7	Br	270°	Same dies. [?Baldwin]. Diameter 21.5-22 mm
4113	3.00	46.3	Br	90°	*Taunton,* Borough. 1667 Taunton ¼d., 'by the constables'. 5.5.12; 5.64.47. BW 227 but I667, obv. and rev. transposed. [?Baldwin]. Same rev. die as 4112; same obv. die as 4114
4114a	2.83	43.6	Br	0°	*Taunton,* Borough. 1667 Taunton ¼d., 'by the constables'. 5.5.12; 5.64.47. BW 228 but I667, obv. and rev. transposed. Nott. Same obv. die as 4113
4114b	2.36	36.4	Br	0°	Same dies. [Baldwin]
4114c	2.33	36.0	Br	0°	Same dies. [?Baldwin]
4114d	2.11	32.5	Br	0°	Same dies. [?Baldwin]
4115a	2.41	37.3	Br	90°	*Taunton,* Borough. 1667 Taunton ¼d., 'by the constables'. 5.5.12; 5.64.47. BW 229 but I667, obv. and rev. transposed. [?Baldwin]. Same obv. die as 4116
4115b	2.32	35.8	Br	90°	Same dies. Baldwin
4115c	2.17 (chipped)	33.4	Br	270°	Same dies. [?Baldwin]
4115d	1.58	24.4	Br	90°	Same dies. [?Baldwin]
4116a	2.54	39.1	Br	180°	*Taunton,* Borough. 1667 Taunton ¼d., 'by the constables'. 5.5.12; 5.64.47. BW 230 but I667, obv. and rev. transposed. Nott. Same obv. die as 4115
4116b	2.49	38.4	Br	0°	Same dies. Baldwin
4116c	1.96	30.2	Br	0°	Same dies. [?Baldwin]
4116d	1.76	27.1	Br	270°	Same dies. [?Baldwin]
4117	1.13	17.5	Br	180°	*Andrews,* Thomas. nd. 5.64.50; A‖TI. BW 232. Nott
4118a	1.82 (chipped)	28.1	Br	90°	*Andrews* (ANDROSSE), Thomas. 1666 ½d. 5.64.50; 5.77. BW 233 but HIS‖HALFE. Nott. Form of surname from 4117
4118b	1.42	21.9	Br	90°	Same dies. [?Baldwin]
4118c	1.33	20.6	Br	270°	Same dies. [?Baldwin]
4119	0.49	7.6	Br	270°	*Barton,* John. 1666. 4.12.2; B‖IM. BW 235. Baldwin

[*continued overleaf*]

PLATE 47

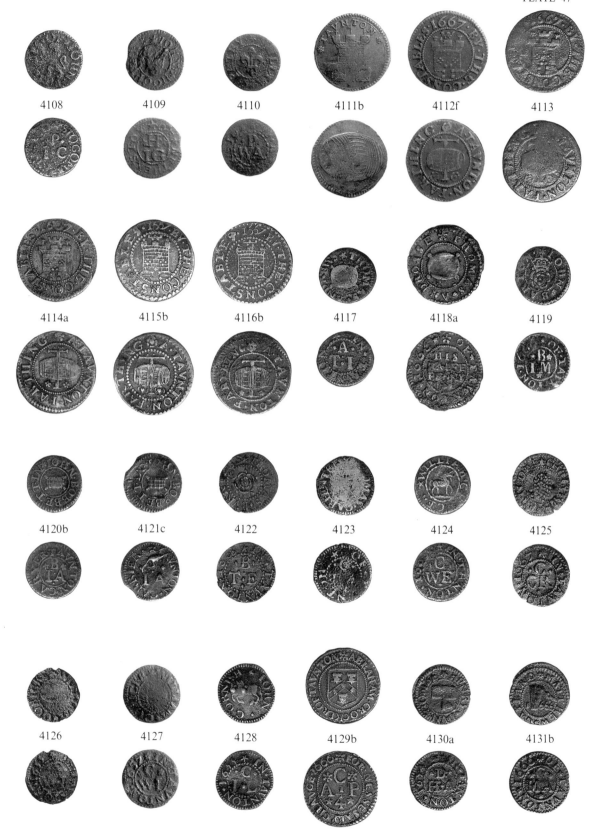

4108 4109 4110 4111b 4112f 4113

4114a 4115b 4116b 4117 4118a 4119

4120b 4121c 4122 4123 4124 4125

4126 4127 4128 4129b 4130a 4131b

Plate 47 (*cont.*)

	Weight			Die	
	g	*gr*		*axis*	
4120a	1.62	25.0	Cu	180°	*Bobbett,* John, carrier (CARYER). nd. 5.64.63; B|IA. BW 237. [Baldwin]. Same obv. die as 4121. Diameter 16-16.5 mm
4120b	1.41	21.8	Cu	0°	Same dies. Nott. Diameter 15 mm
4121a	1.86	28.7	Cu	270°	*Bobbett,* John, carrier. nd. 5.64.63; B|IA. BW 238. Nott. Same obv. die as 4120
4121b	1.21	18.7	Cu	0°	Same dies. [?Baldwin]
4121c	0.79	12.1	Cu	180°	Same dies. [Baldwin]. On the rev. of specimens a-c, listed in weight order, the developing flaw shows they are also in order of striking
4122	0.56	8.6	Br	270°	*Burridge,* Thomas. 1663. 4.12.1 (·THOMAS·BVRRIDGE around); B|TE (·B·|T·E|·; ·IN·TAVNTON·I663 around). BW —; Dickinson 238A. Baldwin
4123	0.84	12.9	Br	180°	*Carpenter,* Thomas. nd. 3.1.15; C|TA. BW 239. Clark 1977. Thomas Carpenter 'clothier' 1657; two leasehold messuages known by the name of the Valiant Soldier, also used as a tavern (Symonds 1911, pp. 58-9)
4124	1.09	16.8	Br	270°	*Chace,* William. 1662. 3.61.3; C|WE. BW 240. Nott. Reading completed from Taunton specimen. Obv. legend starts at 9 o'clock
4125	0.74 (chipped)	11.5	Cu	0°	*Cooke,* Christopher. 1667. 4.9.5; C|CR. BW 242. Nott
4126	0.44 (chipped)	6.8	Br	0°	*Coricke,* William. 1655. 5.83.43; C|WI. BW 243. Nott. Reading confirmed from Taunton specimen. Same obv. die as 4127
4127	0.71	11.0	Br	90°	*Coricke,* William. 1657. 5.83.43; C|WI. BW 244. Nott. Same obv. die as 4126
4128	0.88	13.6	M	180°	*Cornish,* John. 1655. 3.60.20; C|IL. BW 245 but obv. = Horse, rev. = I.L.C. Baldwin
4129a	2.41	37.1	Cu	0°	*Crocker,* Abraham. 1666 ¼d., 'for necessary (NESSESARY) change'. 5.14 Weavers; C|AP|¼. BW 246. [?Baldwin]. Diameter 20.5 mm
4129b	2.10	32.5	Cu	0°	Same dies. Nott. Diameter 20-20.5 mm
4129c	2.10	32.4	Cu	0°	Same dies. [Nott]. Diameter 20.5 mm
4129d	2.09	32.2	Cu	180°	Same dies. [Baldwin]. Diameter 21 mm
4129e	1.87	28.9	Cu	0°	Same dies. [?Baldwin]. Diameter 20 mm
4129f	1.85	28.5	Cu	180°	Same dies. [?Baldwin]. Diameter 21-21.5 mm
4130a	1.16	18.0	M	180°	*Dunscombe,* Henry. 1654. 3.6.42; D|HA. BW 249. Nott
4130b	0.99	15.2	M	180°	Same dies. [?Baldwin]
4131a	1.02	15.8	Br	0°	*Gaylard,* Matthew. 1666. 3.6.46; G|MA. BW 251. [?Baldwin]
4131b	0.90	14.0	Br	0°	Same dies. Baldwin
4131c	0.58	9.0	Br	180°	Same dies. [?Baldwin]
4131d	0.56 (chipped)	8.6	Br	180°	Same dies. [Nott]

TAUNTON (*cont.*)

	Weight		Die		
	g	gr	axis		
4132	0.85	13.2	M	0°	*Glyde,* John. nd. 2.4.7; G|IM. BW 252. Nott. Obv. device confirmed from Taunton specimen
	(chipped)				
4133a	0.88	13.6	Br	180°	*Graye,* Hugh. 1666. 5.64.50; G|HA. BW 253 but HVGH. [Baldwin]. Hugh Graye 'sergeweaver' 1670 (Symonds 1911, p. 57)
	(chipped)				
4133b	0.72	11.1	Br	180°	Same dies. Nott
4134	0.77	11.9	M	180°	*Greggory,* Andrew. 1655. 5.49.1; G|AM. BW 256. Nott
	(chipped)				
4135a	1.10	16.9	Br	180°	*Hossham,* Martin. 1655. 5.51.20; H|MI. BW 258. [Nott]. Diameter 16 mm
4135b	0.98	15.1	Br	180°	Same dies. [?Baldwin]. Diameter 15.5 mm
4135c	0.87	13.4	Br	180°	Same dies. [Baldwin]. Diameter 15-15.5 mm
4135d	0.57	8.8	Br	0°	Same dies. [Baldwin]. Diameter 16-16.5 mm. Struck from flawed obv. die
4136a	1.05	16.2	M	180°	*How,* Roger. 1653. H|RC; H|RC. BW 259. [?Baldwin]
4136b	0.92	14.2	Br	180°	Same dies. Nott
4137	0.62	9.5	Br	90°	*Maber,* Joseph. 1664. 5.14 Clothworkers; M|IM. BW 263. Nott. Date completed from Taunton specimen
	(pierced)				
4138	1.11	17.1	Cu	0°	*Meredith,* John. 1666, 'for necessary change (NECESSARY CHENG)'. 5.7.25; 5.77. BW 264 but NECES|SARY:, obv. and rev. transposed. Nott. Reading completed from Taunton specimen
4139	0.43	6.6	Br	270°	*Munday,* Matthew (MATHEW). nd. 5.57.13; M|MW. BW 267. [Baldwin]. Matthew Monday the elder 'clothier' 1689 (Symonds 1911, p. 63)
	(chipped)				
4140	1.15	17.7	Br	?°	*Munday* (. . .), Matthew (. . .). nd? 5.57.13?; M|MW. *BW 267 (MATHEW.MVNDAY = a woolcomb). Nott. Obverse flat; rev. different from 4139, and from two varieties in Taunton
	(chipped)				
4141	0.98	15.1	Br	0°	*Munden,* Thomas. nd. 5.64.48; M|TE. BW 268. Baldwin [or Spink]
4142a	1.08	16.7	M	0°	*Parry,* Peter, clothworker (CLOTHWORK). 1654. 3.63.24; P P|date. BW 270 but an ibex. Nott
4142b	0.81	12.5	M	0°	Same dies. [Baldwin]
4143a	1.19	18.4	M	180°	*Sprake,* John. nd. 5.65.21; S|IG. BW 282. [Baldwin]. John Sprake dead by 1663 (Symonds 1911, p. 60)
4143b	1.11	17.2	M	180°	Same dies. Nott
	(chipped)				
4143c	0.85	13.1	M	180°	Same dies. [?Baldwin]
4144	0.56	8.6	Br	0°	*Timewell,* Stephen (STEAPHEN). nd. 5.61.10; T|SE. BW 286. Baldwin
4145	0.47	7.2	Br	0°	*Tompson,* Robert. nd. 5.43.35; T|RE. BW 287. Baldwin
4146	1.14	17.6	Br	180°	*Treagle,* George. nd. 5.85.10; T|GF. BW 288. Nott. George Treagle, publisher and bookseller, 1646-53 (Plomer 1907, p. 181)
4147a	1.64	25.3	Cu	90°	*Tubb,* John. 1666. Date; T|IE. BW 289. [Nott]
	(pierced)				
4147b	1.23	19.0	Cu	90°	Same dies. Baldwin
4147c	1.05	16.2	Cu	90°	Same dies. [?Baldwin]
4147d	0.88	13.6	Cu	90°	Same dies. [Nott]
4147e	0.81	12.5	Cu	90°	Same dies. [?Baldwin]

Named signs

4148	1.34	20.6	Br	180°	*Three Widows* (AT THE 3 WIDDOWS): P[urchase], R[ichard]. 1655. P|RE; P|RE. BW 284. Baldwin [or Spink]. Attribution to Richard Purchase at the Three Widows inn from Symonds 1911, p. 60

TAUNTON. Taunton St James parish

The reading is TANTON IAMES

4149	0.77	11.8	Br	180°	*Dawley,* Edward. nd. 5.57.10; D|ET. BW 248. Nott
	(chipped)				

TAUNTON. Taunton St Mary Magdalene parish

The reading is TANTON MAGDALEN on both, the first N in TANTON and the N in MAGDALEN retrograde on 4150

4150	0.93	14.4	Br	0°	*Midleton,* Robert. nd. 5.60.1; M|RE. BW 266 but all N's retrograde except the second in TANTON. [Nott]. Obv. legend starts at 6 o'clock. Same obv. die as 4151
4151a	1.10	17.0	Br	180°	*Midleton,* Robert. nd. 5.60.1; M|RE. BW 266 but N's in MIDLETON and IN retrograde. [?Baldwin]. Same obv. die as 4150
4151b	0.63	9.6	Cu	0°	Same dies. Baldwin

[*continued overleaf*]

PLATE 48

4132   4133b   4134   4135a   4136a   4137

4138   4139   4140   4141   4142a   4143c

4144   4145   4146   4147b   4148   4149

4150   4151b   4152   4153a   4154   4155

Plate 48 (*cont.*)

TAUNTON DEAN (*district*)

The vale in which Taunton is situated, cf. the Somerset hundred of *Taunton and Taunton Dean*, and from 1974 the borough of *Taunton Deane*. The reading is TANTON DEANE

	Weight		Die		
	g	gr	axis		
4152	0.77	11.8	Cu	180°	*Grove,* Jeffrey (IEFFERY). 1664. 5.14 Clothworkers; G|IR. BW 257. Baldwin [or Nott or Spink]

WALCOMBE (Wells St Cuthbert parish)

Exton, Francis *see* 2283/2 (Herts.: Walkern)

WELLINGTON

The reading is WELLINGTON on 4154-6; WILLINGTON on 4153

4153a	1.87	28.9	Cu	180°	*Wellington* (WILLINGTON), [Corporation], Overseers. 1666 ½d., 'for the benefit of the poor (POORE)'. 5.77; 5.77. BW 293. Baldwin. Same rev. die as 4154
4153b	1.77	27.4	Cu	180°	Same dies. [?Baldwin]
4154	2.05	31.7	Cu	180°	*Wellington,* [Corporation], Overseers. 1666 ½d., 'for the benefit of the poor (POORE)'. 5.77; 5.77. BW 292. Nott. Same rev. die as 4153
4155	0.80	12.3	M	0°	*Samford,* Christopher (CRISTOPHER). nd. 5.14 Grocers; S|CA. BW 297. Baldwin. Christopher Sanford gent., grocer (A. J. Monday, see Bidgood 1886, no. 298 n.)

WELLINGTON (*cont.*)

	Weight			Die	
	g	gr		axis	
4156	1.00	15.4	Br	0°	*Samford,* Christopher (CRISTOPHER). nd. 5.14 Grocers; S|CA. BW 297. [Nott]. See 4155
					Wright, Stephen *see* 3933 (Shropshire)

WELLS

See also WALCOMBE. The reading is WELLS on 4157 (IN THE CITIE OF WELLS COVNTY OF SVMMERSET), 4158-9 (CITIE OF WELLS IN THE COVNTY OF SVMMERSET), 4160-1 (CITTIE OF WELLS IN THE COVNTY OF SVMMERSET), 4162-6, 4170; WELLES on 4168-9; WELS on 4167. Note on 4157-61: The arms of the City of Wells are *Silver on a mount vert in base an ash-tree proper between three wells gules* (Scott-Giles 1953, p. 325)

4157	1.00	15.4	Cu	180°	*Wells,* City (CITIE). 1657. 5.14 Wells (IN·THE·CITIE· OF· WELLS around); C W| date (.C·W.|*1657*; · COVNTY · OF · SVMMERSET around). BW —, cf. 300 (CITIE·OF·WELLS·IN·THE). [Nott]. Rev. legend starts at 5 o'clock. Same rev. die as 4158. Turned in the dies
4158a	2.61	40.2	Cu	180°	*Wells,* City (CITIE). 1657. 5.14 Wells; C W|date. BW 300 but *1657*. [?Baldwin]. Rev. legend starts at 5 o'clock. Same obv. die as 4159; same rev. die as 4157. Diameter 18.5 mm
4158b	2.51	38.8	Cu	180°	Same dies. [Nott]. Diameter 17.5 mm
4158c	2.09	32.3	Cu	0°	Same dies. [?Baldwin]. Diameter 17.5 mm
4158d	1.77	27.3	Cu	180°	Same dies. [?Baldwin]. Diameter 18 mm
4158e	1.70	26.2	Cu	180°	Same dies. [Baldwin]. Diameter 17.5 mm
4158f	1.58	24.3	Cu	0°	Same dies. Baldwin. Overstruck on: IOHN·STEW. . . [1657], rev. ·TH. . .OF·BALFAST . . . (BW Ireland 105 or Belfast 1913, 54). Diameter 18.5-19 mm
4158g	1.52	23.4	Cu	180°	Same dies. [?Baldwin]. Diameter 18-18.5 mm
4158h	1.40	21.5	Cu	180°	Same dies. [?Baldwin]. Diameter 18-19 mm
4158i	1.15	17.8	Cu	180°	Same dies. [Baldwin]. Diameter 17-17.5 mm
4159	1.86	28.6	Cu	180°	*Wells,* City (CITIE). 1657. 5.14 Wells; C W|date. BW 300 but *1657*. Baldwin [or Spink 1971]. Rev. legend starts at 5 o'clock. Same obv. die as 4158
4160a	2.23	34.4	Br	270°	*Wells,* City (CITTIE). [16]69. 5.14 Wells; 5.60.5 (C W). BW 301. Nott. Same rev. die as 4161. Diameter 21.5 mm
4160b	2.22	34.2	Br	0°	Same dies. [Spink, *NCirc* Sep. 1976, 7667]. Diameter 21-21.5 mm
4160c	2.16	33.3	Br	90°	Same dies. [Baldwin]. Diameter 20 mm
4160d	1.83	28.3	Br	180°	Same dies. [?Baldwin]. Diameter 21-21.5 mm
4160e	1.51	23.3	Br	90°	Same dies. [Baldwin]. Diameter 20 mm
4161a	2.39	36.9	Br	0°	*Wells,* City (CITTIE). [16]69. 5.14 Wells; 5.60.5 (C W). BW 301. [Baldwin]. Same rev. die as 4160
4161b	1.88	29.0	Br	0°	Same dies. [?Nott]
4161c	1.80	27.7	Br	0°	Same dies. [?Baldwin]
4161d	1.60	24.6	Br	0°	Same dies. [Nott]
4162a	1.01	15.6	Br	180°	*Andrews,* William. 1651. W A; W A. BW 302. [Baldwin]. Same obv. die as 4163
4162b	0.91	14.0	M	180°	Same dies. Baldwin
4163	1.10	17.0	Br	180°	*Andrews,* William. 1651. W A; W A. BW 302. [?Baldwin]. Same obv. die as 4162
4164a	1.18	18.3	Cu	0°	*Andrews,* William. 1651. W A; W A. BW 302. [Baldwin]
4164b	0.88	13.5	Cu	0°	Same dies. Nott
4165a	0.99	15.2	Cu	0°	*Davidge,* John. 1652. I D; I D. BW 304. Nott
4165b	0.50	7.7	Br	180°	Same dies. [Baldwin]
4166a	1.02	15.8	M	0°	*Midleham,* James. 1666. I M (···|I M|···; ·IAMES·MIDLEHAM· around); 5.32.9
	(chipped)				(·WELLS·I666·· around). BW —, cf. 306 (IN·WELLS); Gray 1915, 306a. Baldwin
4166b	0.82	12.7	M	0°	Same dies. [Baldwin]
4167	1.18	18.2	Br	180°	*Towse,* Tristram. 1655. T T; date. BW 309. Nott
4168a	1.27	19.6	M	180°	*Warmall,* Robert. 1664. R W; R W. BW 310. [?Baldwin]. Diameter 16-17 mm. See also 4170
4168b	1.03	15.9	M	180°	Same dies. Nott. Diameter 15.5-16.5 mm
4168c	0.79	12.2	M	180°	Same dies. [?Baldwin]. Diameter 16-16.5 mm
	(chipped)				
4169a	1.04	16.0	M	90°	*Warmall,* Robert. 1664. R W; R W. BW 310. [Baldwin]
4169b	0.85	13.2	M	270°	Same dies. [?Baldwin]
4170	0.81	12.6	Cu	180°	*Warmer,* Robert. 1660. R W; R W. BW 311. Baldwin. See also 4168-9

Named signs

Three Swans: ?W—, S— *see* 'WEL' (Uncertain I)

[*continued overleaf*]

PLATE 49

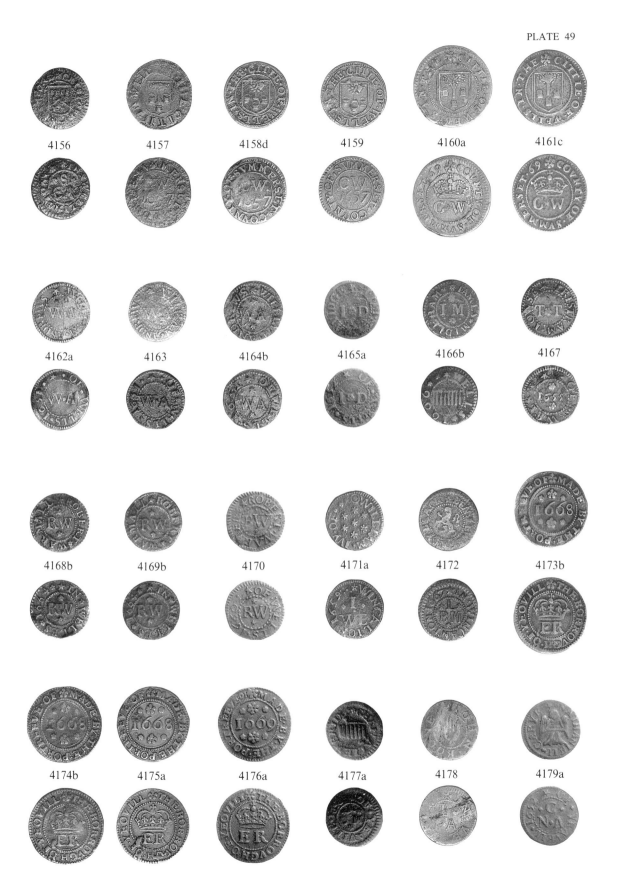

4156 4157 4158d 4159 4160a 4161c

4162a 4163 4164b 4165a 4166b 4167

4168b 4169b 4170 4171a 4172 4173b

4174b 4175a 4176a 4177a 4178 4179a

Plate 49 (*cont.*)

WESTON / WESTON BAMPFYLDE / WESTON IN GORDANO / WESTON SUPER MARE / WESTONZOYLAND

	Weight		Die	
	g	*gr*	*axis*	

Coulson, Thomas *see* 2312/1 (Herts.)
Hancock, Thomas *see* WESTBURY (Wilts.)

WINCANTON

The reading is WINCALTON on 4171, cf. *Wincaulton* 1291 (Ekwall 1960, p. 522); WINCANTON on 4172

| 4171a | 1.60 | 24.6 | Cu | 180° | *Ivy,* William. 1659. 2.4.13; I\|WE. BW 319. Baldwin. The obv. legend incorporates a ring and pellet (i.e. a full moon?) |
| 4171b | 1.20 | 18.5 | Br | 180° | Same dies. [?Nott] |

Named signs
| 4172 | 1.49 | 23.0 | Br | 0° | *Black* [*Lion*] (AT Y^EBLACK): Lewes, Ben—. 1667. 3.11; L\|BM. BW 321. Baldwin |

WINSCOMBE

Jones, William *see* 1764 (Glos.: Winchcombe)

YEOVIL

The reading is YEAVELL on 4179-82, 4185, 4187, with IN SOMERSET on 4181; YEOVELL on 4178, 4188-90, with IN SOMERSET on 4188-90; YEOVILL on 4173-6; YEAVILL on 4177, 4183; EYEAVELL on 4184, EYEAVILL on 4186, cf. *Yeouil or Euill* (Morden 1695)

4173a	2.24	34.6	Cu	270°	*Yeovil,* Borough (BORROVGH) (The Portreeve). 1668. Date; 5.60.5 (E R). BW 326 but PORTREEVE·OF. [?Baldwin]. Same rev. die as 4174-5
4173b	1.76	27.1	Cu	270°	Same dies. [?Baldwin]
4173c	1.34	20.7	Cu	270°	Same dies. [?Baldwin]
4174a	1.68	25.9	Cu	0°	*Yeovil,* Borough (BORROVGH) (The Portreeve). 1668. Date; 5.60.5 (E R). BW 326 but PORTREEVE·OF. [?Baldwin]. Same rev. die as 4173, 4175
4174b	1.39	21.4	Cu	0°	Same dies. [?Baldwin]
4174c	1.11	17.2	Cu	0°	Same dies. [Nott]
4175a	1.81	27.9	Cu	180°	*Yeovil,* Borough (BORROVGH) (The Portreeve). 1668. Date; 5.60.5 (E R). BW 326 but PORTREEVE·OF. [Baldwin]. Same rev. die as 4173-4
4175b	1.72	26.5	Cu	180°	Same dies. Nott
	(pierced)				
4175c	1.70	26.3	Cu	90°	Same dies. [Baldwin]
4175d	1.68	25.9	Cu	180°	Same dies. [?Baldwin]
4175e	1.47	22.6	Cu	180°	Same dies. [?Baldwin]
4175f	1.43	22.1	Cu	90°	Same dies. Nott
4175g	1.23	19.0	Cu	180°	Same dies. Nott
4175h	1.07	16.5	Cu	90°	Same dies. [Nott]
4175i	0.98	15.2	Cu	180°	Same dies. Nott
4176a	1.51	23.2	Cu	180°	*Yeovil,* Borough (BORROVGH) (The Portreeve). 1669. Date; 5.60.5 (E R). BW 327. Baldwin
4176b	1.19	18.4	Cu	180°	Same dies. [?Baldwin]
4176c	1.18	18.2	Cu	180°	Same dies. [Baldwin]
4176d	1.16	17.9	Cu	180°	Same dies. [?Nott]
4176e	1.13	17.4	Cu	180°	Same dies. [?Baldwin]
4176f	0.97	14.9	Cu	0°	Same dies. [Nott]
	(chipped)				
4177a	1.50	23.2	Br	180°	*Allembridge,* Christ—. 1656. 5.82.4; A|CM. BW 328. Nott. Christopher Allambridge of Yoavell, grocer (Vis. Som. 1672, p. 202)
4177b	1.21	18.6	Br	180°	Same dies. [?Baldwin]
4178	1.02	15.7	Br	270°	*Boone,* John. nd. 3.6.1; B|IA. BW 330. Nott
4179a	1.15	17.7	M	180°	*Carye,* Nathaniel (NATHANIELL). 1652. 3.10.6; C|NA. BW 331. Baldwin. Same rev. die as 4180
4179b	1.07	16.5	M	180°	Same dies. [?Nott]

YEOVIL (*cont.*)

	Weight			Die	
	g	*gr*		*axis*	
4180	1.01	15.6	Br	180°	*Carye,* Nathaniel (NATHANIELL). 1652. 3.10.6; C|NA. BW 331. [?Baldwin]. Same rev. die as 4179
4181	0.79	12.2	Br	0°	*Clarke,* Joseph. nd. 3.10.17; C|II. BW 332 but THE. Baldwin
4182	0.58	9.0	Br	180°	*Cosbey,* John. 1667. 5.43.30; I C. BW 333 but COSBEY. Nott
4183	1.02	15.7	Br	0°	*Daniell,* William. 1653. 4.15.4; D|WM. BW 334. Baldwin. Reading completed from Taunton specimen
4184	0.97	15.0	M	90°	*Hayne,* John. 1652. 3.11 (· IOHN · HAYNE around); H|ID (· H · |I · D; · OF · EYEAVELL · I652 around). BW —, cf. 335; Dickinson 335A. Spink 1973. Obv. legend starts at 2 o'clock
4185a	1.43 (chipped)	22.1	M	180°	*Haynes,* Philip (PHILLIP). 1655. 3.108.27; P H. BW 336. [?Baldwin]. Diameter 16.5 mm
4185b	1.24	19.1	M	0°	Same dies. [?Nott]. Diameter 15.5 mm
4185c	1.19	18.3	M	180°	Same dies. Brand [or Seaby 1960+]. Diameter 16 mm
4185d	0.75 (chipped)	11.5	Br	0°	Same dies. [Baldwin]. Diameter 16.5-17 mm
4186	0.96	14.9	Br	0°	*Moore,* George. nd. M|GE; M|GE. BW 337. Baldwin [or ?Nott]
4187a	0.98	15.1	Br	0°	*Moore,* Richard. 1668. 3.53.20; M|RD. BW 338. [?Nott]
4187b	0.74	11.3	Br	0°	Same dies. Baldwin
4188a	0.90	13.9	M	180°	*Seward,* Ambrose. nd. 1.44; S|AA. BW 339. [?Baldwin]. Same rev. die as 4189. Struck off-centre
4188b	0.89	13.7	M	180°	Same dies. Nott
4189	1.26	19.4	Br	90°	*Seward,* Ambrose. nd. 1.44; S|AA. BW 340. [?Baldwin]. Same obv. die as 4190; same rev. die as 4188
4190	1.35	20.8	M	90°	*Seward,* Ambrose. nd. 1.44; S|AA. BW 340. Nott. Same obv. die as 4189

'SOMERSET and DORSET'

Pitman, John *see* 975 (Dorset: Sherborne)

ADDENDUM

AYLSHAM (Norfolk)

| 4191 | 0.33 (worn, chipped) | 5.1 | Cu | 270° | *Haukins,* Michael (MICHAELL). 1666. 5.83.1; M H. BW 7 (ALSHAM); BW 104 (Marsham) but HAVKINS = shuttle, ALSHAM; BW Yorks. 232 (Masham) but O. = shuttle, ALSHAM. Seaby [1974 ex Glendining 6.3.74 lot 285 ex Hird]. Identified as BW Yorks. 232 (obv. a man making candles, rev. MASHAM), but shapes in chief and in base of a fesswise charge are the 'ghosts' of chisel marks on rev.; shuttle and first letter of place-name confirmed from die-duplicate found Brandon (Suffolk) in or before 1993. BW Norfolk 104 derives from a raid on Yorkshire. See Monks forthcoming |

PLATE 50

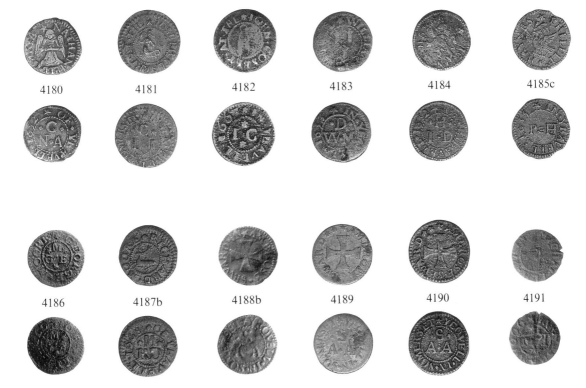

4180   4181   4182   4183   4184   4185c

4186   4187b   4188b   4189   4190   4191

INDEX OF FINDS

INDEX OF PLACES OF ISSUE

This index includes the counties represented in Part IV, and named signs

INDEX OF TRADES AND OTHER DESCRIPTIONS

Only trades named on the tokens or in the notes are indexed; other tradesmen may be identified through the Classified index of types. Officials responsible for issuing tokens will be found in the index of issuers.

INDEX OF ISSUERS

Persons are indexed by a standardized form of surname, normally the commonest London form as counted by Bardsley (1901), although Bartholomew (1972, for local names), Reaney (1976, 1991), Cottle (1978), and the current London telephone directory have been consulted also. The actual readings when different are added within brackets in capitals; references are provided from these readings unless they would have been immediately adjacent. Abbreviated forenames are silently extended, except for 'Will' which could stand for names other than William. Indexed also are the following rare forenames, defined as names absent from Withycombe (1977): America, Blythe, Clare (m.), Conway, the theatrical Tamerlane, Twyford, Violet (m.), Wormley, and the biblical Anchor (?), Onesiphorus, and Sidricke if it stands for Shadrach. Corporate issuers are indexed by place, and collected under 'Corporations' and 'Parishes'. Other collective headings are 'Bailiffs', 'Overseers...', and 'Poor'. In addition there are entries for the exceptional legends A BRASSE HALFE PENNY, ANNO DOM: I669, FEARE GOD HONOR THE KING, MADELY WOOD YEILDS COLE THATS GOOD, NOE WANT WHERE THESE ARE, QVONDAM ESQVIRE, RECEIVE THE CROWN IN EVERY TOWN, TAKE THESE THAT WIL ILE CHAING THEM STIL, and in Latin CREDE SED CAVE, and (?) MALLIA CADREENE.

INDEX OF LETTERS IN OBVERSE AND REVERSE TYPES

Groups of two or three letters are alphabetized according to the first, i.e. the forename initial. (Surnames, and the initial where a token does not give the surname, are of course to be found in the index of issuers.) Triangles of letters are read in the order ₁ ² ₃, i.e. forename of husband — surname — forename of wife, which probably was the contemporary way of reading them. On 3986, however, the letters I L E form an inverted triangle, perhaps following the earlier custom of setting the wife's initial below. On 3872-3 (H M C) and 4087 (R M V) the wife's initial is apparently above. The incongruous letters M C M for Margaret Mangles (3024), W B for Joseph Braban (3075: E G also appears), might be explained from their business or family history; whereas A A I on 3782 was simply an error, corrected to I A A in a later state of the die. On 3892 there is space for a wife's initial, but only E D is present.

A A A	3981		C T S	3351
A A I	3782 [in error for I A A]		C W	4157-61
A B	3074, 3135		C Y H	3603
A C P	4129			
A D	3487-8		D B	3788 (*D B*)
A D I	3147-8		D C	3513
A F	3648		D D S	3613
A G M	4134		D P	3186
A H	3689, 3842-3		D P K	3716
A H A	3689		D R	3063
A I I	3857		D T E	3210
A L	3221-2, 3272, 3705		D Y	3716 [i.e. Duke of York]
A M	3176-7, 3629			
A M E	4008		E A	3373
A M S	3706-7		E A A	4095
A P	4028		E A I	3676
A R	4069-70		E B	3494
A S A	4188-90		E B A	3139
A T	3732		E B E	3072-3
A W A	3409-10		E B M	3313-14
A W M	3851		E B R	3048
			E C	3140, 3607, 3913, 4019
B	3995, 4099-4101		E C E	3241, 3395, 3404
B A	3365		E D	3102-3
B B	3304-6, 3598		E D –	3892 (third letter missing)
B H	3161, 3916		E D T	4149
B H A	3570-2		E F	3874-6
B L M	4172		E G	3075, 3877
B M M	3091		E G K	3640-1
B R S	3263		E H	3157, 3778-9
B T E	3209		E H A	3160
B W A	3352-5		E H M	3165
			E L I	3797-8
C	3319-20, 4044		E M F	3251
C A M	4177		E M M	3898-9
C B	3510, 3946-54, 3999		E N E	3180
C C A	3322-4		E O	3342-3
C C R	4125		E P	3462
C H M	3264		E P E	3717
C M	4072		E P I	3989
C O	3665-75		E P M	3344
C R	3366-7		E Q ?I	3093
C R F	3990		E R	3887, 4173-6
C S	3052-9		E R D	3620-1
C S A	4155-6		E R M	3998

SYLLOGE OF COINS OF THE BRITISH ISLES

SYLLOGE OF COINS OF THE BRITISH ISLES

Published by the British Academy, except Nos. 8 and 34 published by the Trustees of the British Museum, and Nos. 16, 31, 33, 38, 43 and 44 published by Spink & Son Ltd.